C L A X O G R A P H Y

The Art

Of Jazz Photography

CLAXOGRAPHY

With texts by William Claxton and James Gavin

By William Claxton

Nieswand
Verlag

Acknowledgements

Thanks to all of the jazz musicians,
composers, and arrangers in the world;
without them there would be no
Claxography.
Special thanks to my wife, Peggy,
for her talent and insight in the editing
of my work; and to my son, Chris,
for his love and support.
Much appreciation to James Gavin for
his words; and to Jens Nieswand and
Ingo Wulff, who made this book possible.

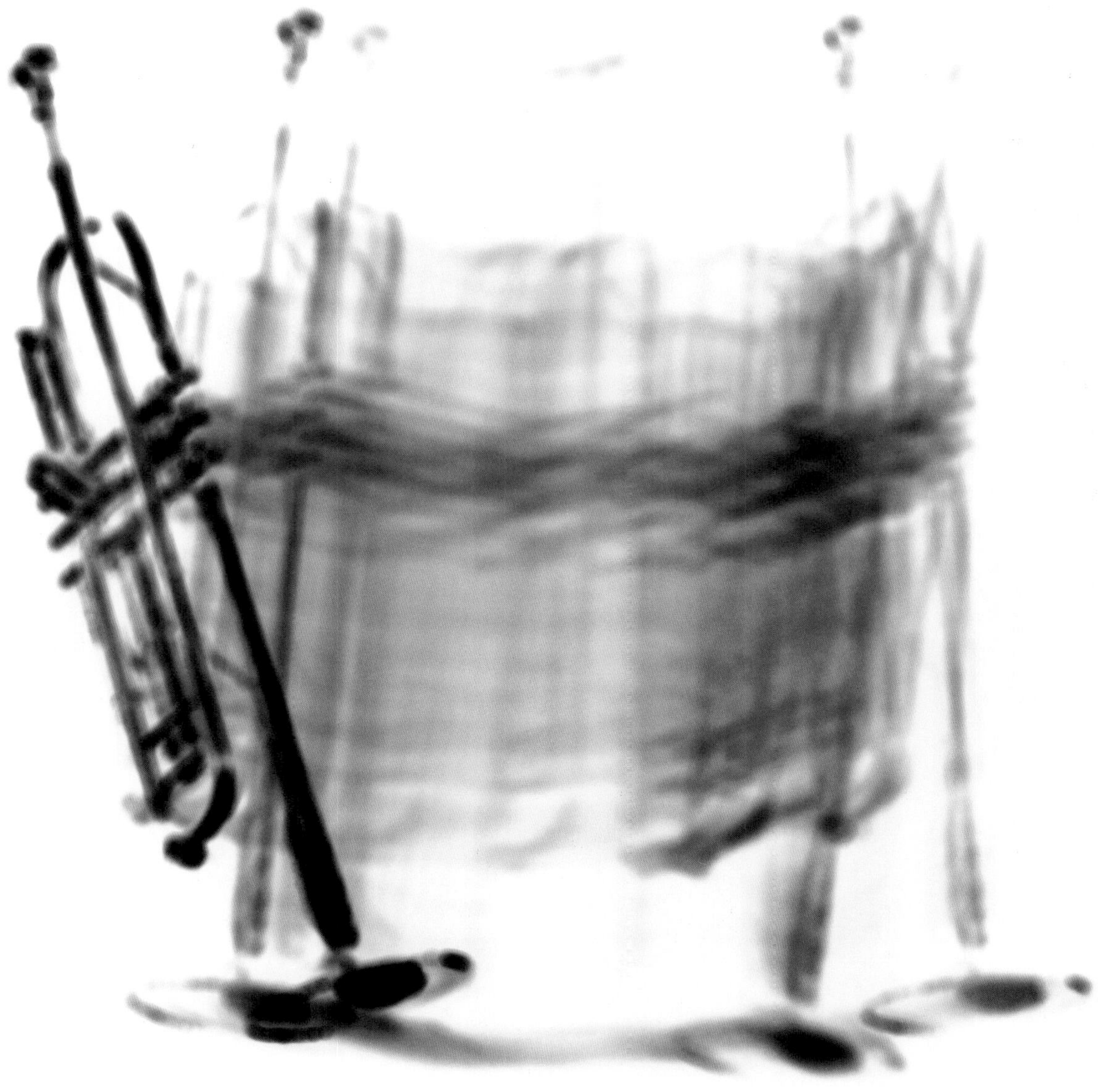

Dancing Trumpets · 1954

Growing up in California, William Claxton spent his time collecting 78s by Duke Ellington, Lena Horne, Count Basie, and Tommy Dorsey. As he pasted their pictures into scrapbooks, Claxton yearned to become a part of their world.

By the time he started photographing musicians himself, he looked for ways to define them as people, not just as performers. He wanted to capture the innate drama in their lives, the fun, the anxiety, the eternal youthfulness. He learned to do all this and more in the 1950s, when his album covers for Pacific Jazz Records reflected a sound born of beach-side jazz clubs and balmy California nights. Today, after decades of award-winning jacket photos, magazine layouts, books, and exhibitions, it's safe to call Claxton the most celebrated photographer in jazz history. *Claxography* offers a fresh look at his work: nearly all its pictures appear here for the first time.

Claxton is a photojournalist. He makes his subjects comfortable enough to lower their guard, then freezes their most telling moments. The greatest revelations occur when he takes musicians away from the stage. He caught a strung-out Art Pepper in the harsh light of day, immediately after the saxophonist had finished a one-year jail term for drug possession; the pain of withdrawal is etched in his handsome face. The Washington, D.C. sax player and mailman Buck Hill brings his horn along on his letter route, lightening the step of some neighborhood kids. After a show at the Brooklyn Paramount, a pensive Sarah Vaughan sits in her gown in a back stairwell of the theater, too tired to paste on a smile.

At recording sessions Claxton hangs out with the players first, letting them get used to his presence. Then he goes to work. Recalled the late Shorty Rogers: "You'd finish taking a chorus, and you'd open your eyes and the first thing you'd see would be Bill, clicking away."

Born in 1927 in Pasadena, California, he began his career as a hobby. While studying psychology at UCLA,* he haunted local jazz clubs with his camera: a 4 x 5 Speed Graphic, obsolete even then. "When I worked," he says, "holding that big, clunky camera up to shoot with flash bulbs

*UCLA: University of California Los Angeles

and dangling extension cords, friends would laugh at me and remark that I looked like a crime photographer: a young, tall, and skinny WeeGee."

One night in 1952 Claxton went to the Haig in Los Angeles to shoot the Gerry Mulligan Quartet with Chet Baker. There he met Dick Bock, who was recording the show to inaugurate Pacific Jazz, his new company. Book took him on as art director, house photographer, and partner. This was near the dawn of the LP, when record covers held vast artistic potential; while scouting for ideas, Claxton created his style. "Most of the jazz photography before me showed sweaty musicians with shiny faces in dark, smoky little bars," he says. "That was jazz to most people. But being on the West Coast, I wanted to bring out the fact that musicians here were living in such a health-conscious environment. So I purposely put them on the beach or in the mountains or on the road in their convertibles."

He also conveyed their sex appeal. His classic pictures of a T-shirted, stunning Chet Baker played a major role in the trumpeter's fantasy image. (That look became fashion in the 80s, when photographer Bruce Weber adapted it for his Calvin Klein advertisements.) Claxton even brought out the sensual connotation of the instruments. A jazzman's horn, he says, is like "an extra appendage" – an idea made explicit in 1994, when MCA Music hired him to design the photo of his choice for Black History Month. He took a black male model onto a rooftop in the hot sun, stripped him down, covered him with oil, and had him press a gleaming trumpet against his chest.

Claxton has endless stories about his pictures. He went to a Hollywood record studio in 1954 to photograph the fabled Joe Albany, an unsung pioneer of bop piano and a notoriously eccentric ex-junkie. He found the pianist "a mostly sweet, intelligent, dopey kind of guy," except in the demonic glimpse included here. The next year he made an outlaw of Jack Sheldon for the cover of his "Get Out Of Town" album. Late at night Claxton drove him to a back alley in Hollywood; turned his headlights on Sheldon, who toted a trumpet case; and *voilà* – instant fugitive.

On a set at Paramount for the filming of the Red Nichols story "The Five Pennies," Claxton spotted a prop infant in an unchildlike resting place. He christened it "Jazz Baby." In 1992 he encountered a grown-up jazz baby in Diana Ross, who asked him to shoot her as she rehearsed some standards for the TV special "Diana Ross Sings Jazz and Blues: Stolen Moments." Ross wanted to look like a real jazz artist. There she stands in the studio – made up to look natural, dressed up to look dressed down.

Other shots are just as indelible: Shorty Rogers grinning in his children's treehouse; Pete Jolly cornered by pianos in a warehouse; Jackie Cain and Roy Kral in the recording studio – the smartest, hippest young couple in jazz; Dinah Washington mugging outrageously during her "Bitter Earth Revue" at Ciro's in Hollywood.

A word about the title of this book. Since Claxton started documenting the jazz life, musicians have found various ways to welcome him into their fraternity. In 1956 Shorty Rogers wrote and recorded "Clickin' with Clax"; Al Cohn followed suit that year with "Sound Claxton!" Then in 1990, a young Canadian sax player named Dan St. Marseille called Claxton to ask if he would photograph him for his first CD. He added that he had very little money and probably couldn't afford him. "I met with him and heard him play," says Claxton. "He was so sincere and such a good musician that I agreed to shoot his picture for just the cost of my materials. We agreed that sometime when he was rich and famous he would hire me and pay my normal fee."

One night Claxton went to hear St. Marseille in a Los Angeles jazz club. Onstage, the player announced his new composition: "Claxography (The Art Of Jazz Photography)." Then he gave Claxton the framed manuscript – and a name for this volume. It's the right term for a gallery of images that resonate like the coolest jazz solo.

James Gavin, New York City, 1995

James Gavin's profiles of pop and jazz personalities appear in the *New York Times* and the *Village Voice*. His forthcoming biography of Chet Baker will be published throughout the U.S. and Europe.

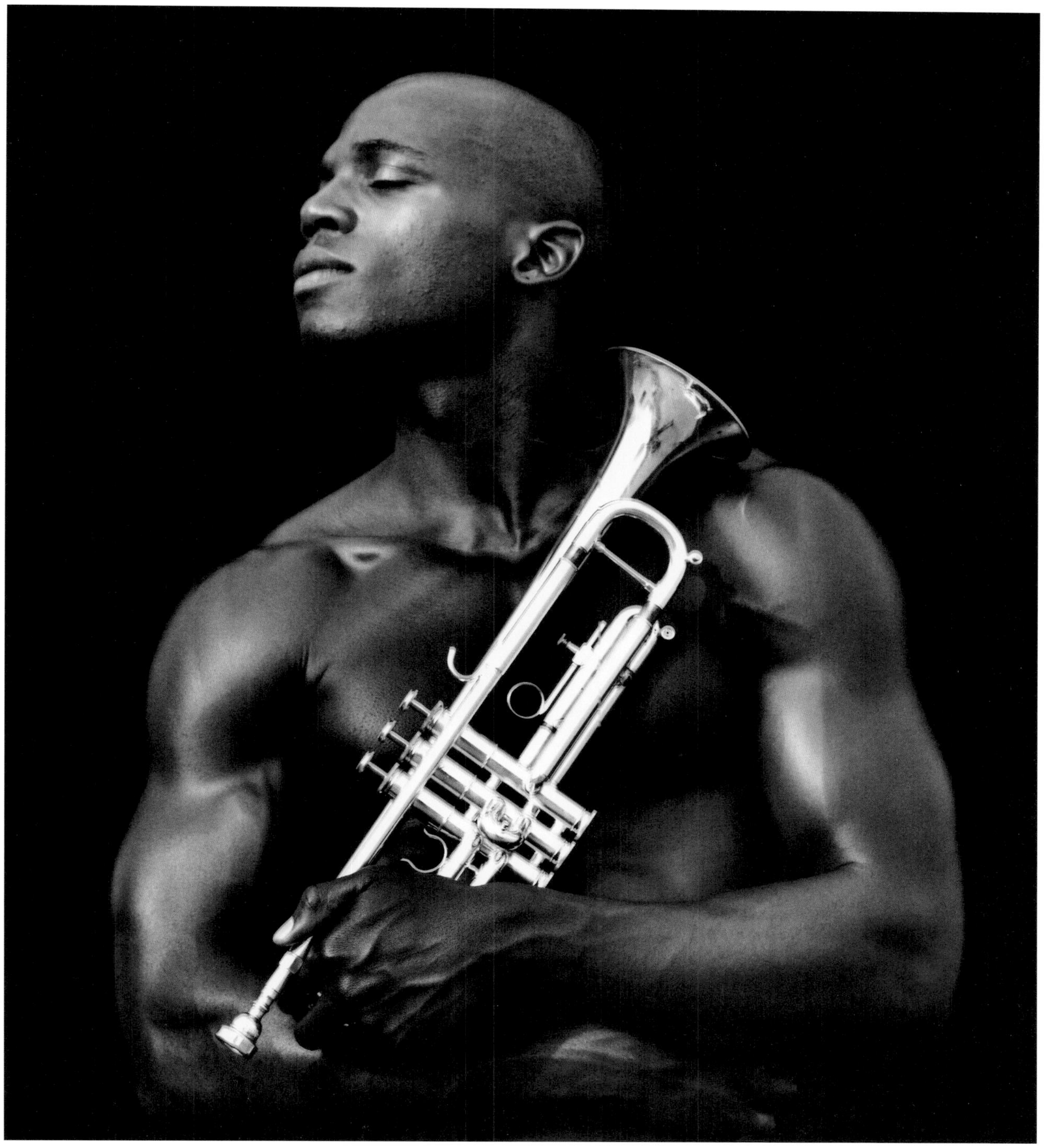

Black Music Month poster
MCA Records · 1993
Model: Billy Brown

Why photograph jazz musicians? I've been asked that a few times. First, and most important, I love their music. But I am also fascinated by the diverse qualities they possess. They have an ingenuousness, a sort of open, innocent attitude. Yet at the same time they display a strong discipline in their dedication to their craft. And I also admire their individualism: Their differences in character and their musical expression.

I am just as intrigued by the movements and body language of musicians while they play. I study them carefully before photographing them, much like I would watch a dancer, an actor, or even an ordinary person performing an ordinary task. I note how their faces and bodies reflect or catch the light; when and at what angles they look their best. I do all this, of course, while listening to their playing. In a sense, I listen with my eyes.

When I feel that I have a visual grasp on the subject, I press the shutter release, and I usually know instantly whether or not I have captured that perfect moment in time. Later, when I look at my proofs, I try to decide, "Did I get *that* shot or not?" Usually I did, and it's a great and satisfying feeling. But as to whether that specific shot will become an important photograph, only time will tell. Frequently I'm asked by record producers to "be sure to shoot a 'classic'!" I usually answer, "I can't promise that, but if you *record* a 'classic', I'll try to shoot one!"

In the photographic studio, where the subject must pose for a preconceived picture idea, a whole different set of circumstances arises. We each bring something to the shoot: The subject brings his physical being, his attire and his instrument; I bring my experience and some sort of plan as how I'm going to photograph them. First of all, I must establish a rapport with my subjects. Right away I let them know that I'm aware of their work. Then I try to win their trust: to let them know that I won't take a bad picture of them; and then if by some strange fate I do, no one will ever see it. I hate ugly pictures of anybody. I am dedicated to beauty. I know there is beauty in all kinds of human beings. So, the act of finding and capturing that beauty is relatively easy for me.

Photographing a jazz *star* in, say, 1955 for a record cover with its 12 x 12" LP format was a relatively simple and delightful experience: The cover concept would be discussed along with the artist's wardrobe to be worn; the artist and I would meet at a suitable location and shoot the cover.

Nowadays, working with the 5 x 5" CD format (my canvas has been miniatured), there are many meetings, discussions, faxes exchanged with creative directors, art directors, the artist's attorneys, managers, agents and the record company executives. Then there are wardrobe fittings, makeup people, hairstylists and groomers. I always preferred to have the jazz artist alone all to myself where we can create a more intimate photograph.

Later in the darkroom, I have a chance to discover and create all over again. Occasionally the shot I thought was so great is not all that fabulous. Perhaps another frame is more interesting when blown up, and an entirely new and exciting image begins to appear through the developer on the print paper. That's a visual surprise that can be rewarding.

The photographs in this collection span 1952 (Oscar Pettiford and Harry "Sweets" Edison) to 1995 (Mark Isham and Marcus Miller). I have tried to select images for their photographic merit rather than for the star status of the musician. So you will see a Memphis street musician in 1960 next to an important and influential jazz player-composer. The international languages of jazz and photography need no special education or sophistication to be enjoyed. In my book, Young Chet, I stated that "Photography is jazz for the eye." All I ask you to do is listen with your eyes.

William Claxton, Beverly Hills, 1995

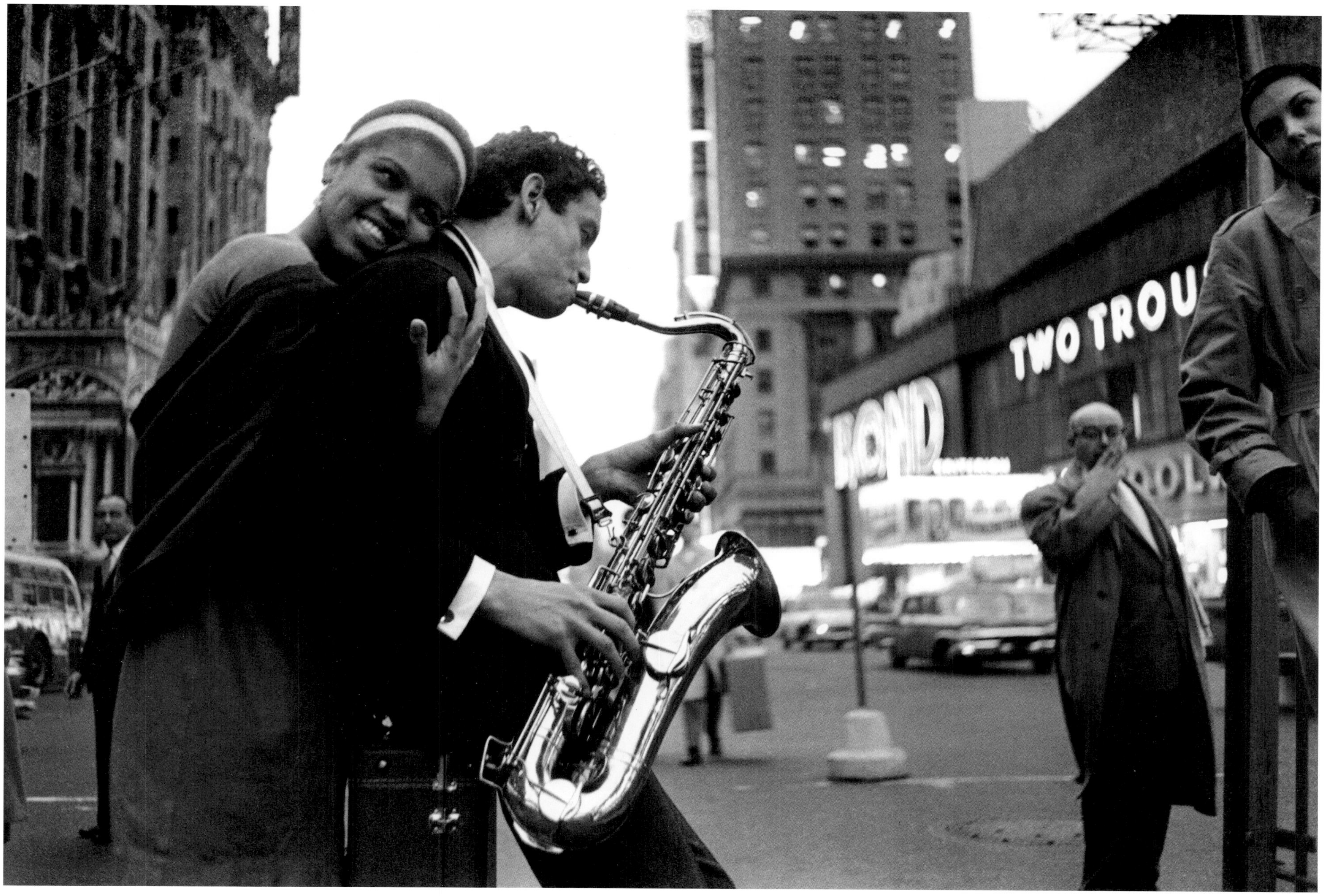

Times Square New York City · 1960

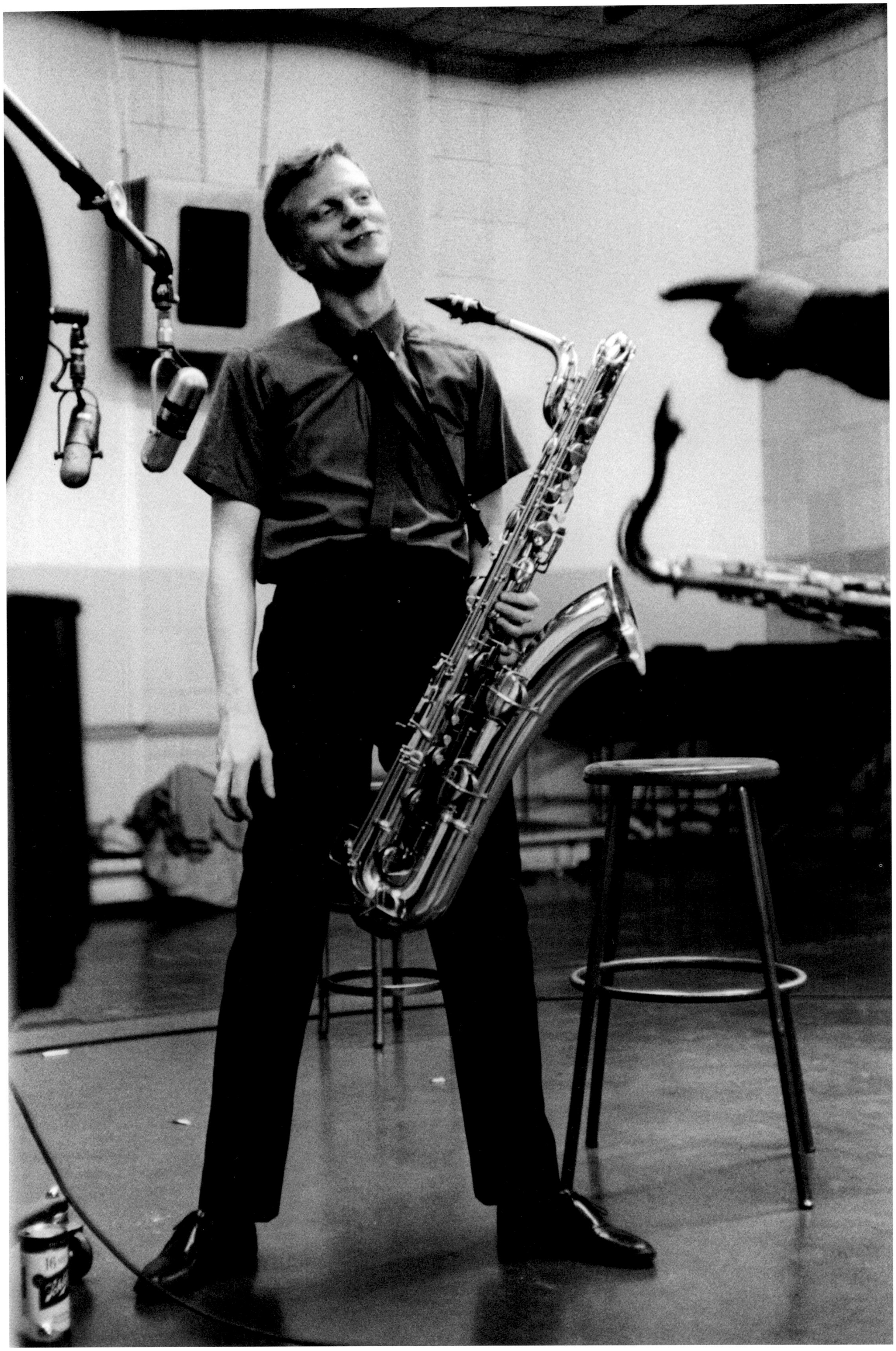

▶
Miles Davis
Los Angeles · 1957

Gerry Mulligan
Hollywood · 1958

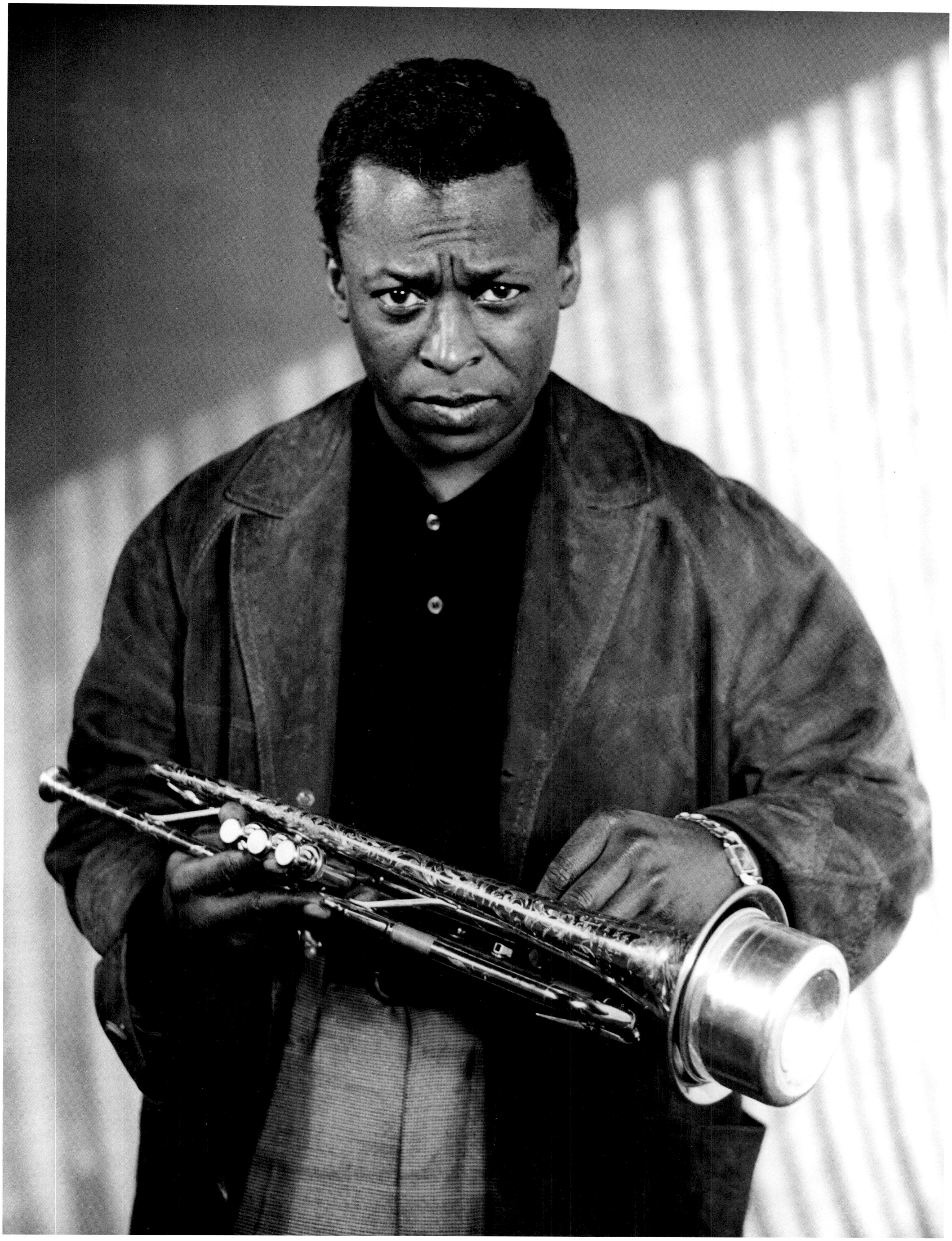

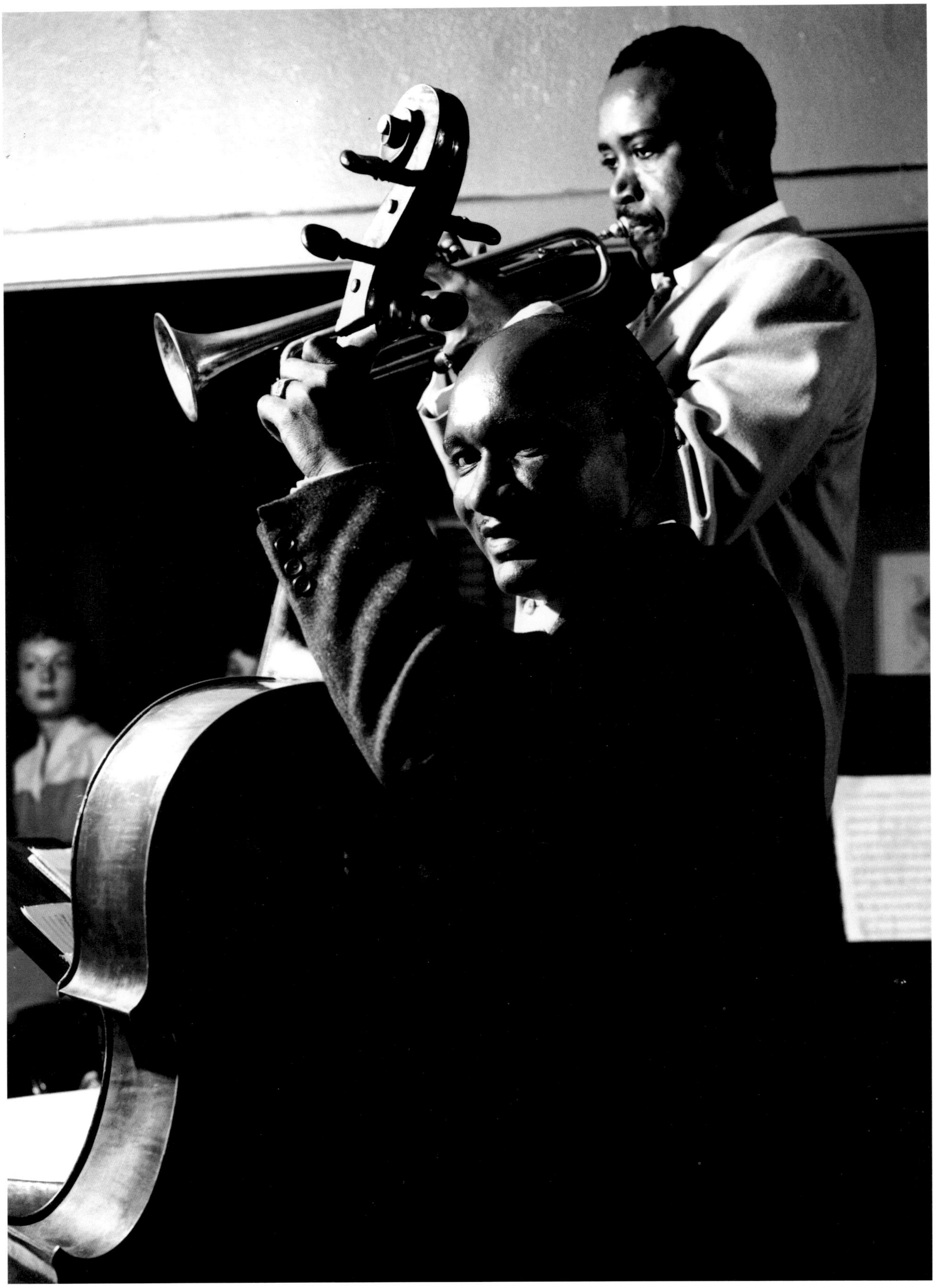

 Oscar Pettiford and Harry "Sweets" Edison Los Angeles · 1952

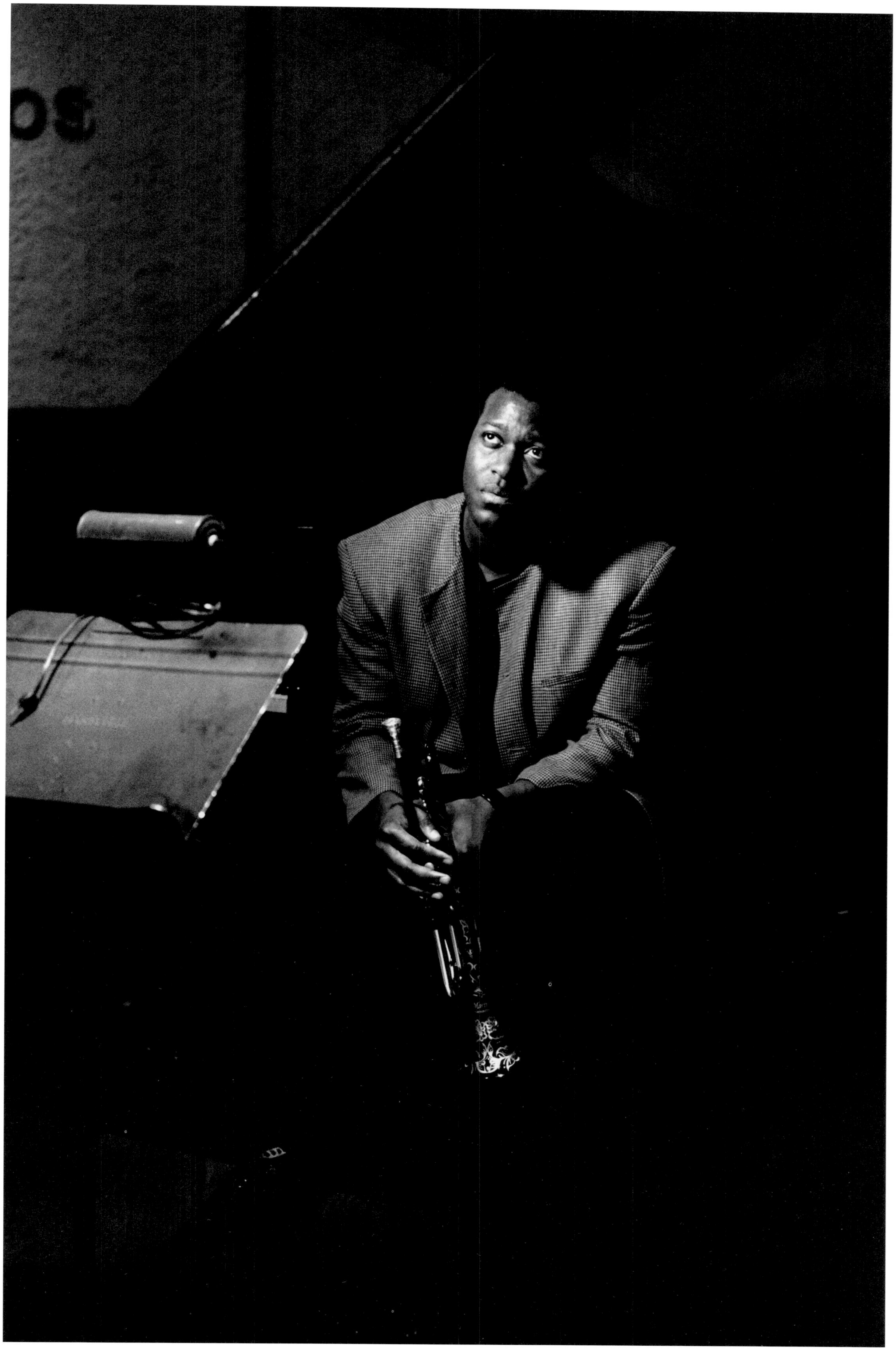

Wallace Roney
New York City · 1994

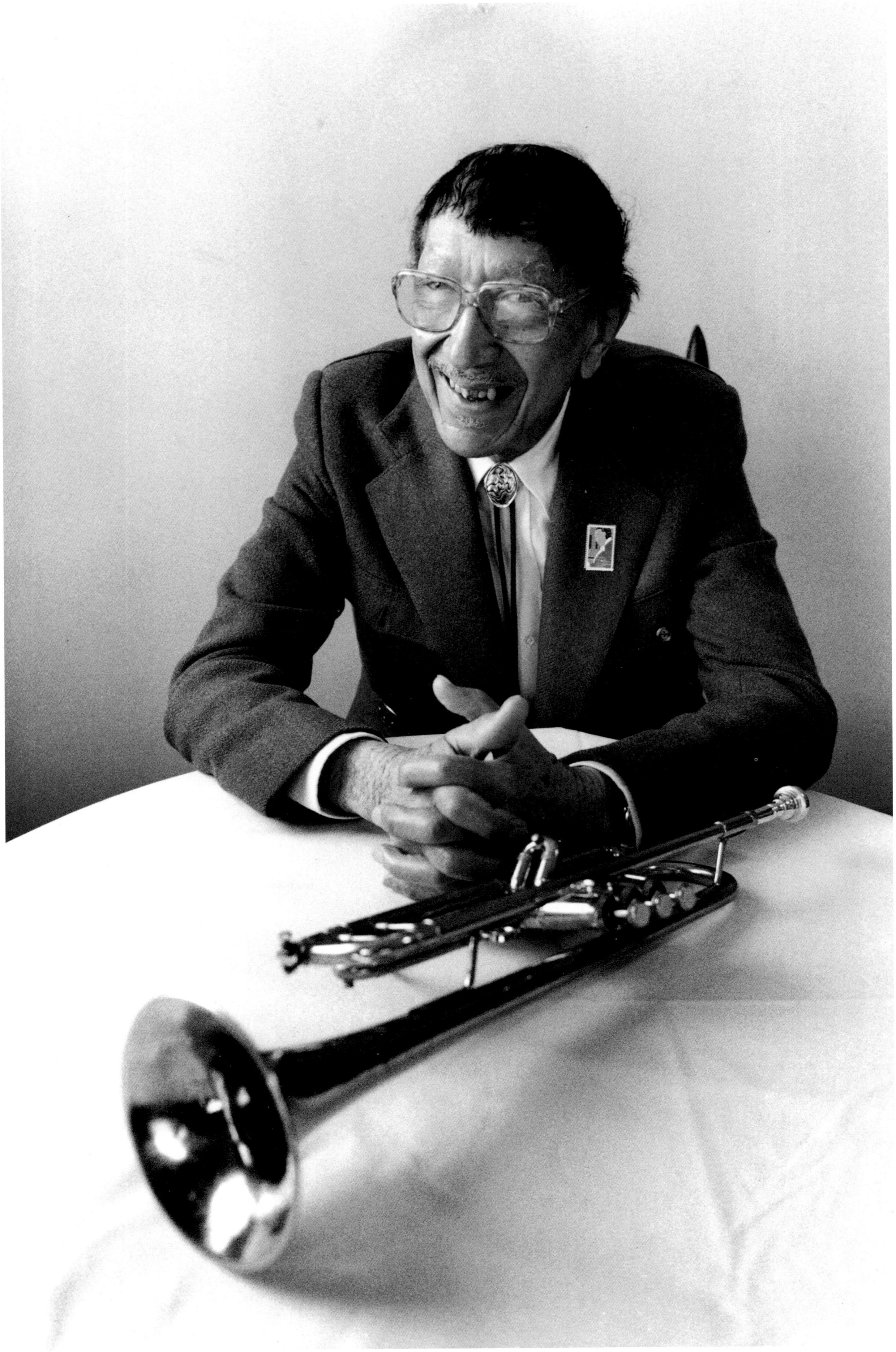

Doc Cheatham
Harlem, New York City
1989

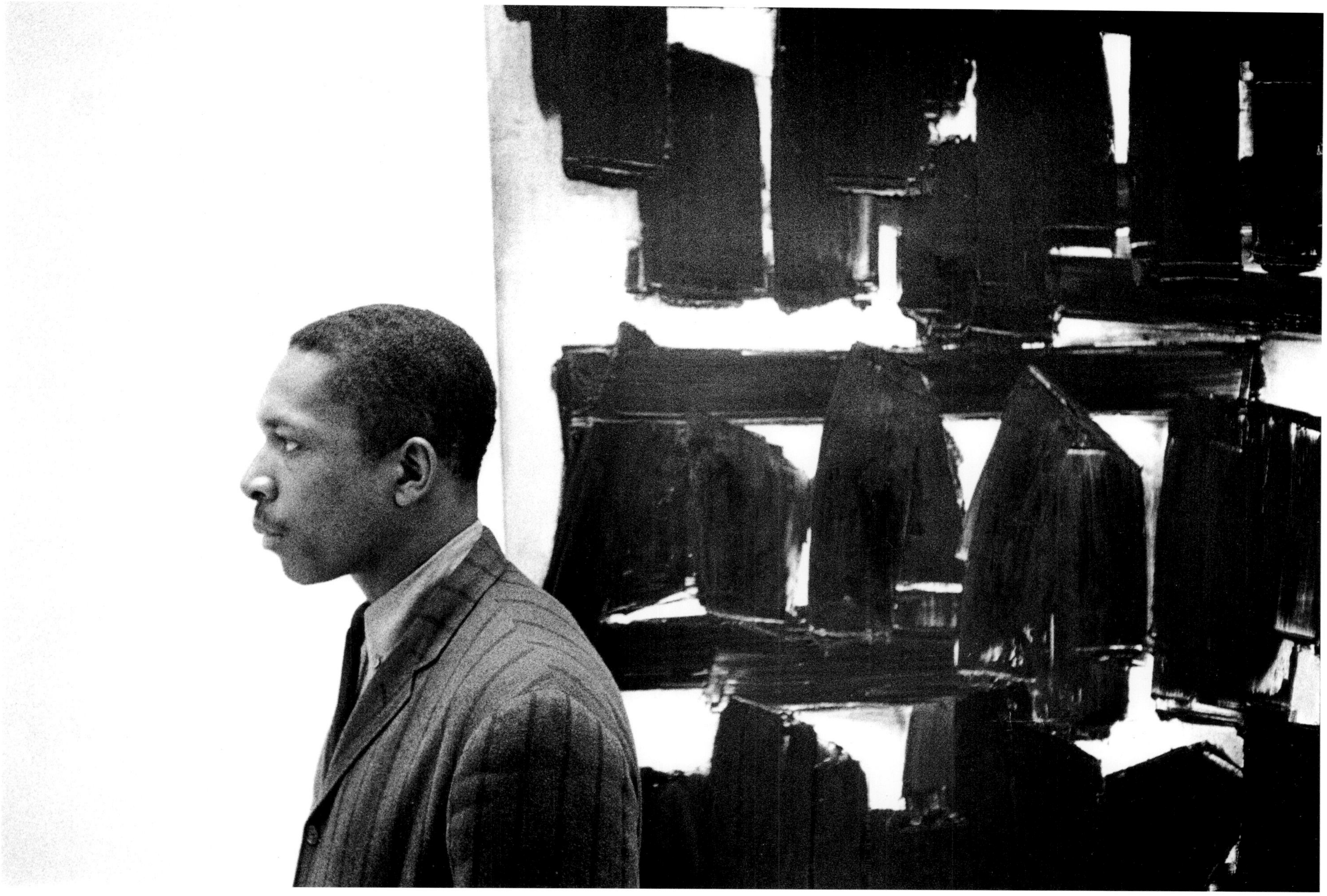

John Coltrane New York City · 1960

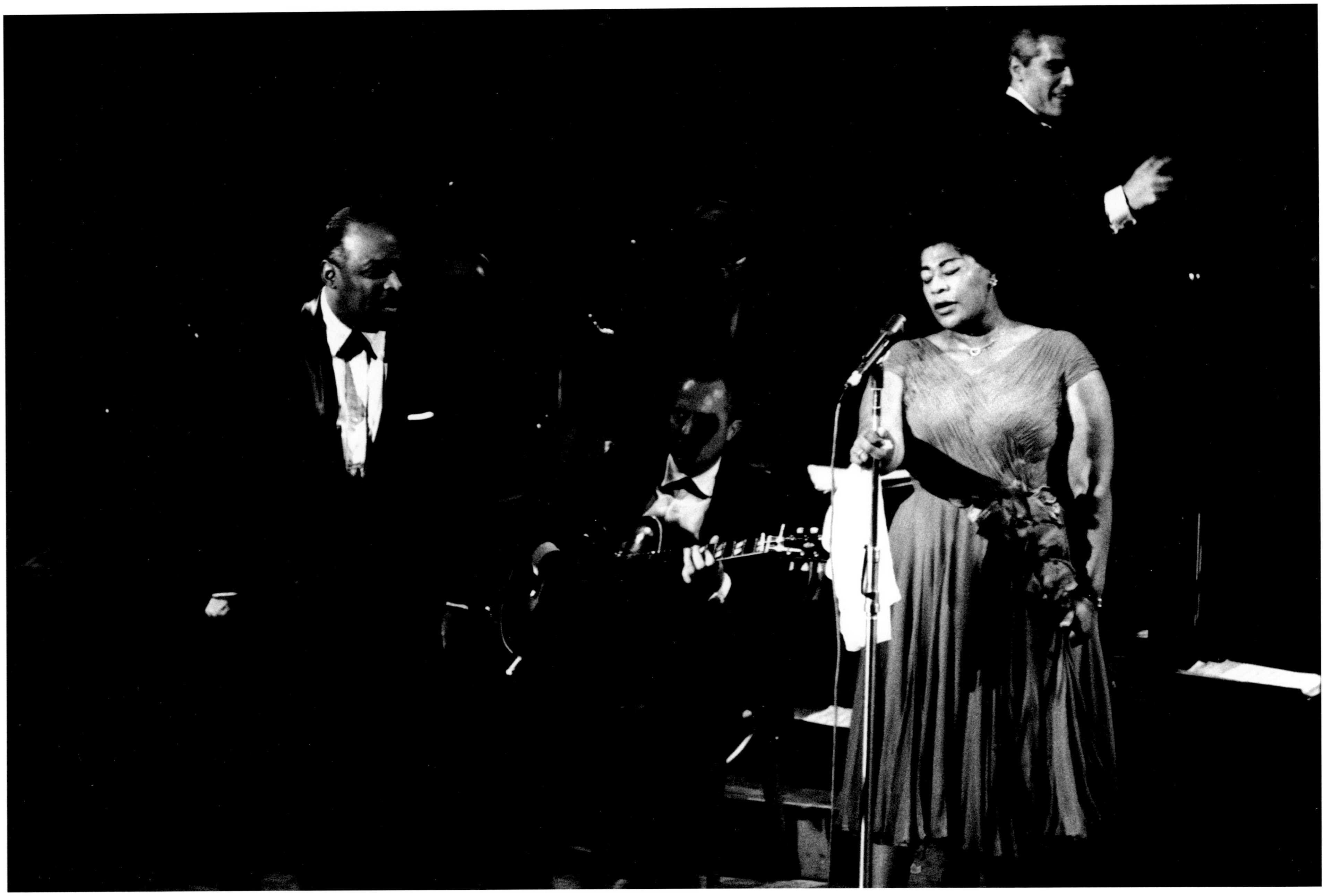

Ella Fitzgerald, Count Basie, Herb Ellis, Lou Levy New York City · 1959

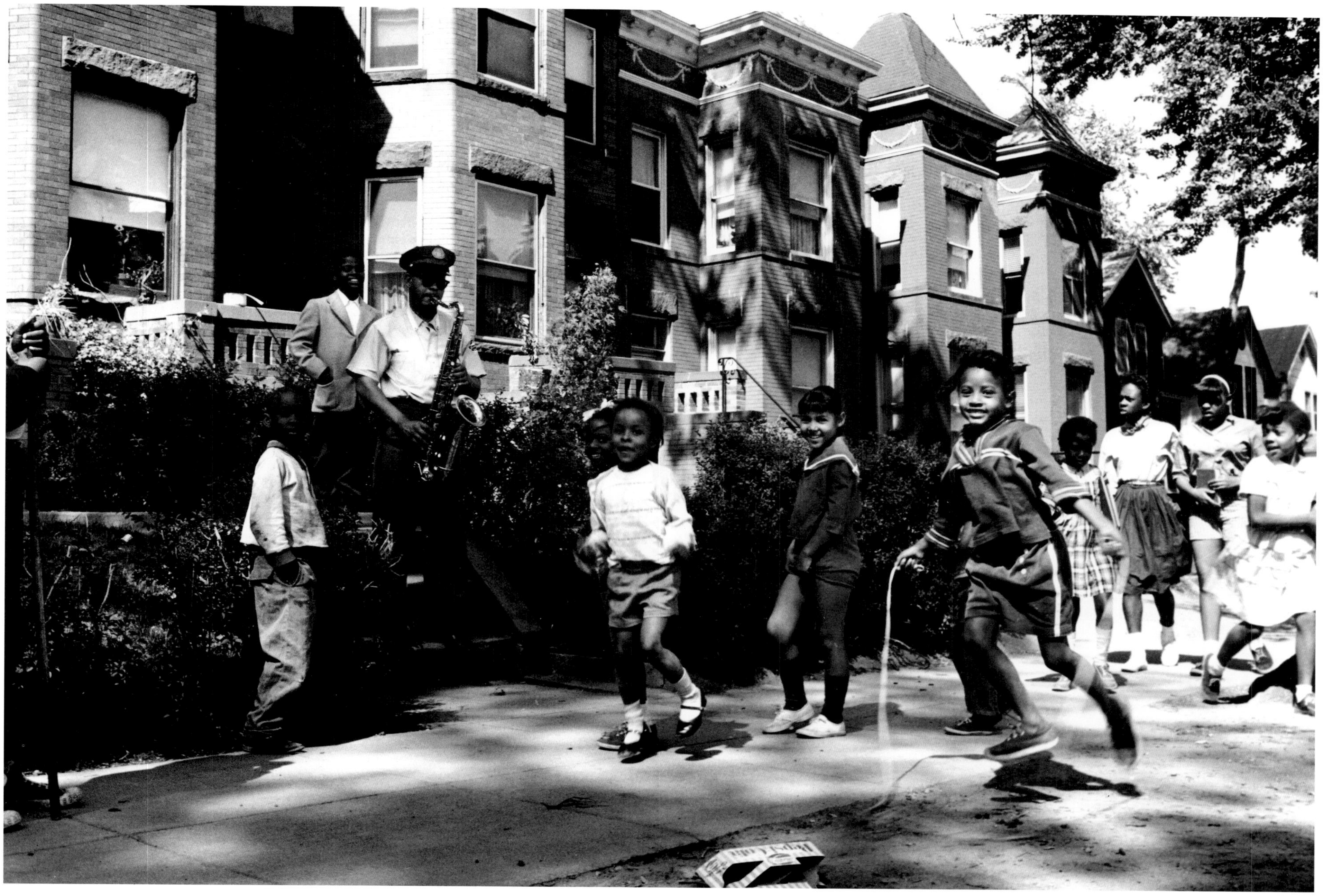

Buck Hill, the jazz postman Washington D.C. · 1960

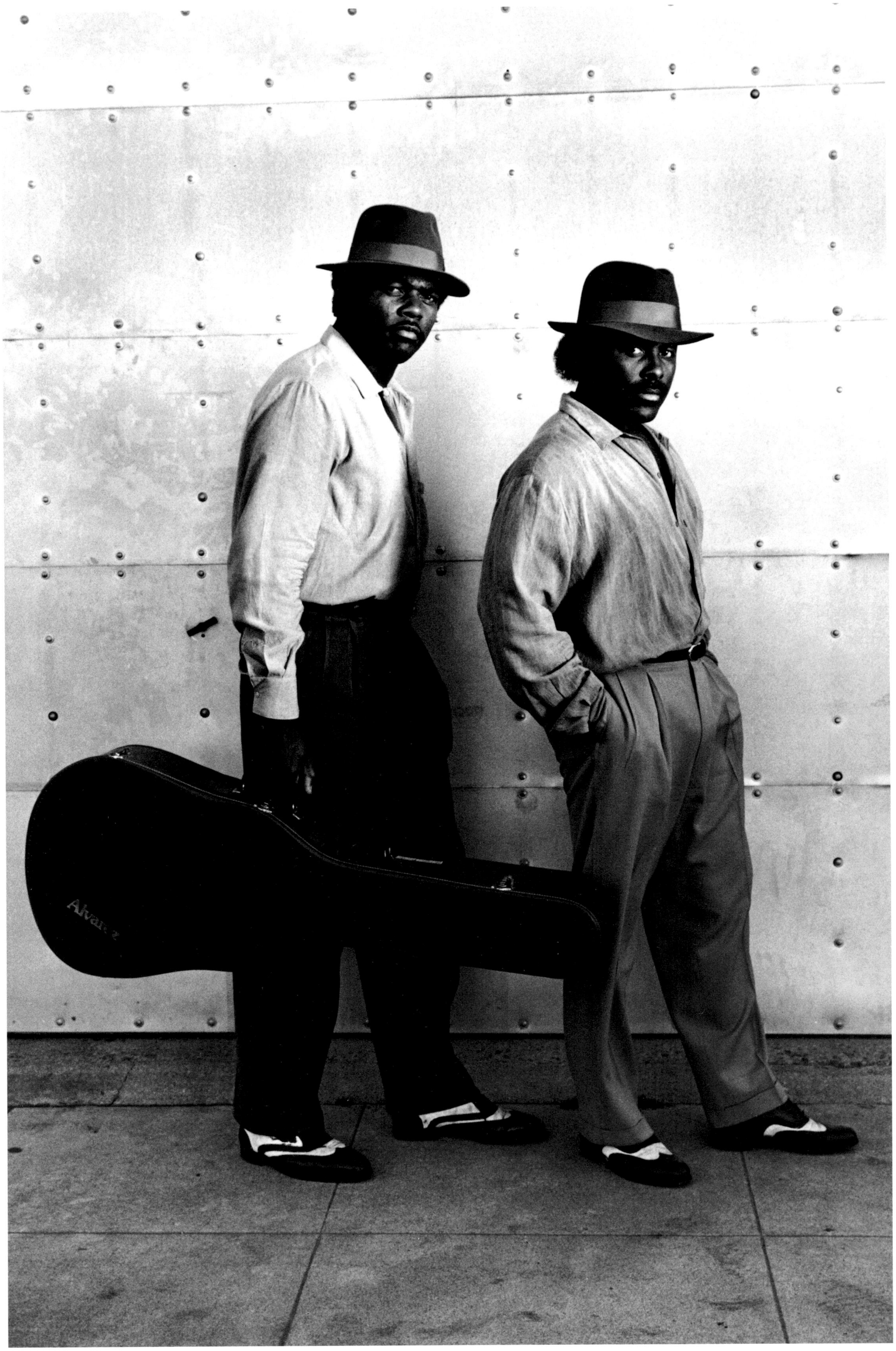

Terry Evans *(left)*
and Bobby King
Los Angeles · 1990

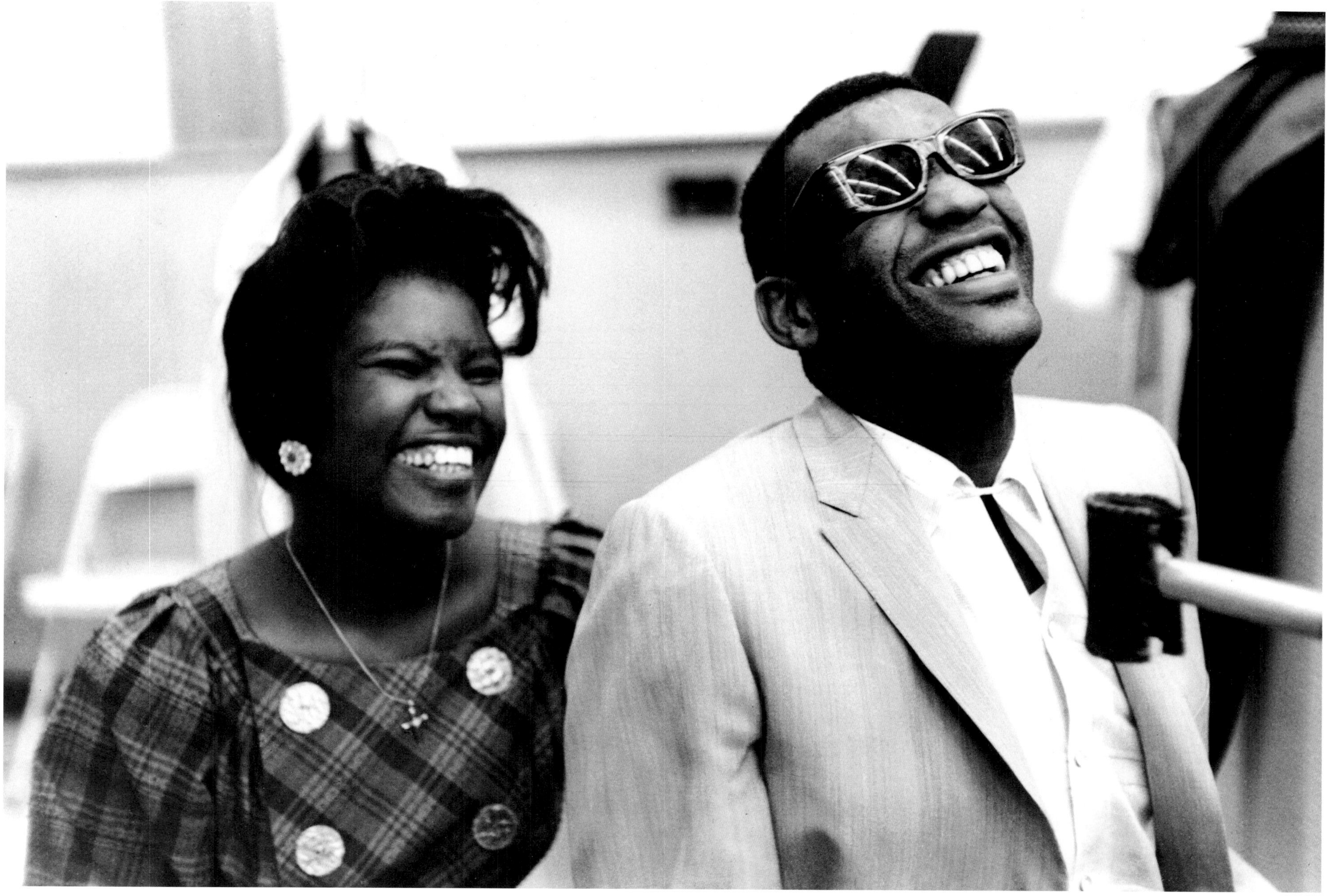

Ray Charles with a Raylette Hollywood · 1959

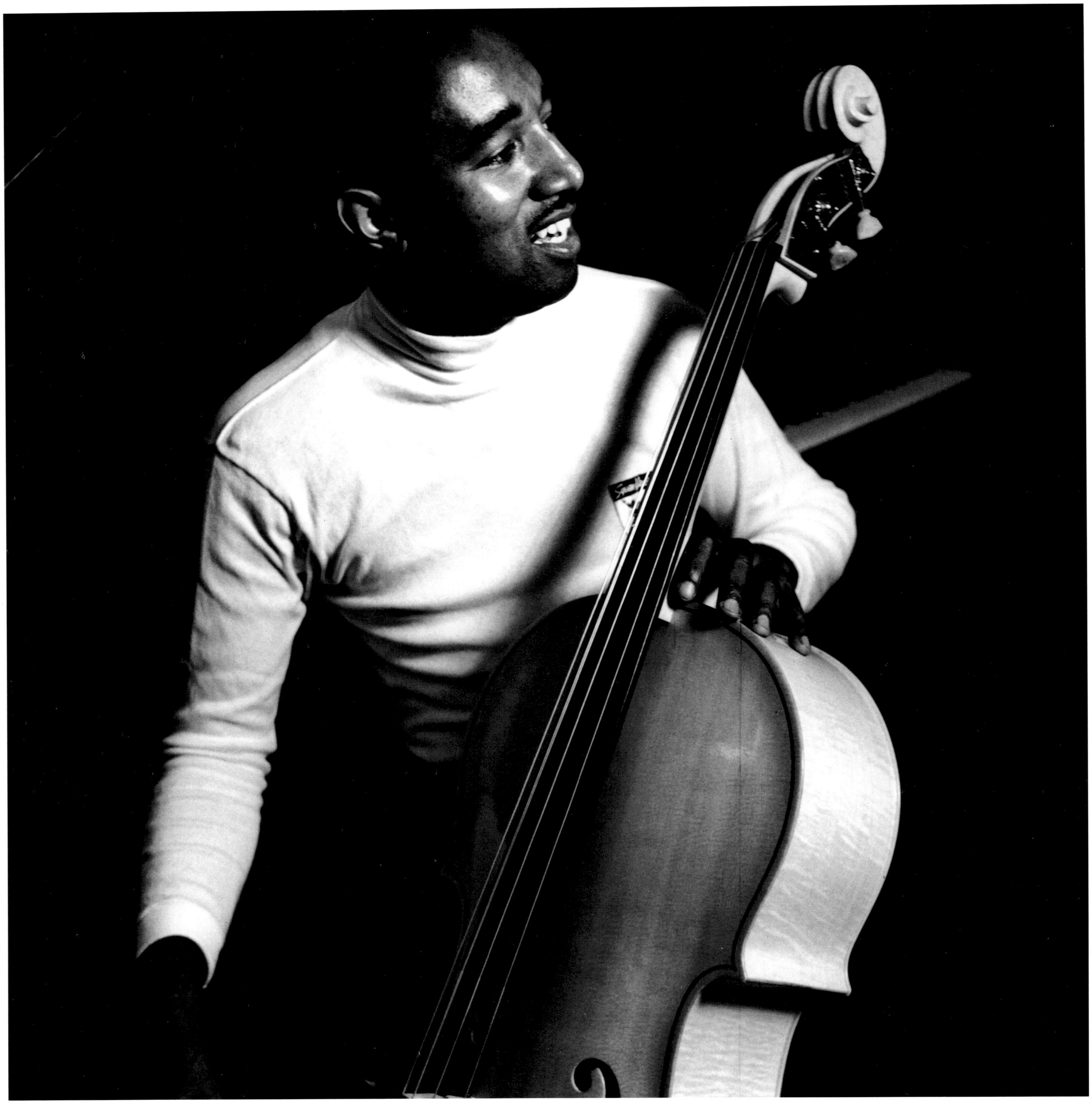

 Ray Brown Hollywood · 1957

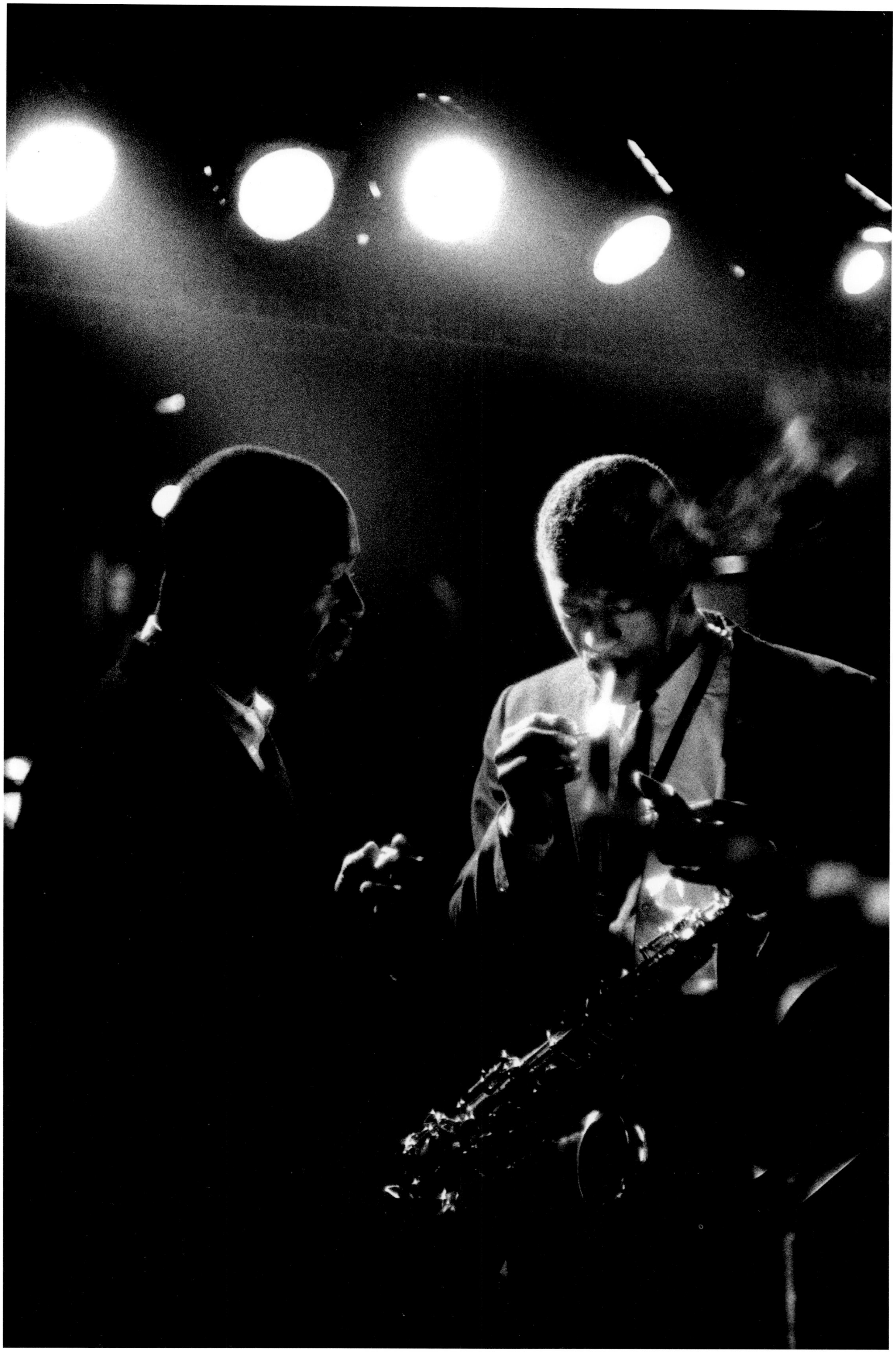

Backstage, the Metronome
New York City · 1960

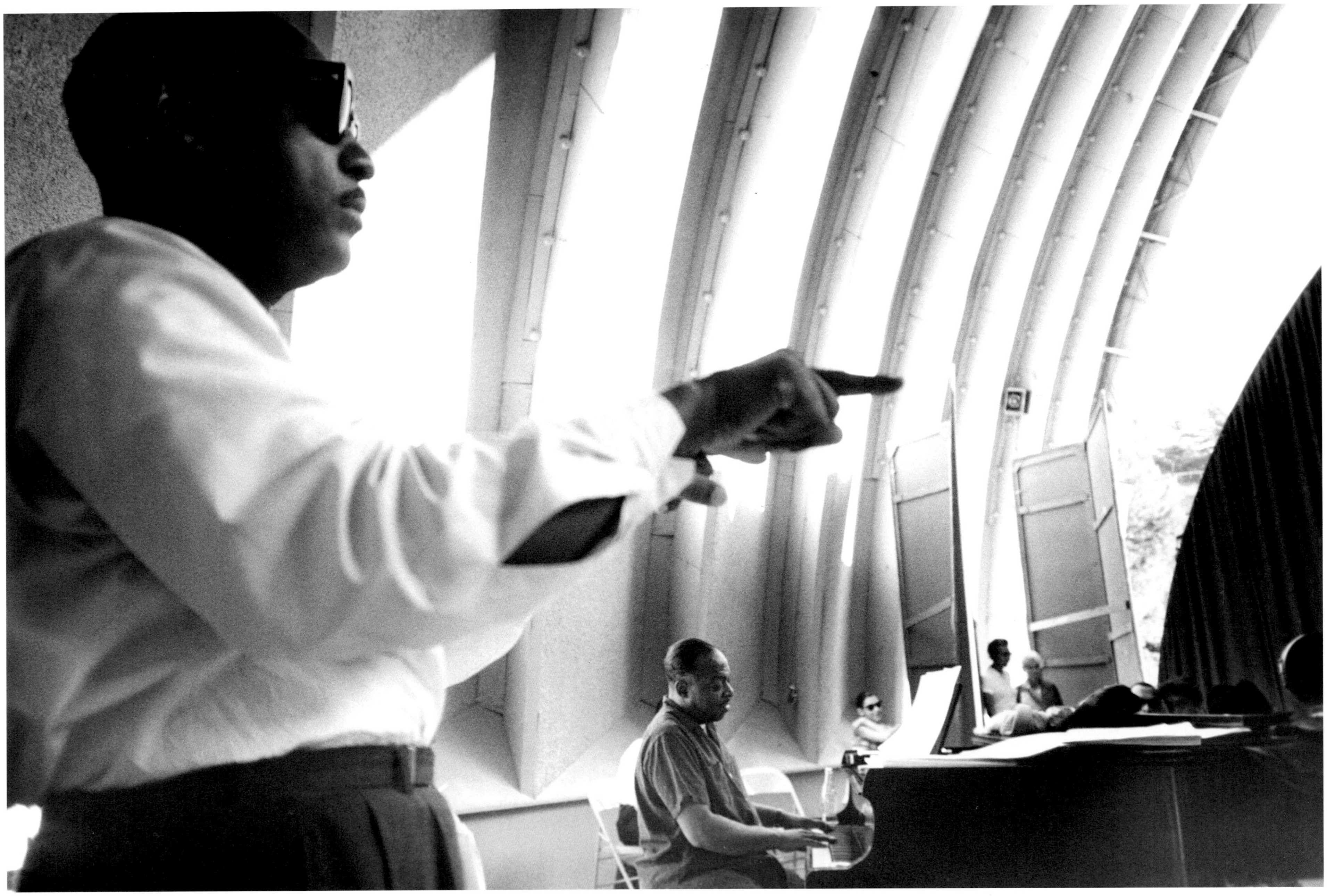

 Benny Carter with the Count Basie Band Hollywood · 1959

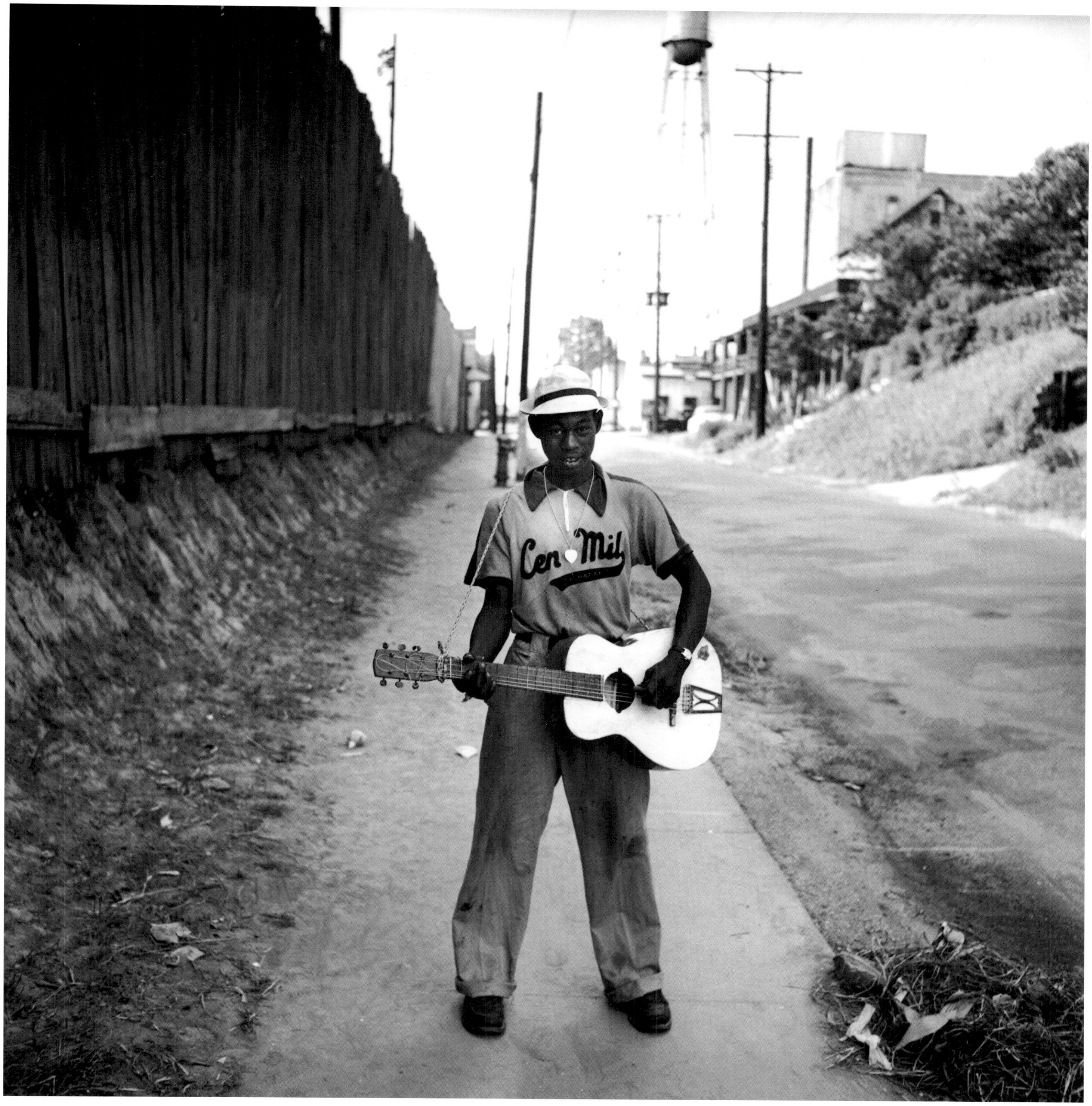

Joe L. Person, street musician Memphis · 1960

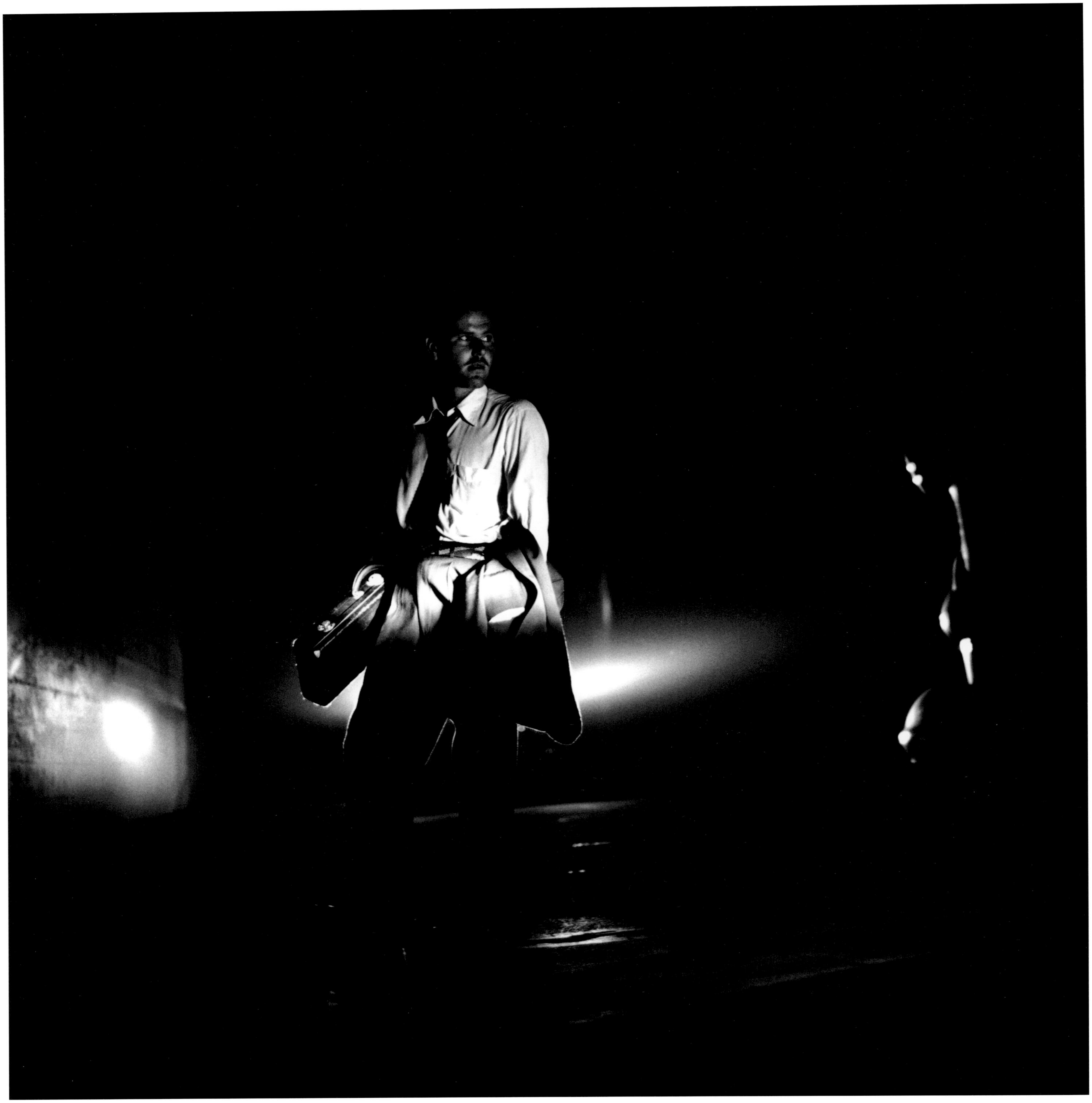

 Jack Sheldon Hollywood · 1955

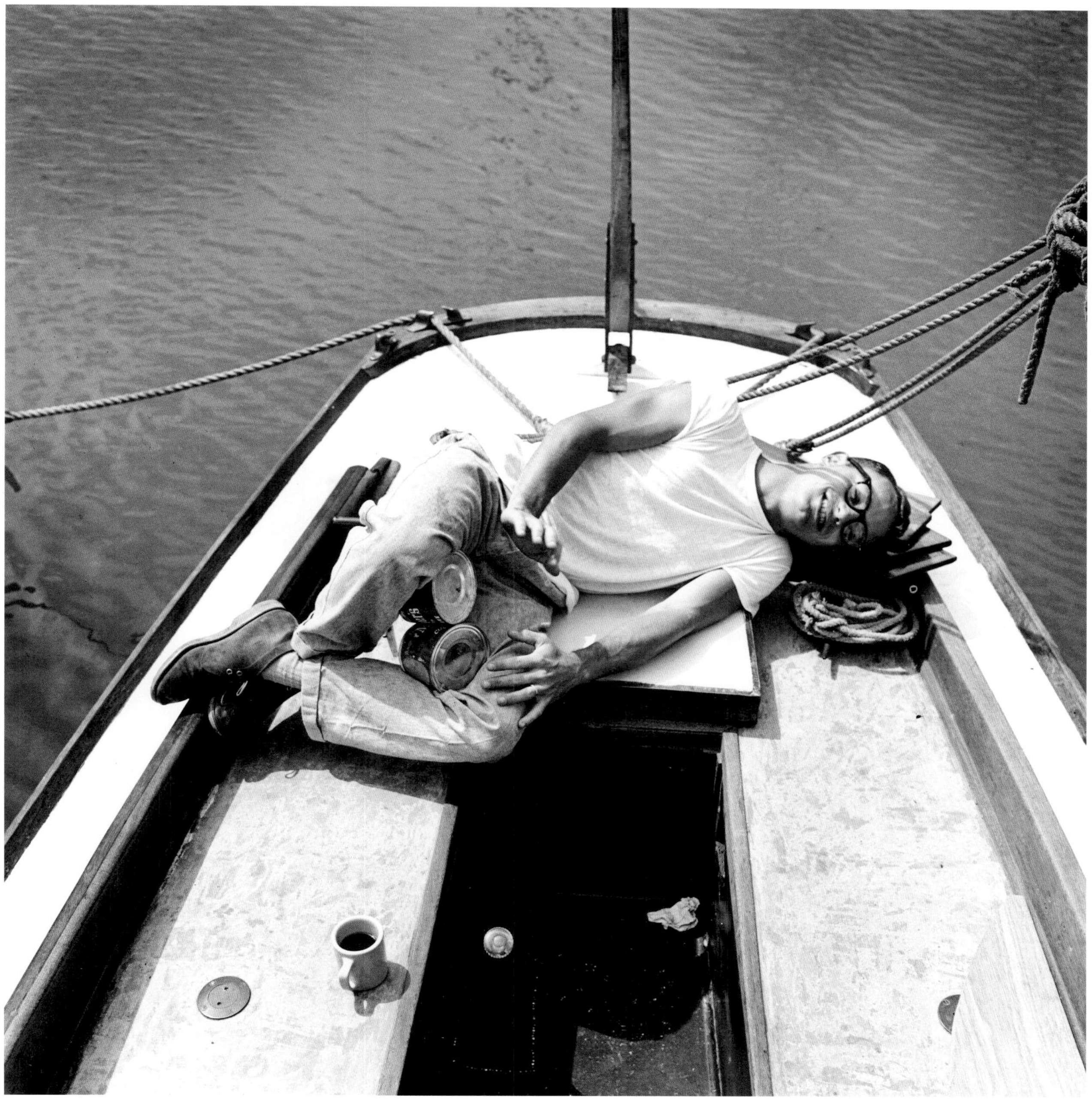

Cal Tjader Sausalito · 1955

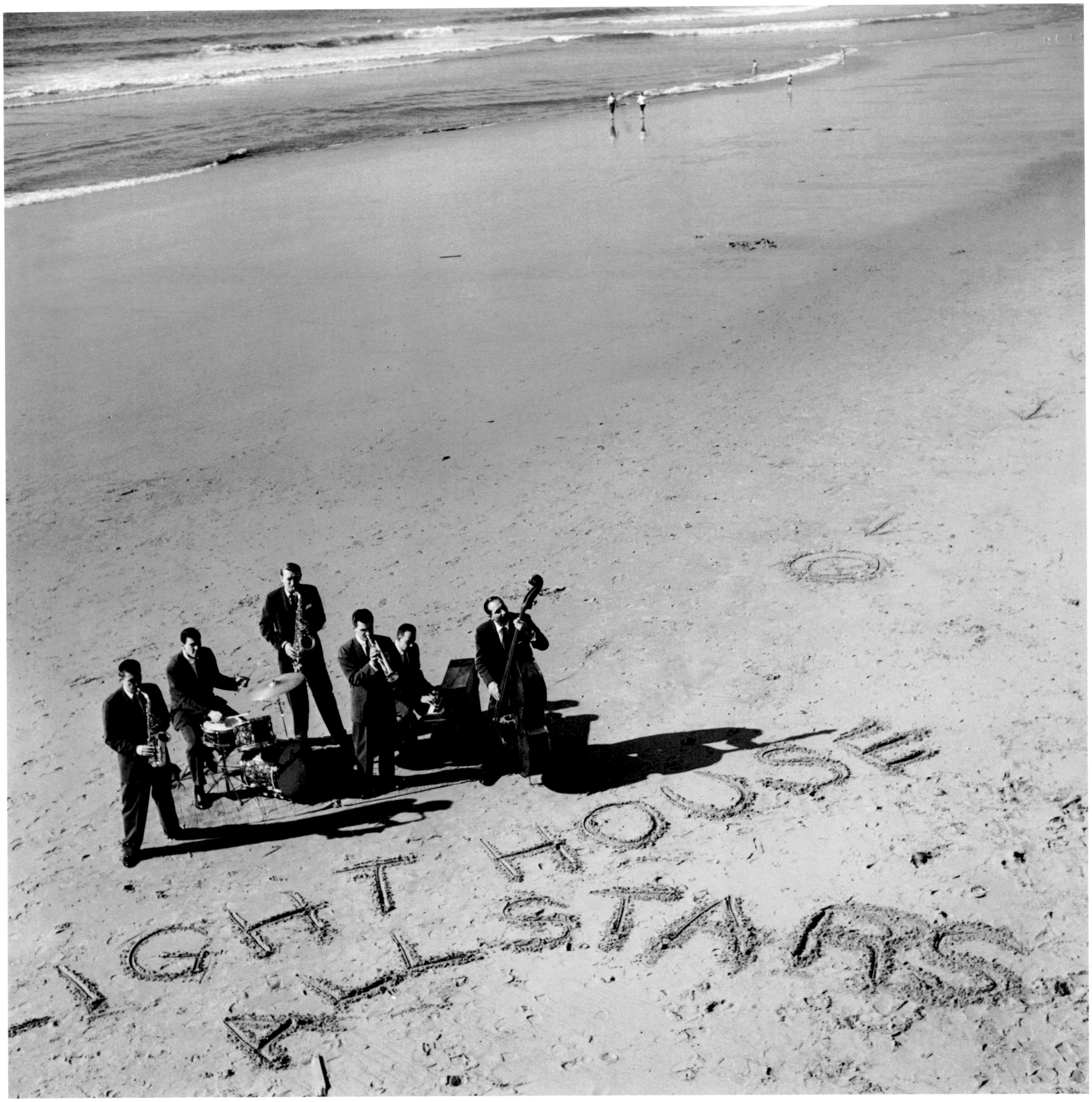

The Lighthouse Allstars Hermosa Beach · 1955

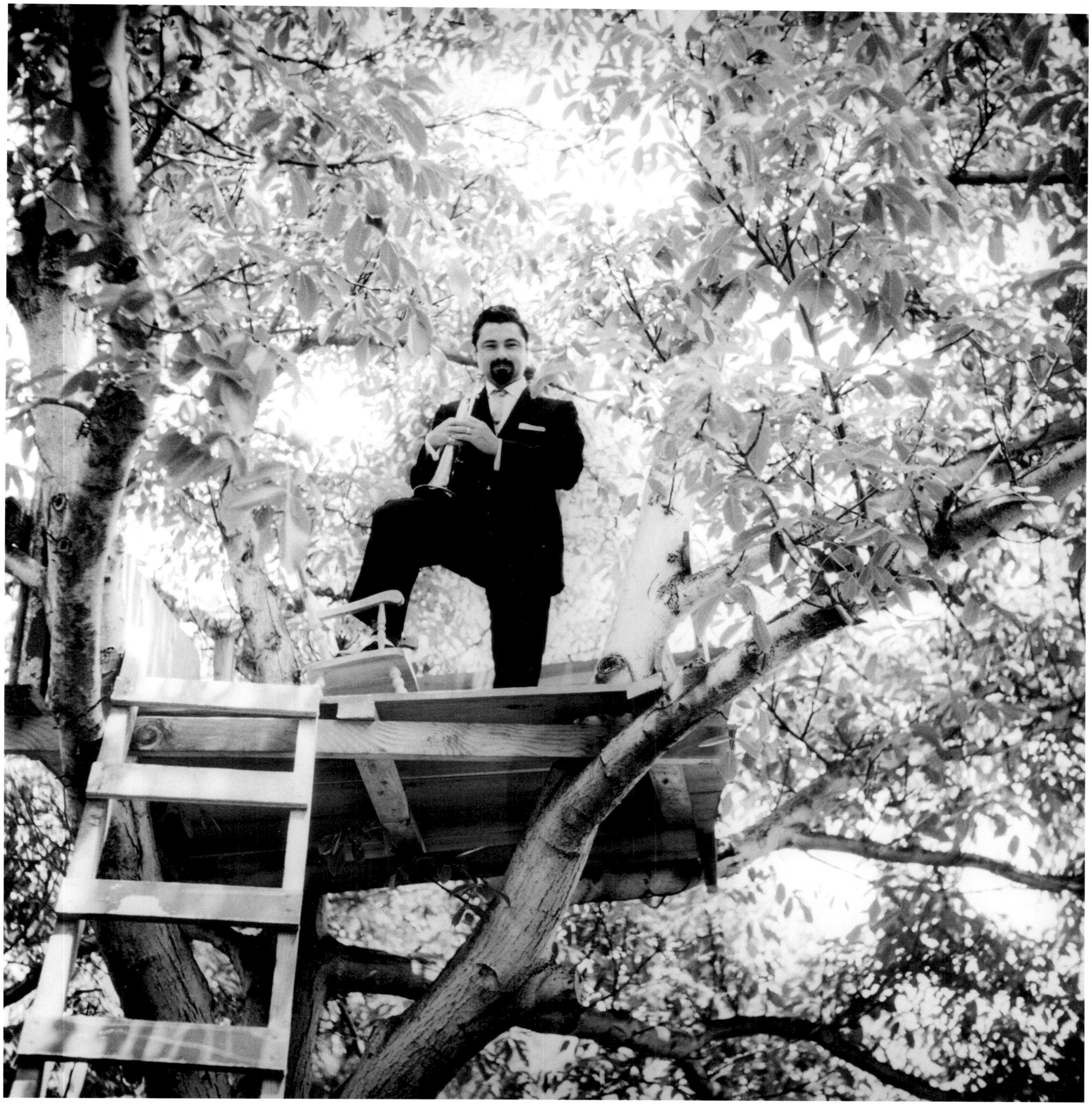

Shorty Rogers North Hollywood · 1955

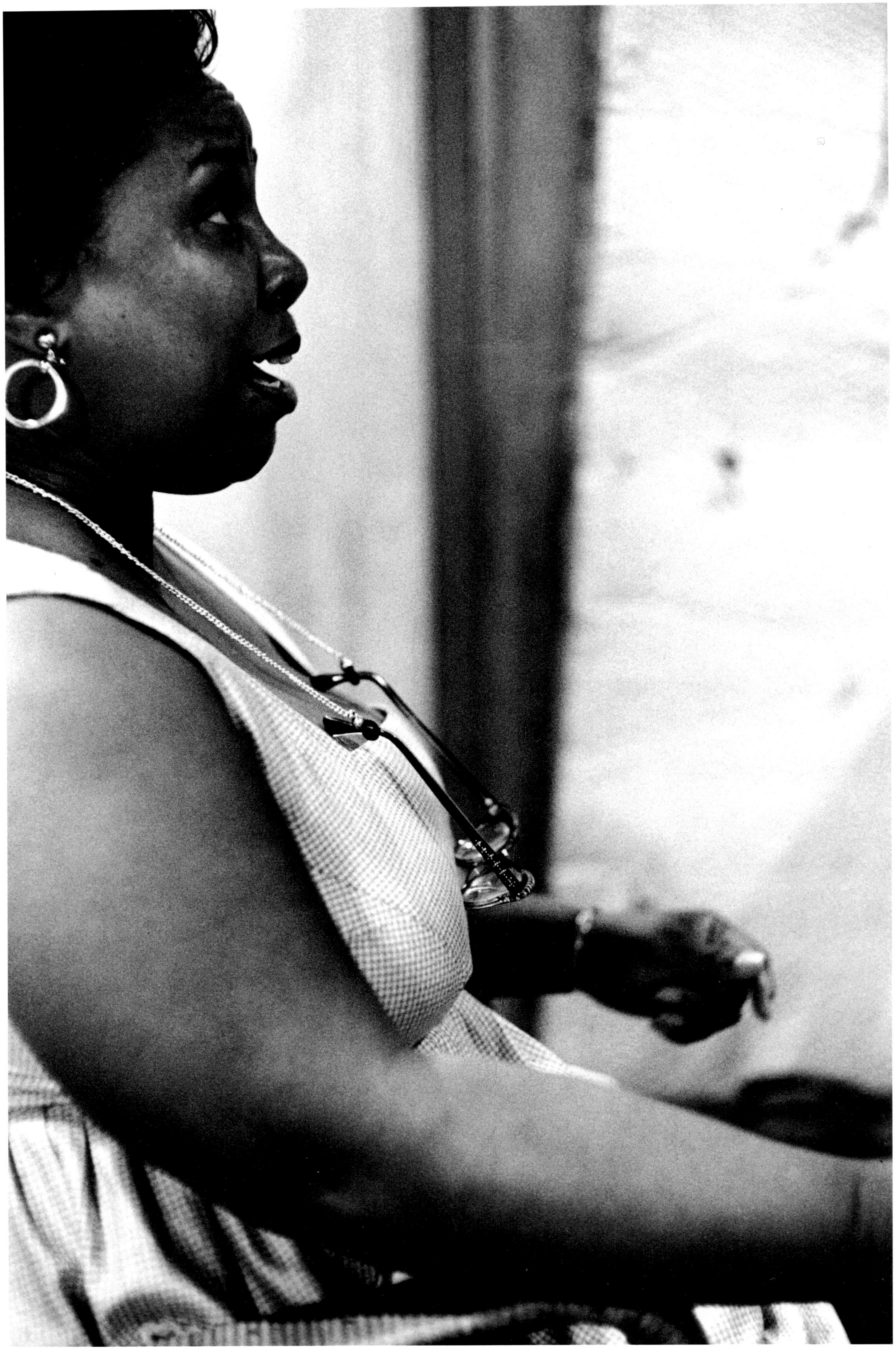

Helen Humes
Los Angeles · 1955

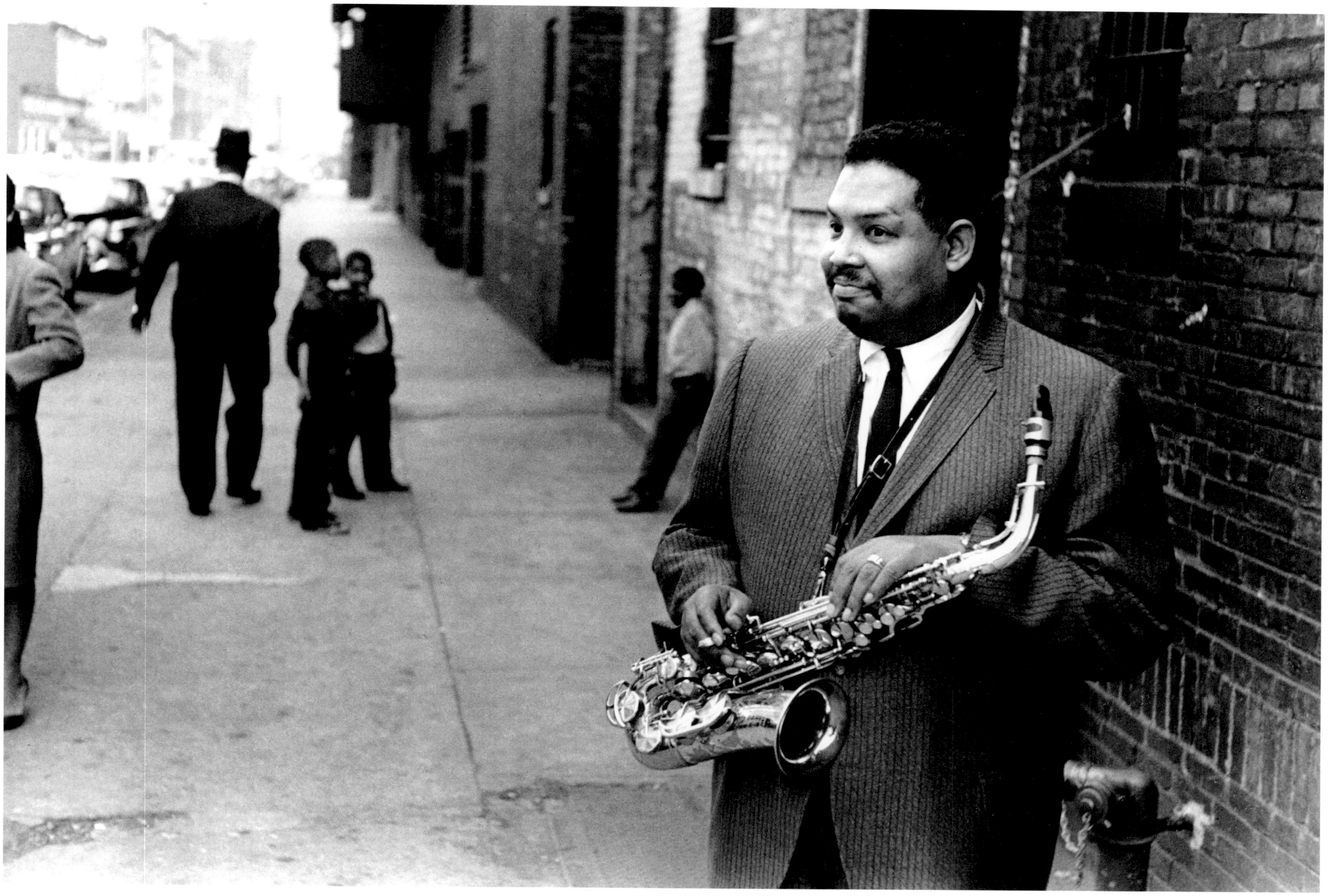

"Cannonball" Adderley New York City · 1960

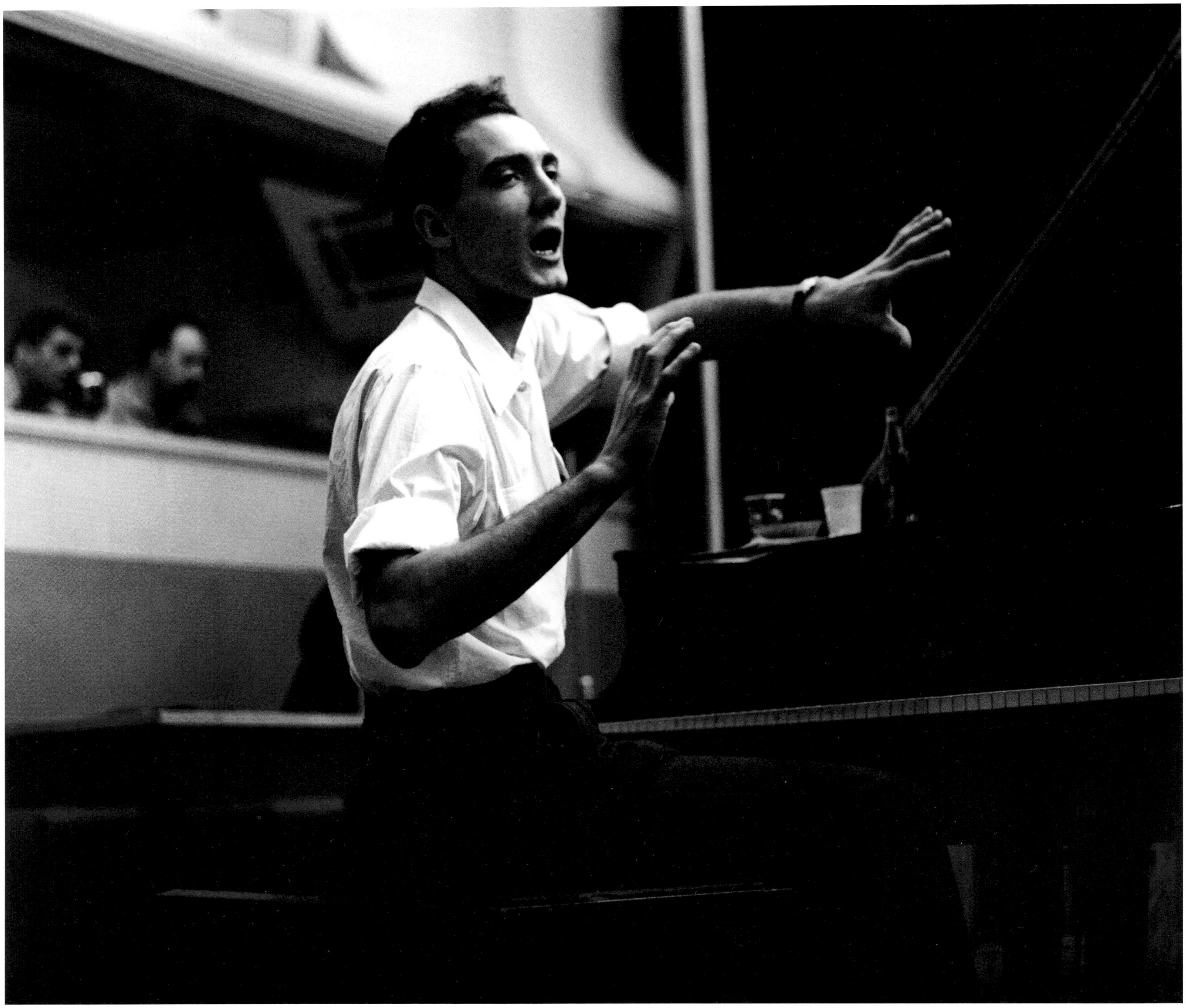

 Walter Norris Hollywood · 1954

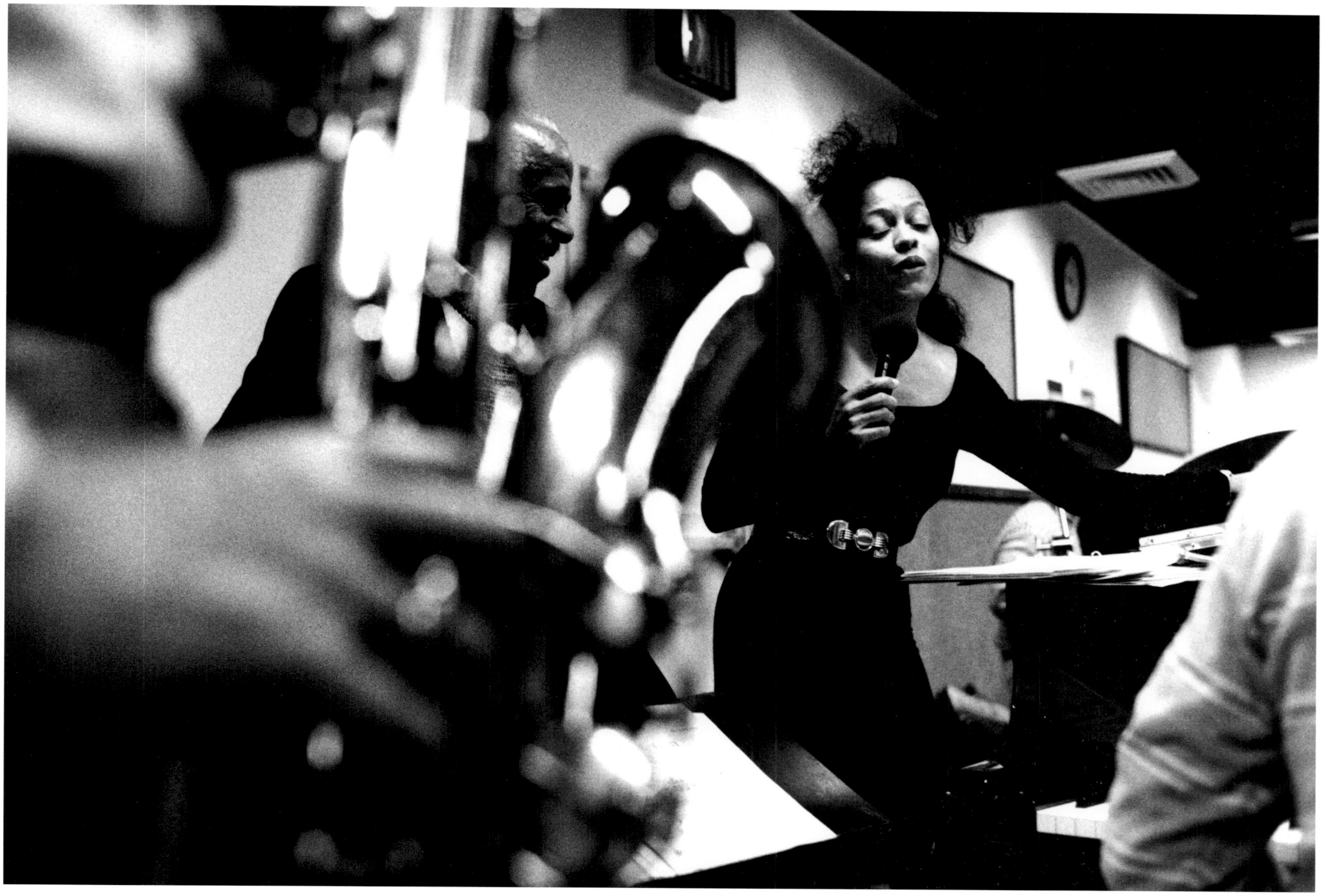

Diana Ross New York City · 1993

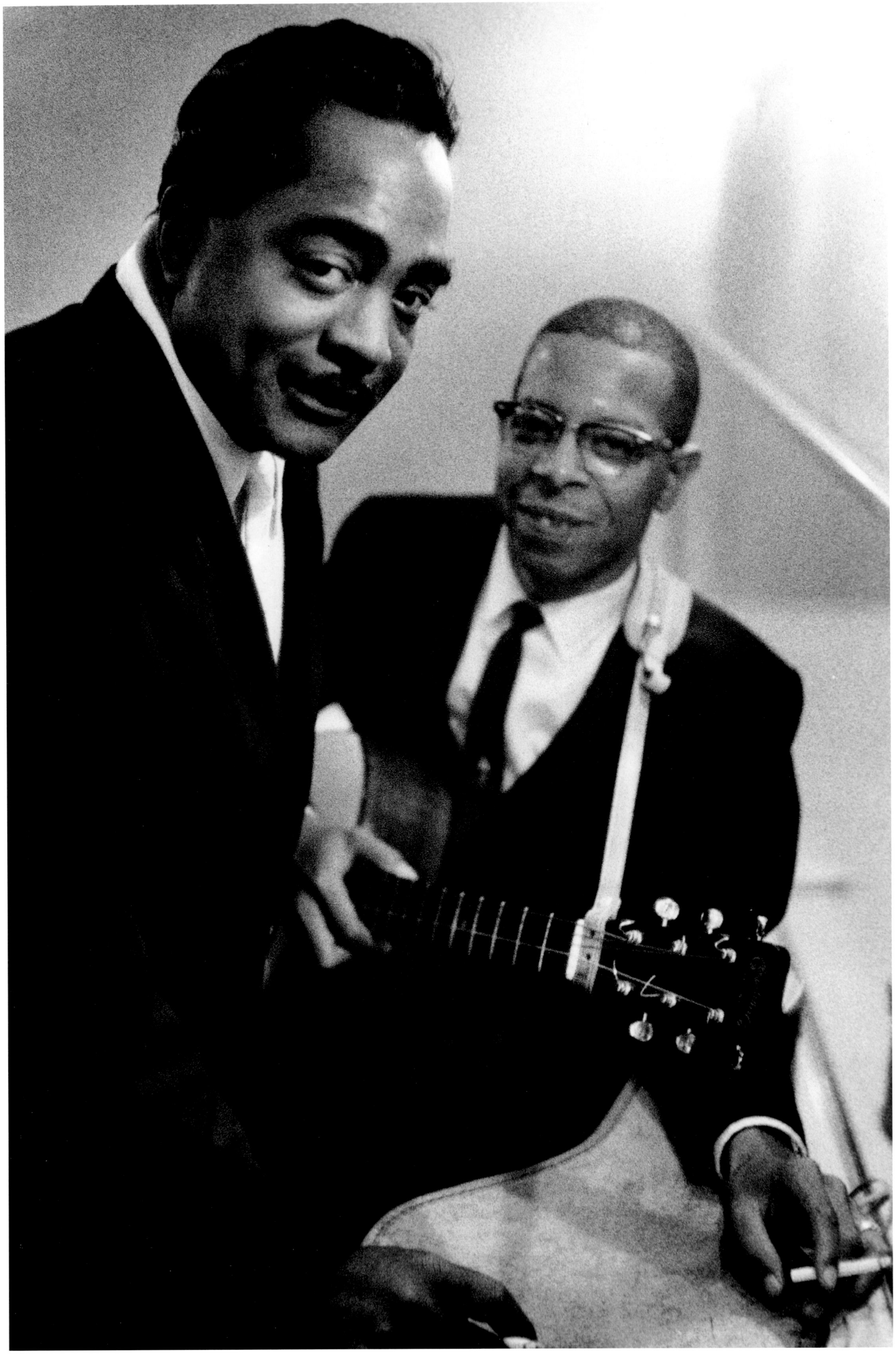

Jimmy Witherspoon
and Sonny Kenner *(guitar)*
Hollywood · 1960

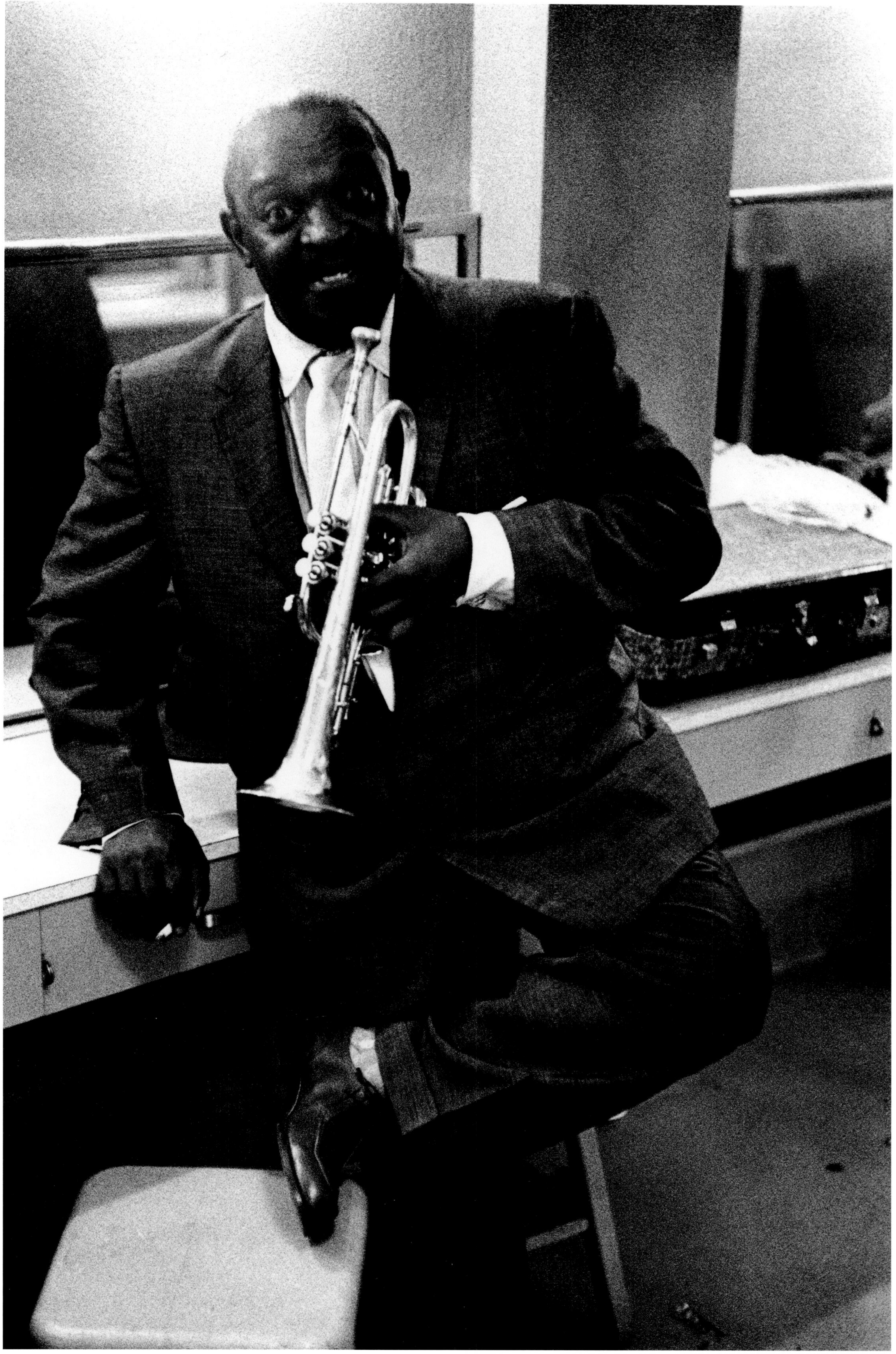

Rex Stewart
Hollywood · 1960

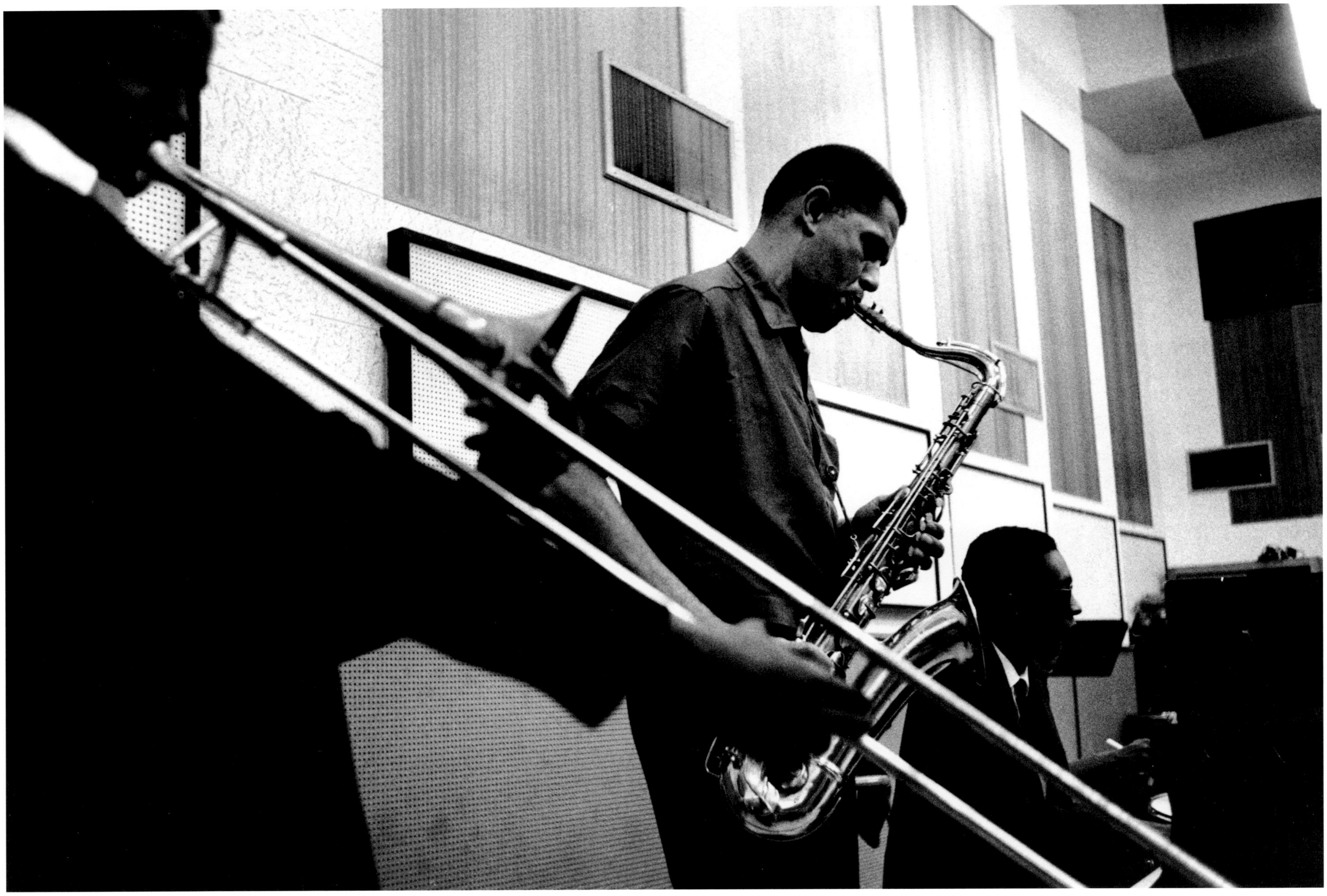

 Dexter Gordon, Dolo Coker ***(piano)*****, Martin Banks** ***(trombone)*** Hollywood · 1957

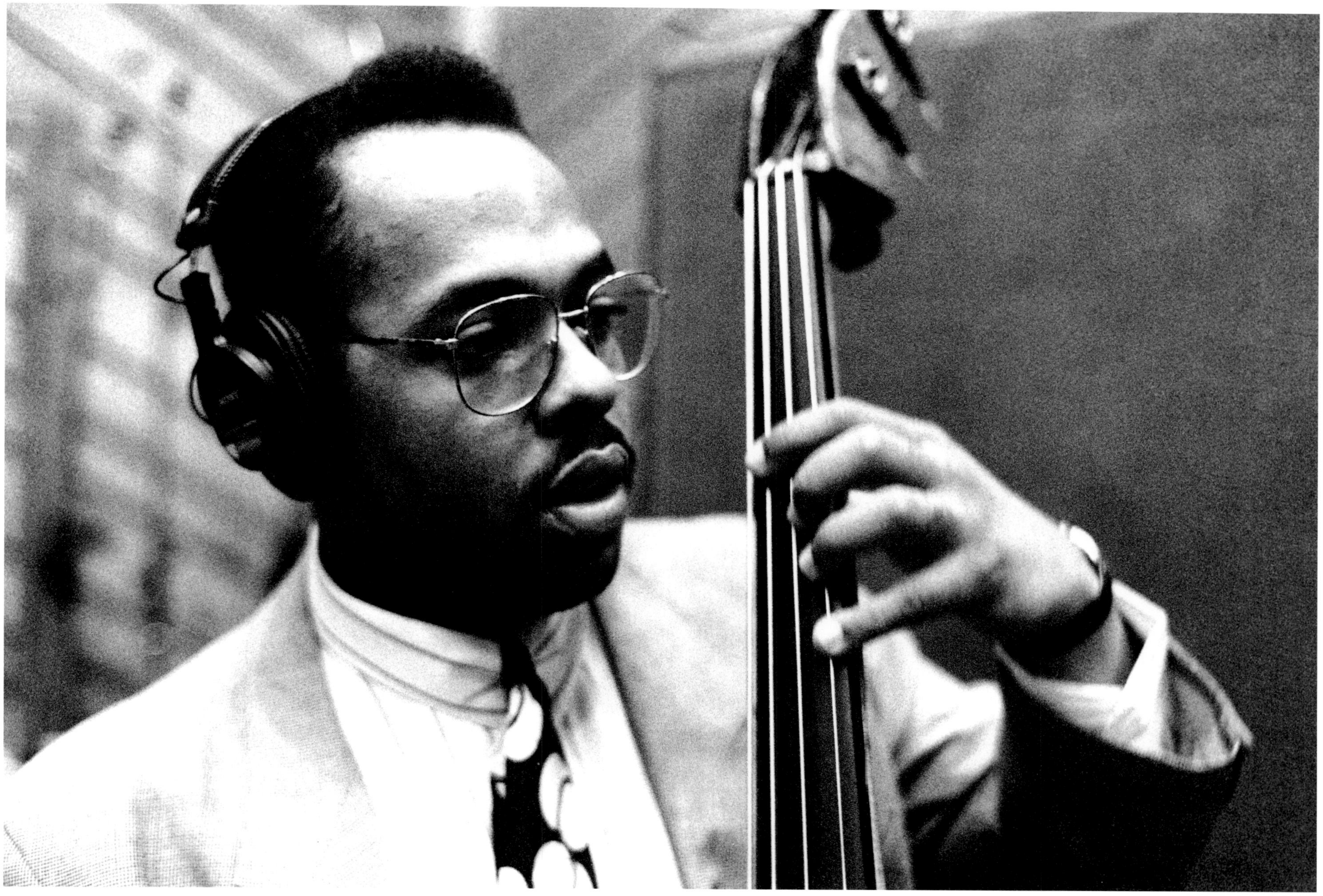

Christian McBride New York City · 1993

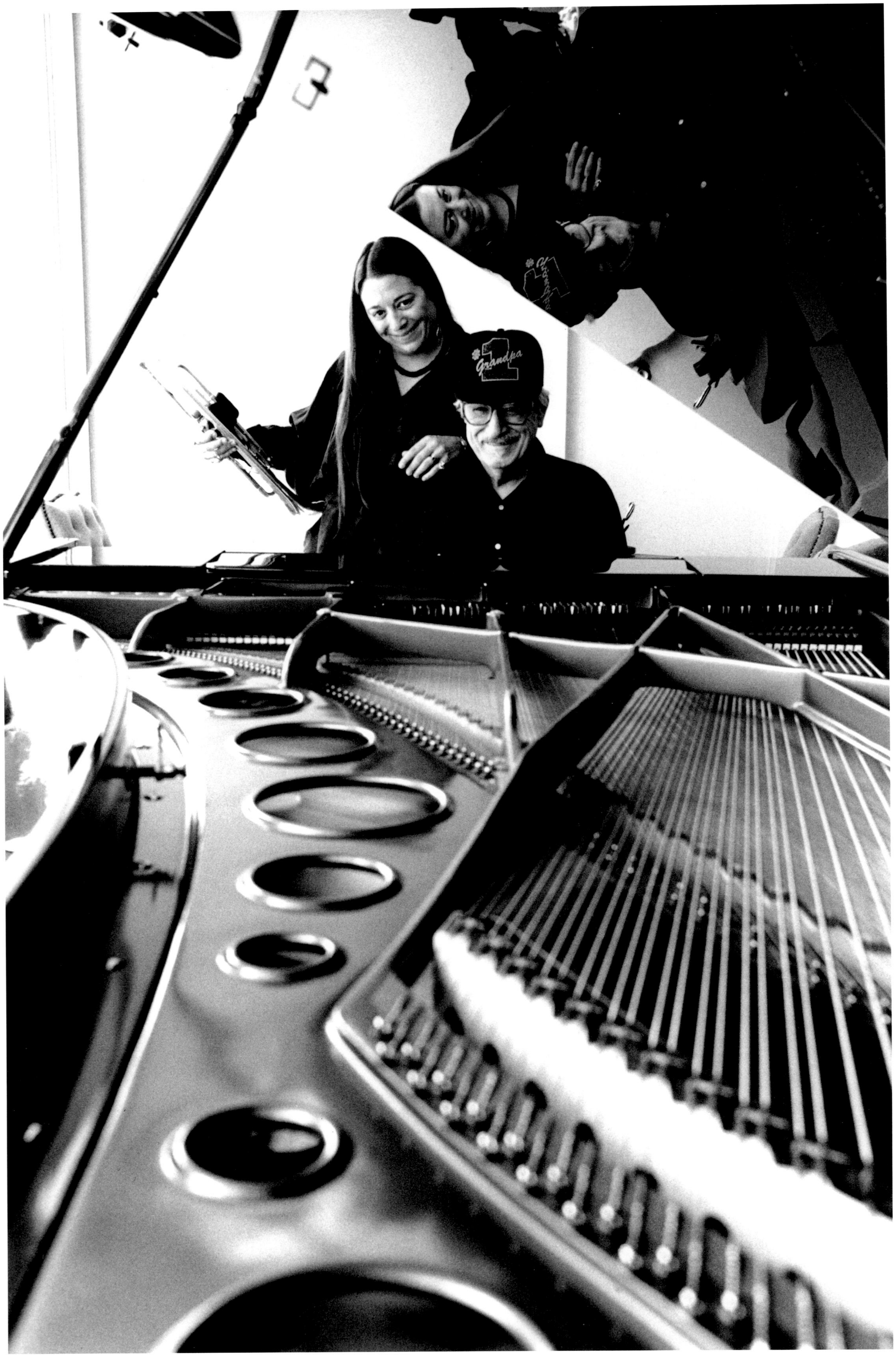

Stacy Rowles *(trumpet)*
and Jimmy Rowles
Los Angeles · 1990

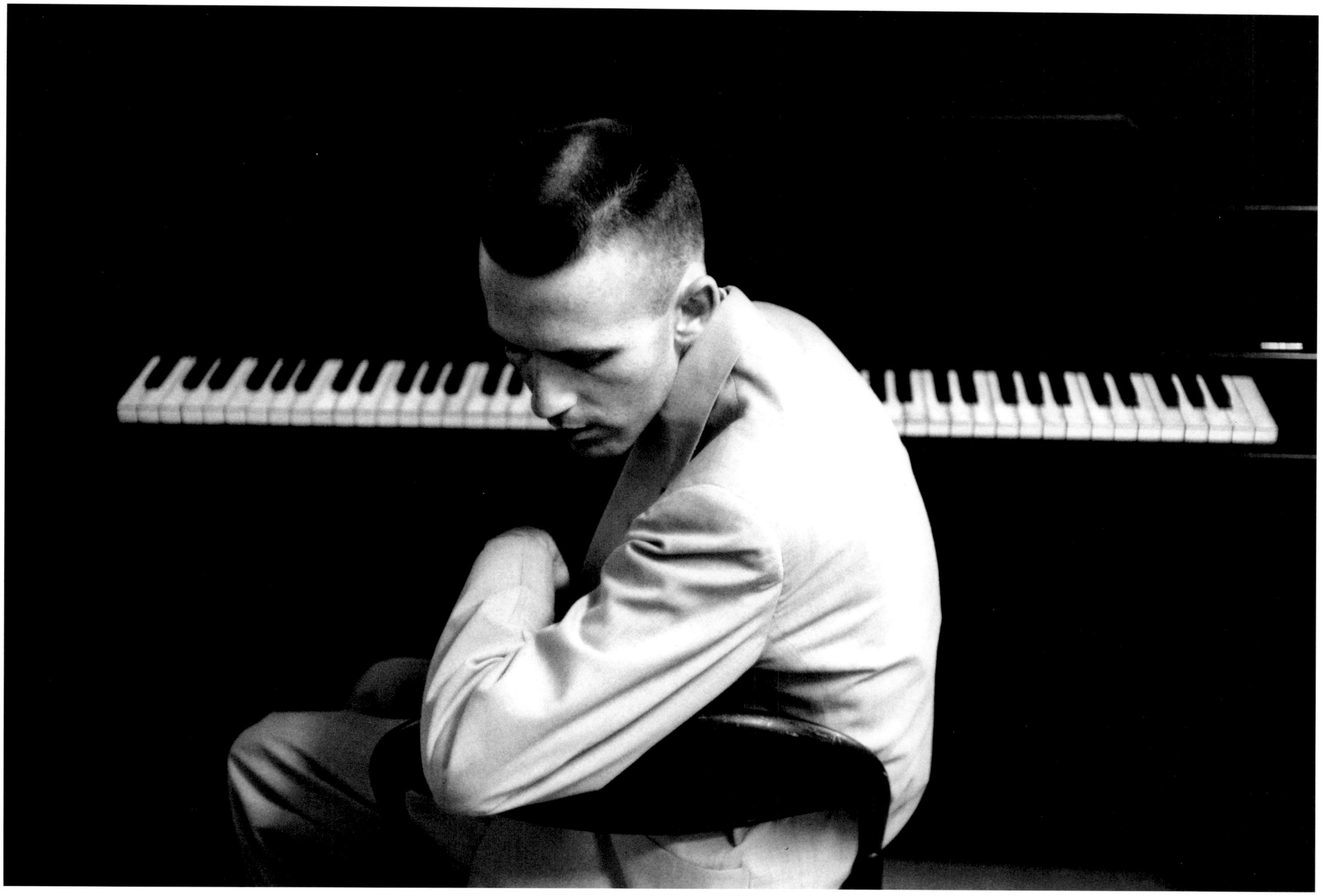

Young pianist Washington D.C. · 1960

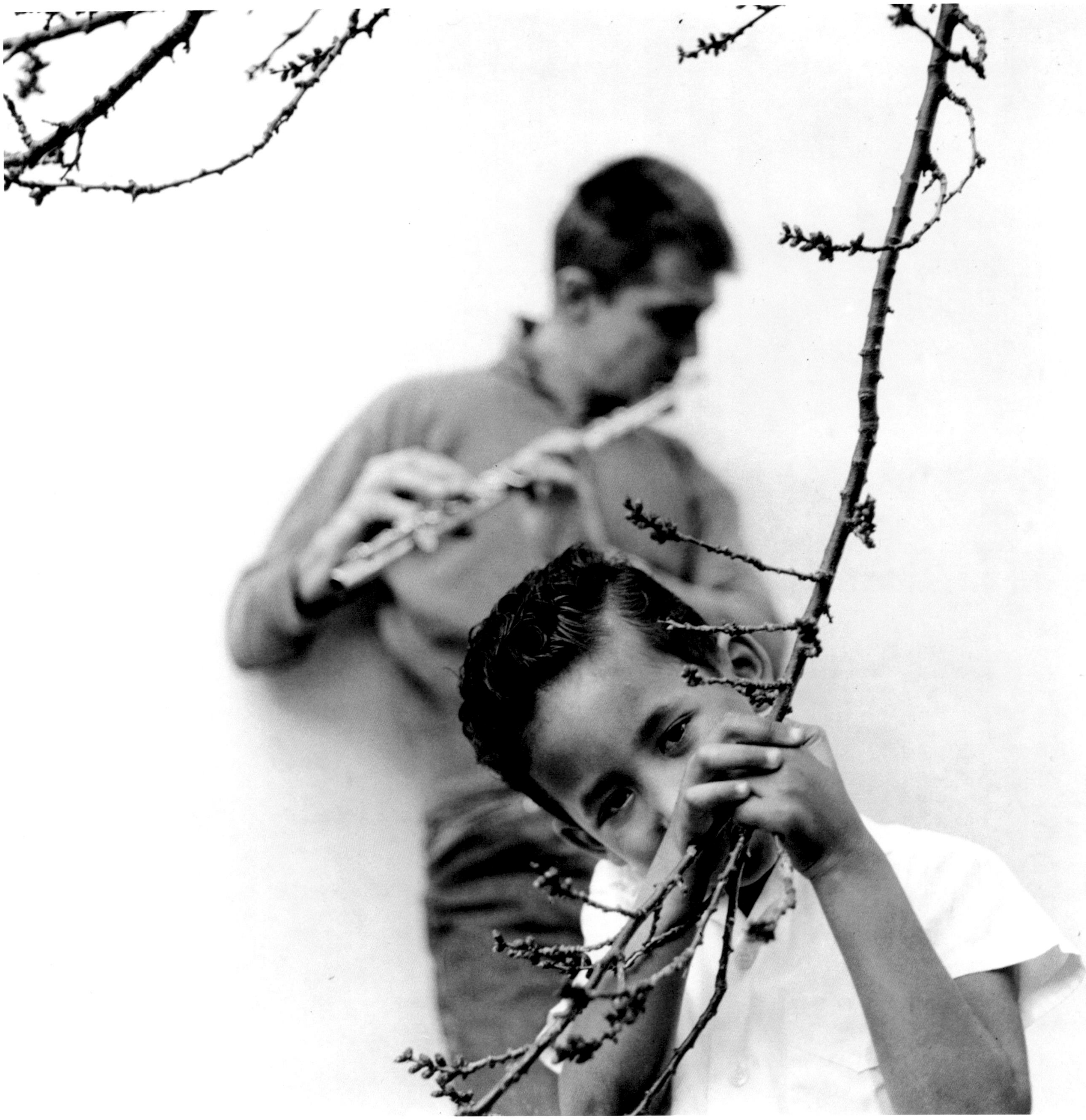

 Bud Shank and young boy North Hollywood · 1956

Art Pepper Los Angeles · 1956 ▶

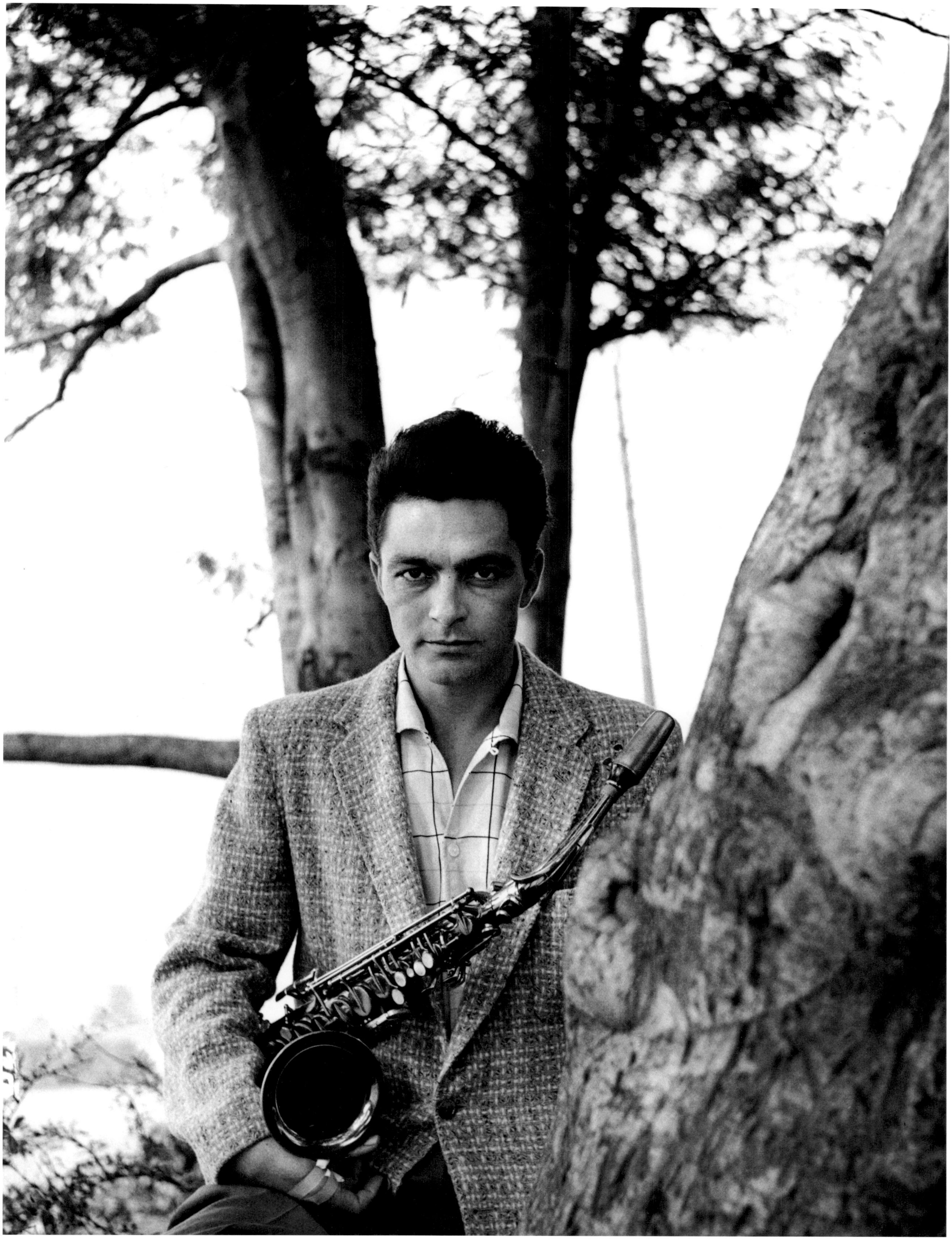

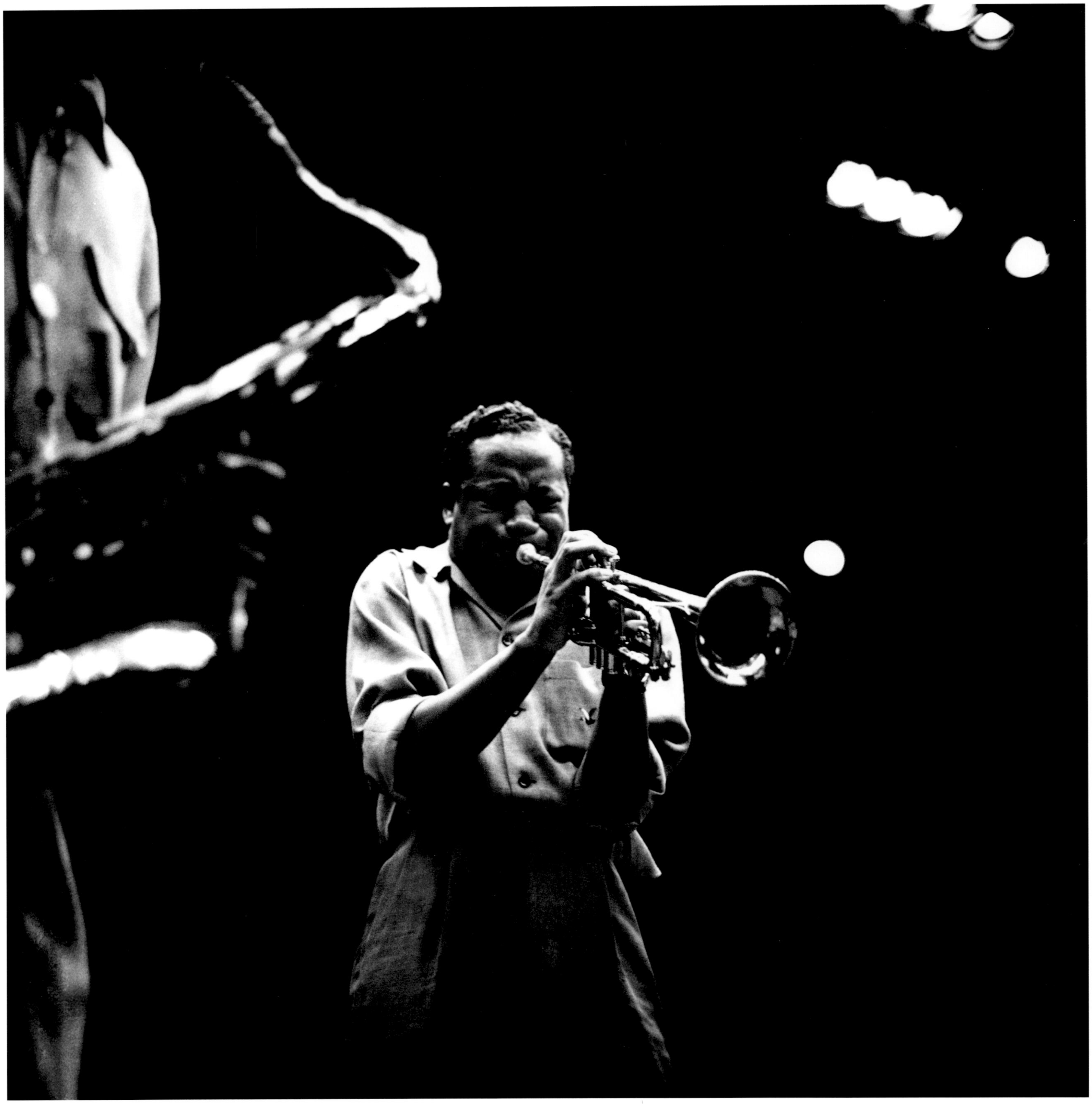

 Clifford Brown Hollywood · 1954

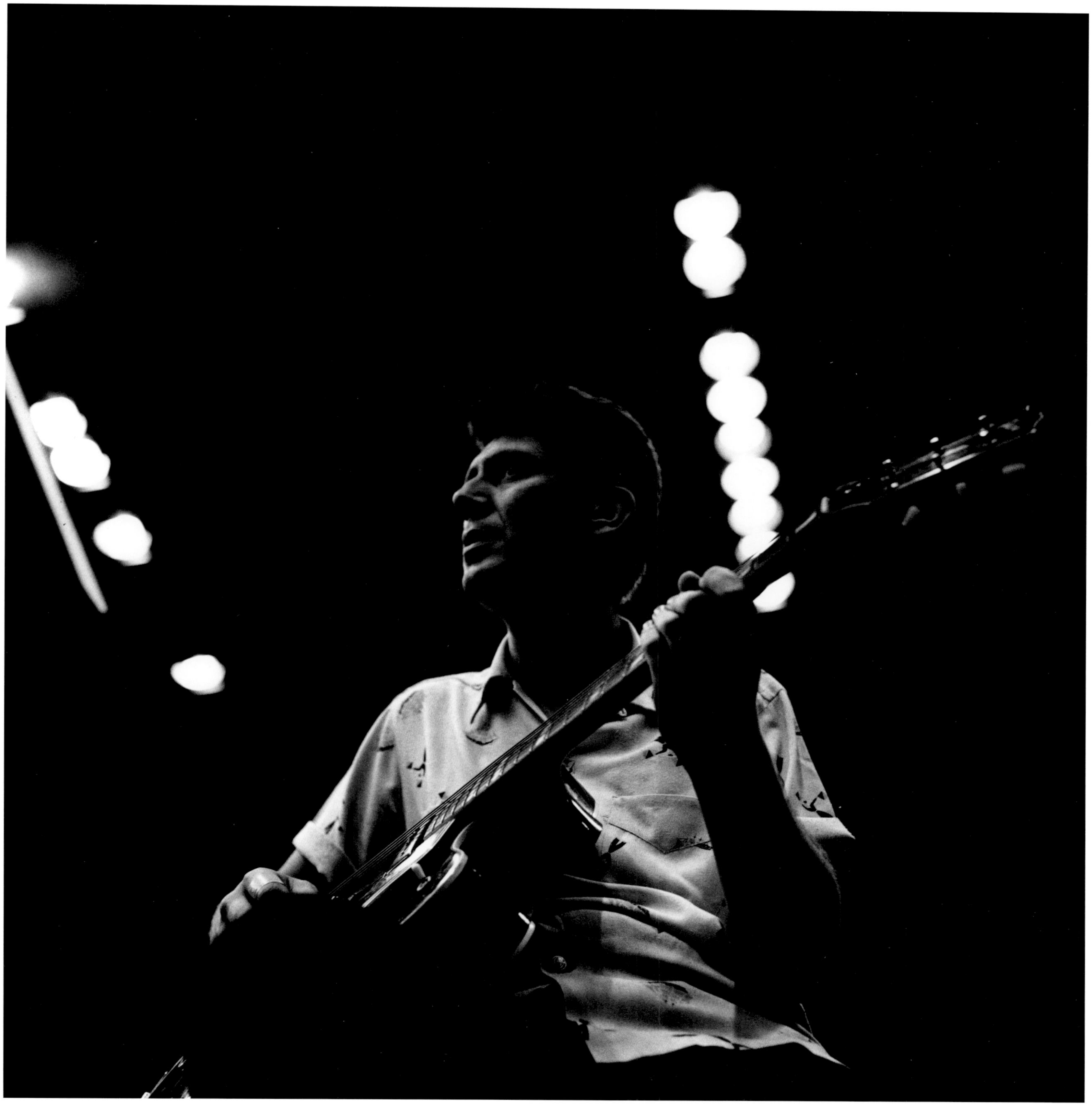

Tal Farlow Hollywood · 1956

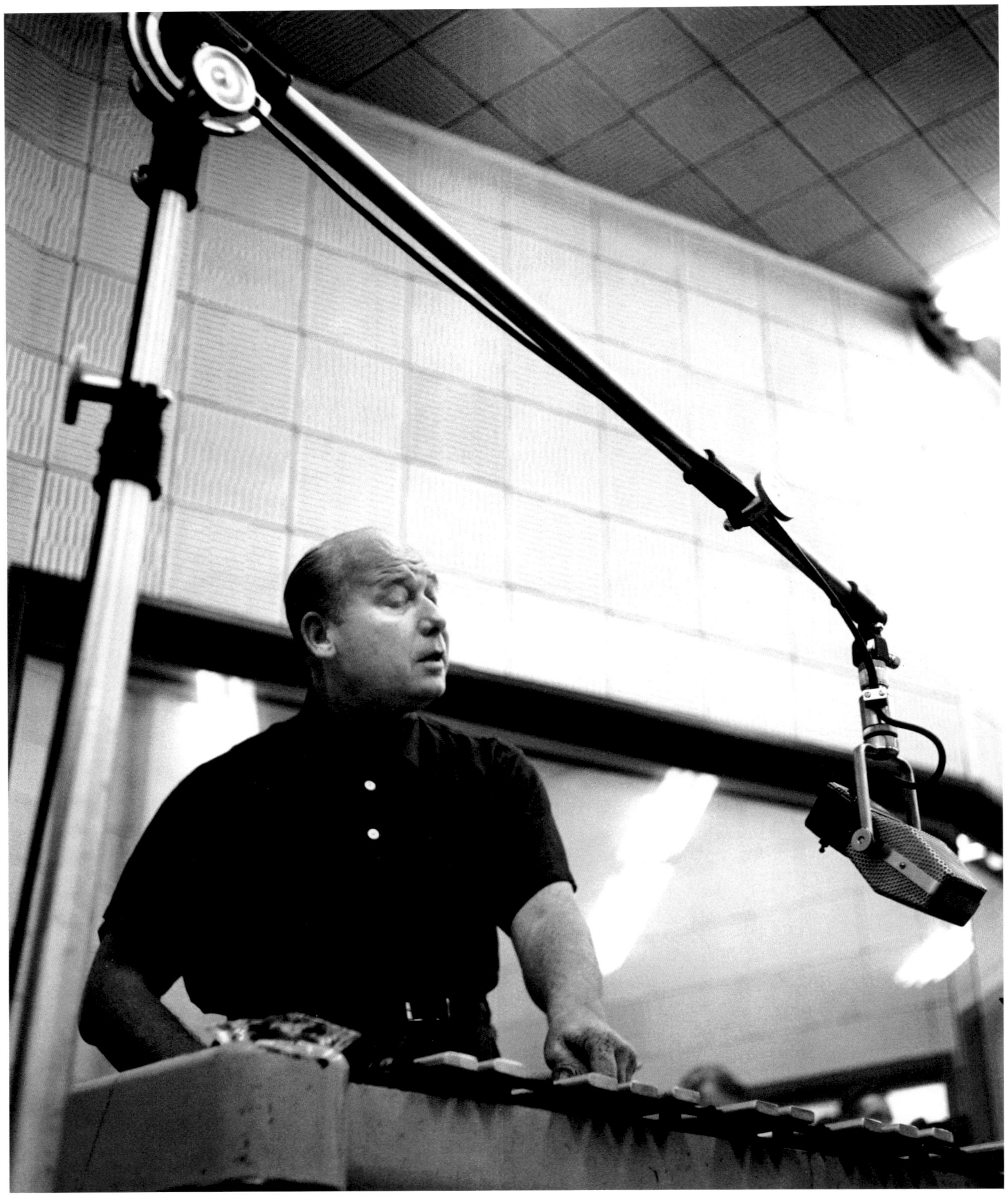

Red Norvo Hollywood · 1954

▶
Zoot Sims and Kenny Drew
Hollywood · 1955

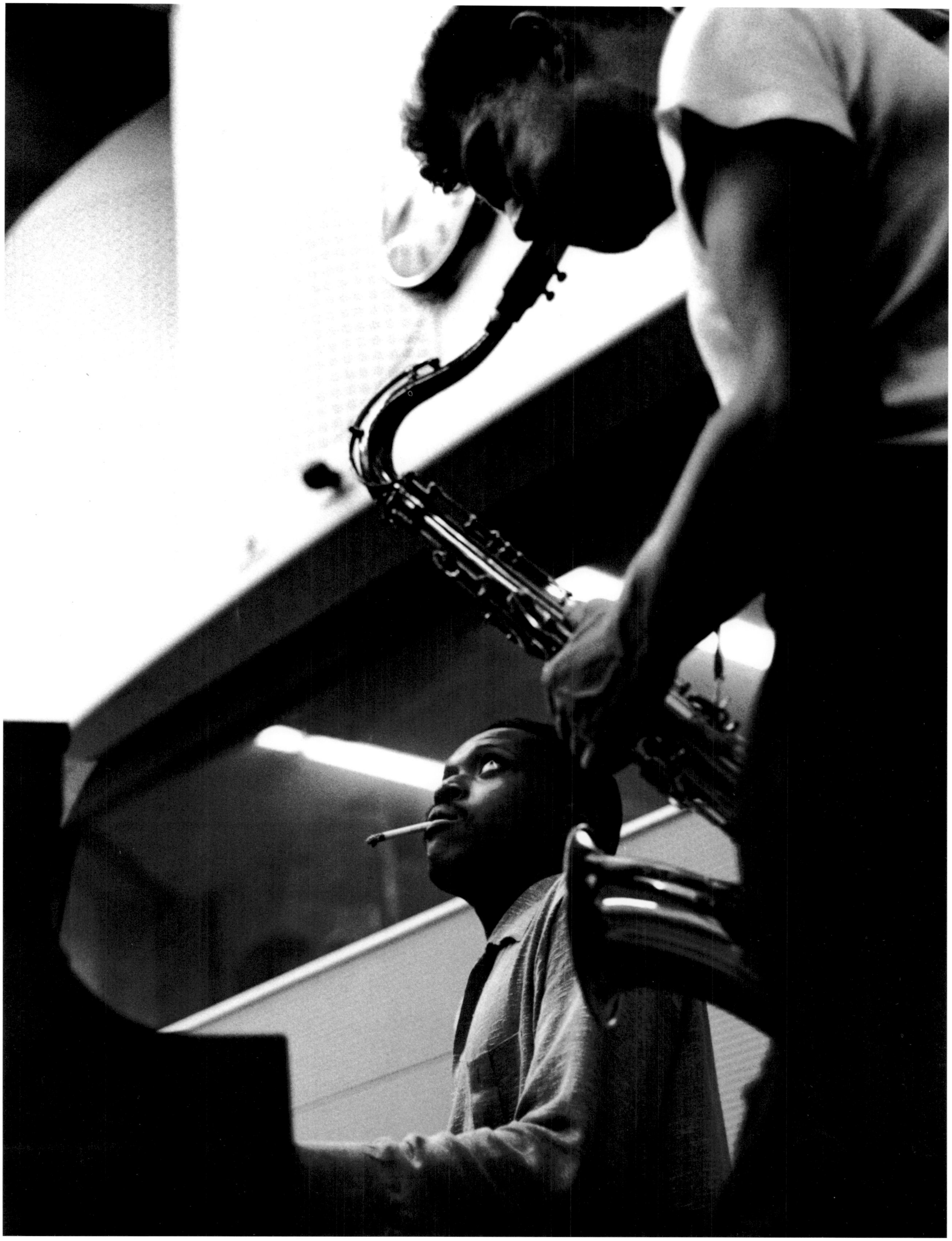

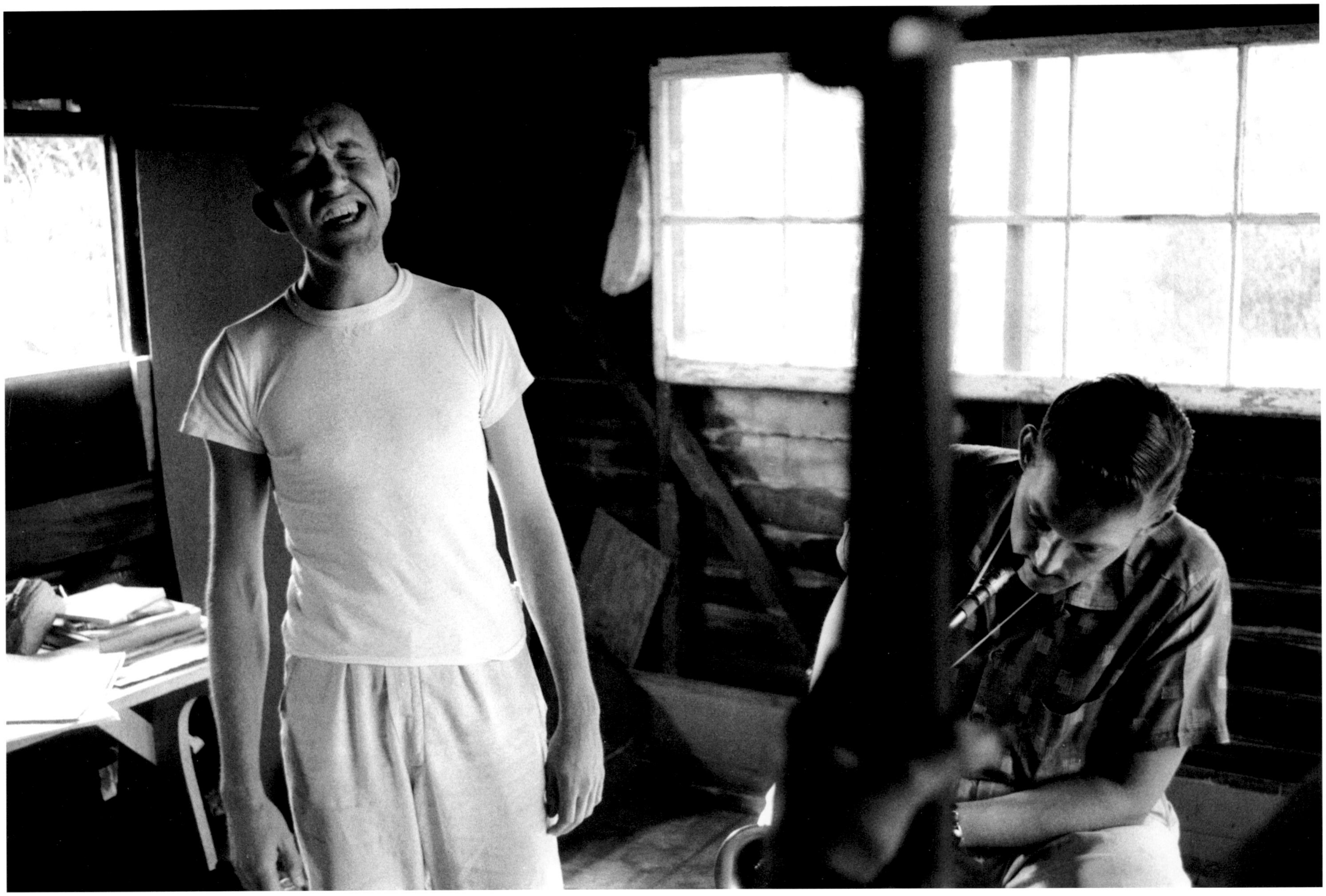

 Bob Dorough and Bob Hardaway ***(tenor sax)*** Los Angeles · 1957

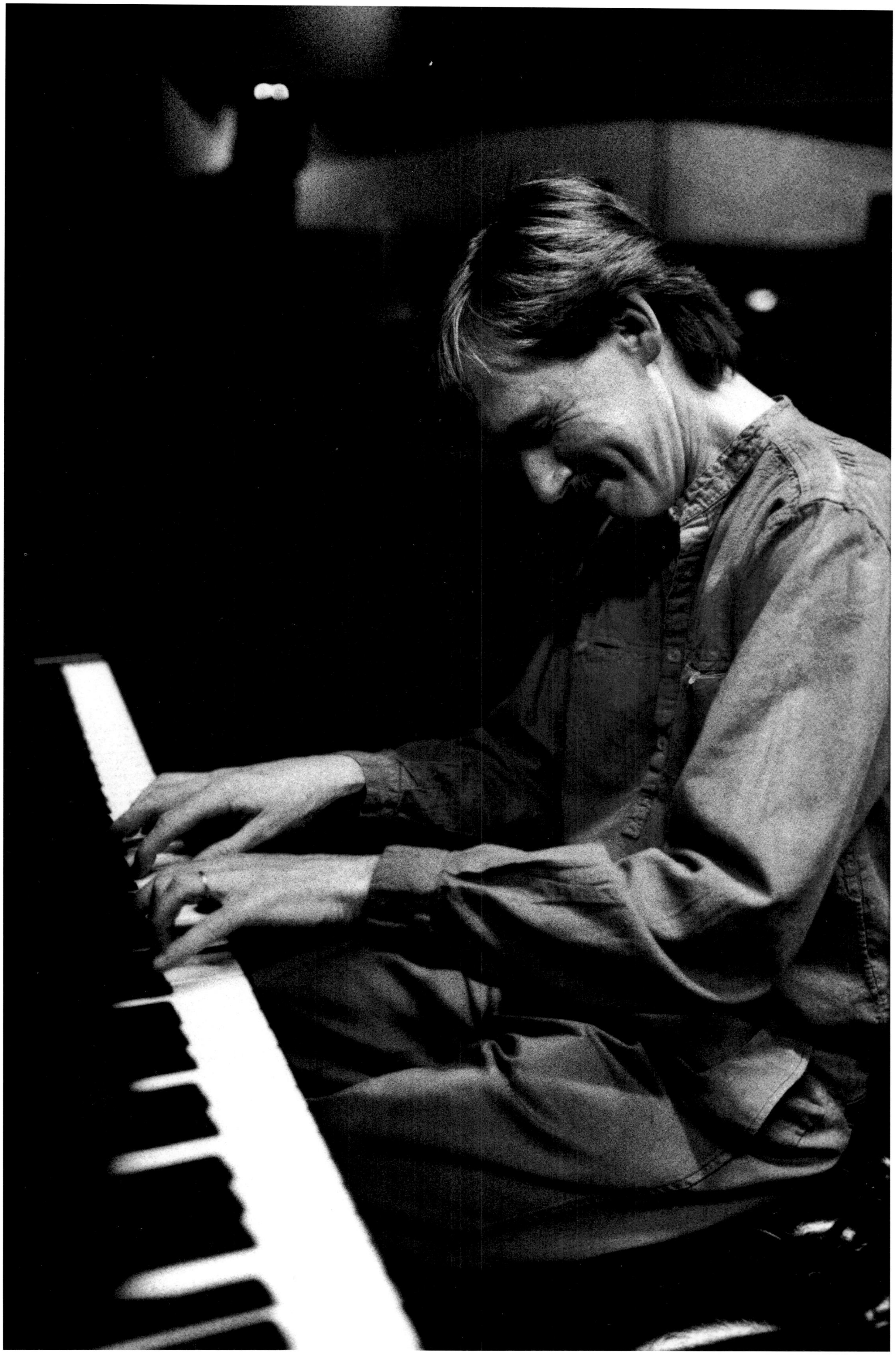

Alan Broadbent
Los Angeles · 1994

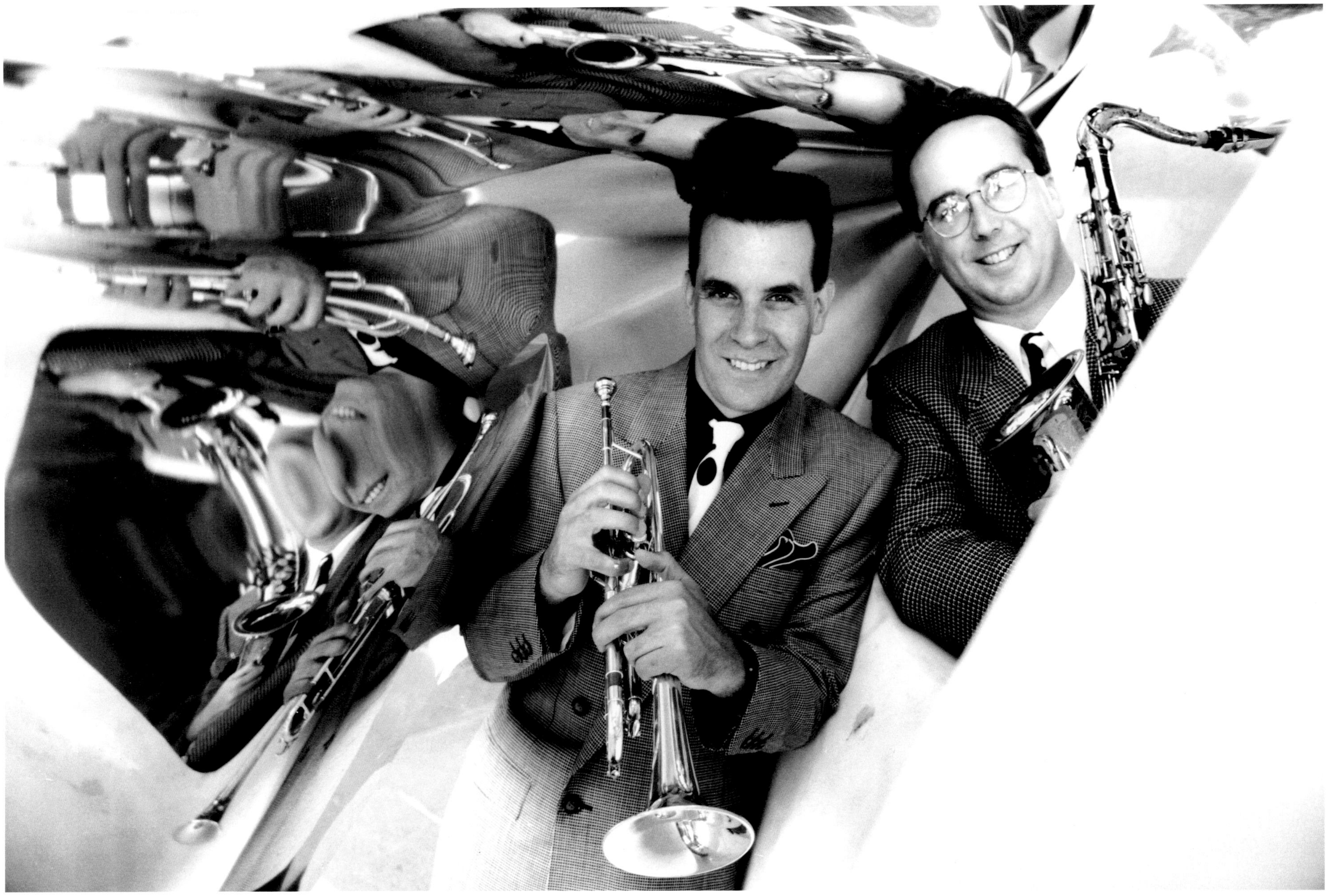

 Dan St. Marseille *(tenor sax)* and Larry Gillespie *(trumpet)* Beverly Hills · 1992

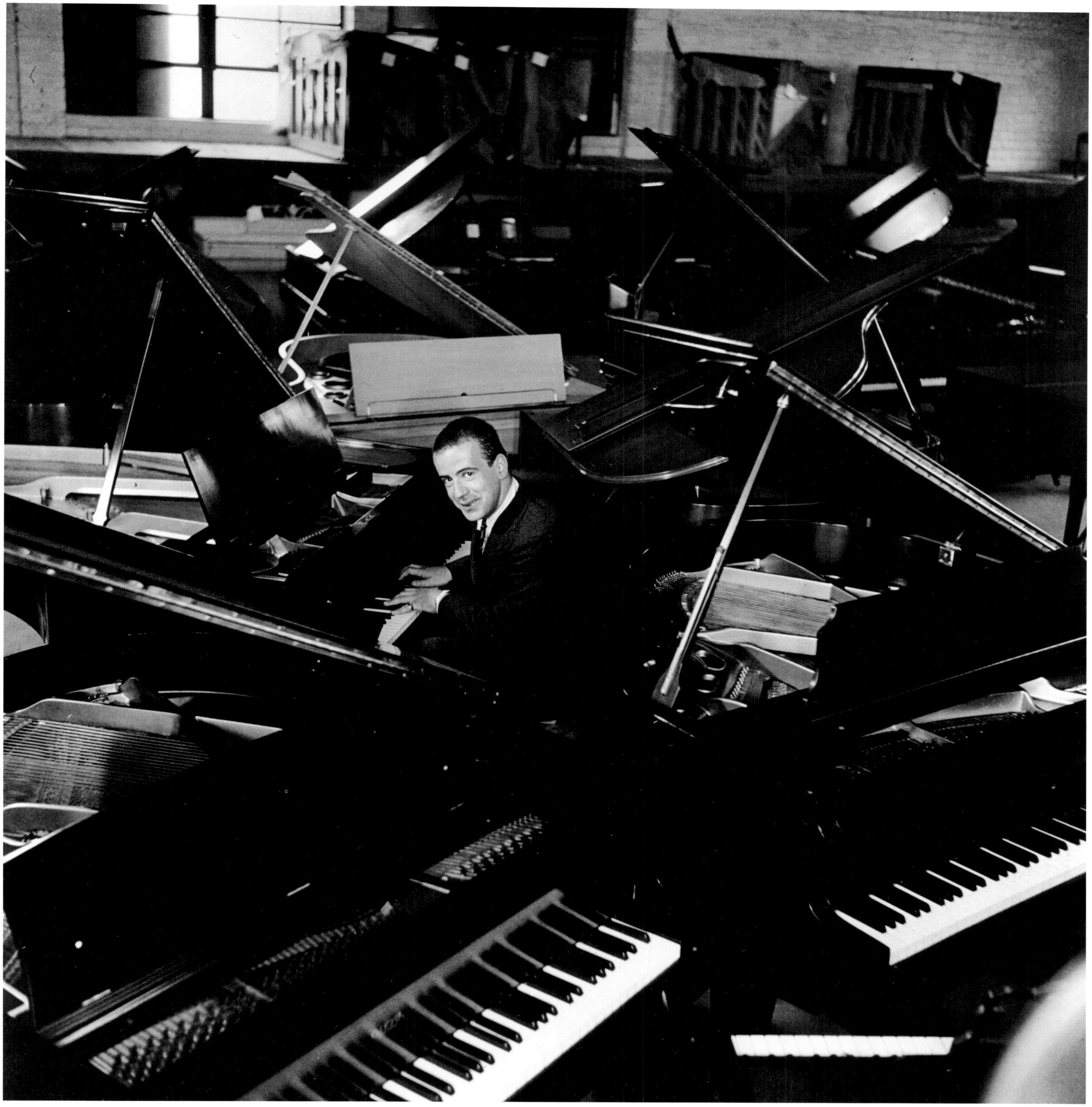

Pete Jolly Los Angeles · 1956

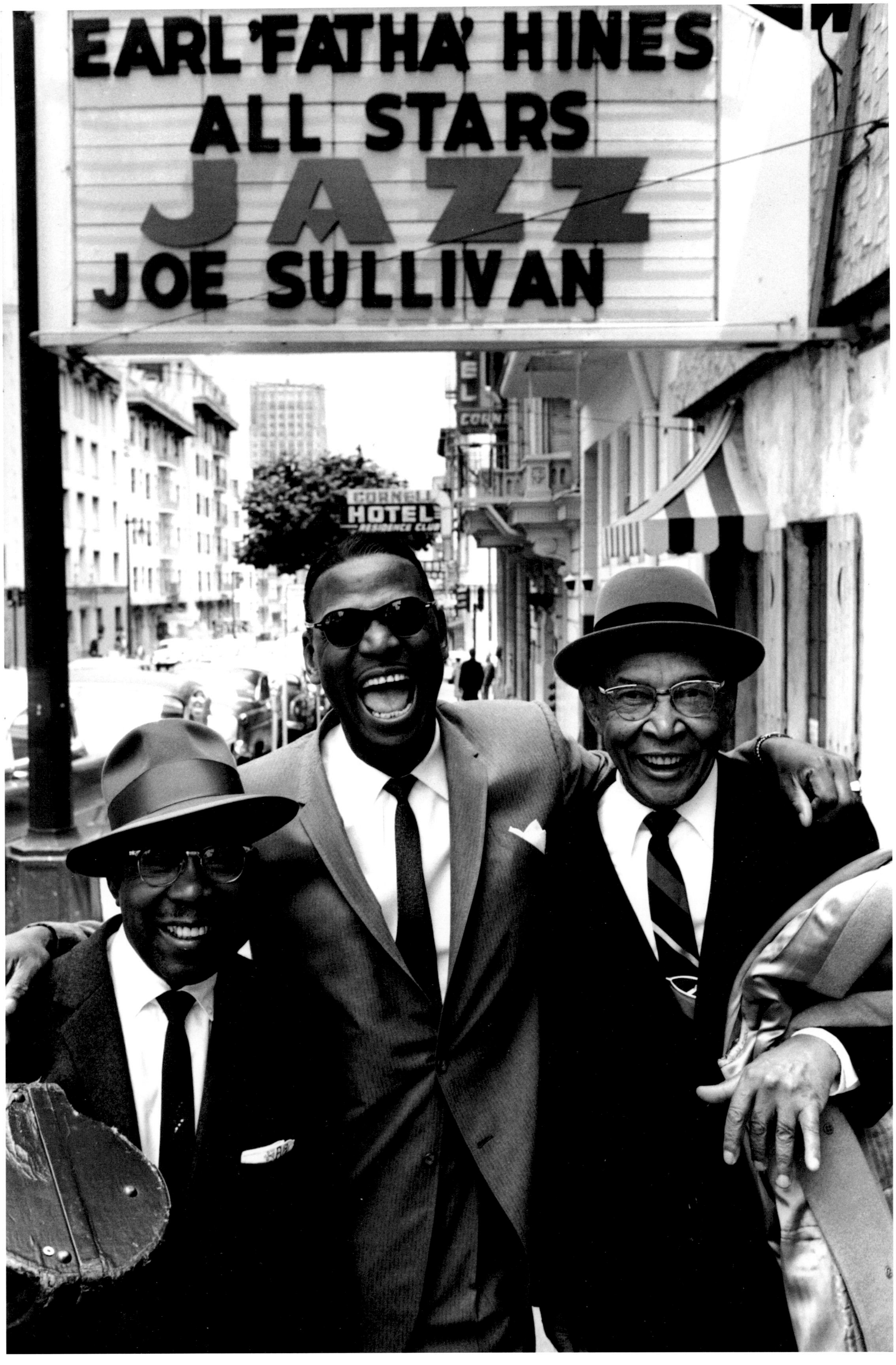

Earl "Fatha" Hines *(center)*,
Jimmy Archey *(left)*,
Pops Foster *(right)*
San Francisco · 1960

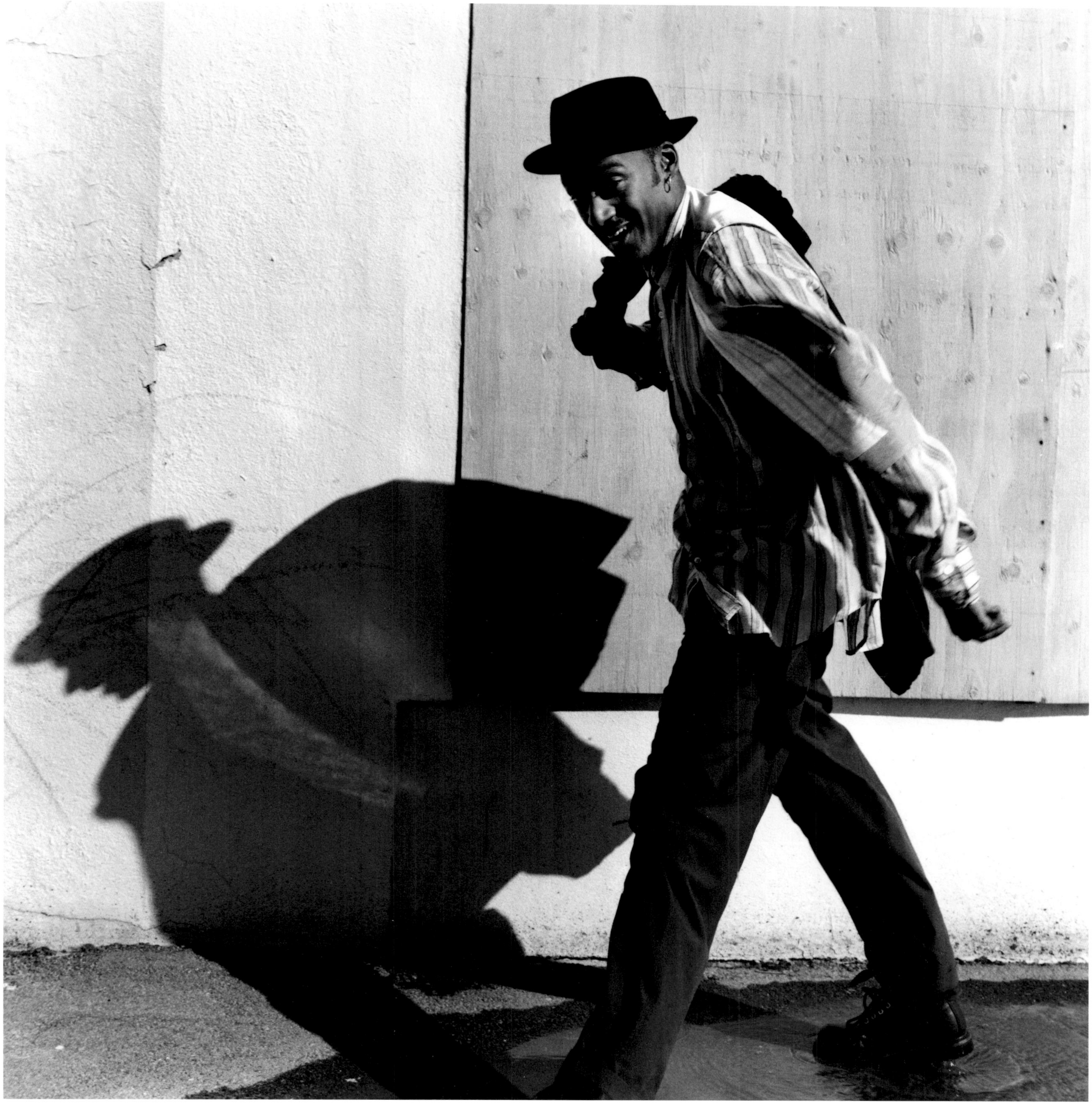

Marcus Miller Santa Monica · 1995

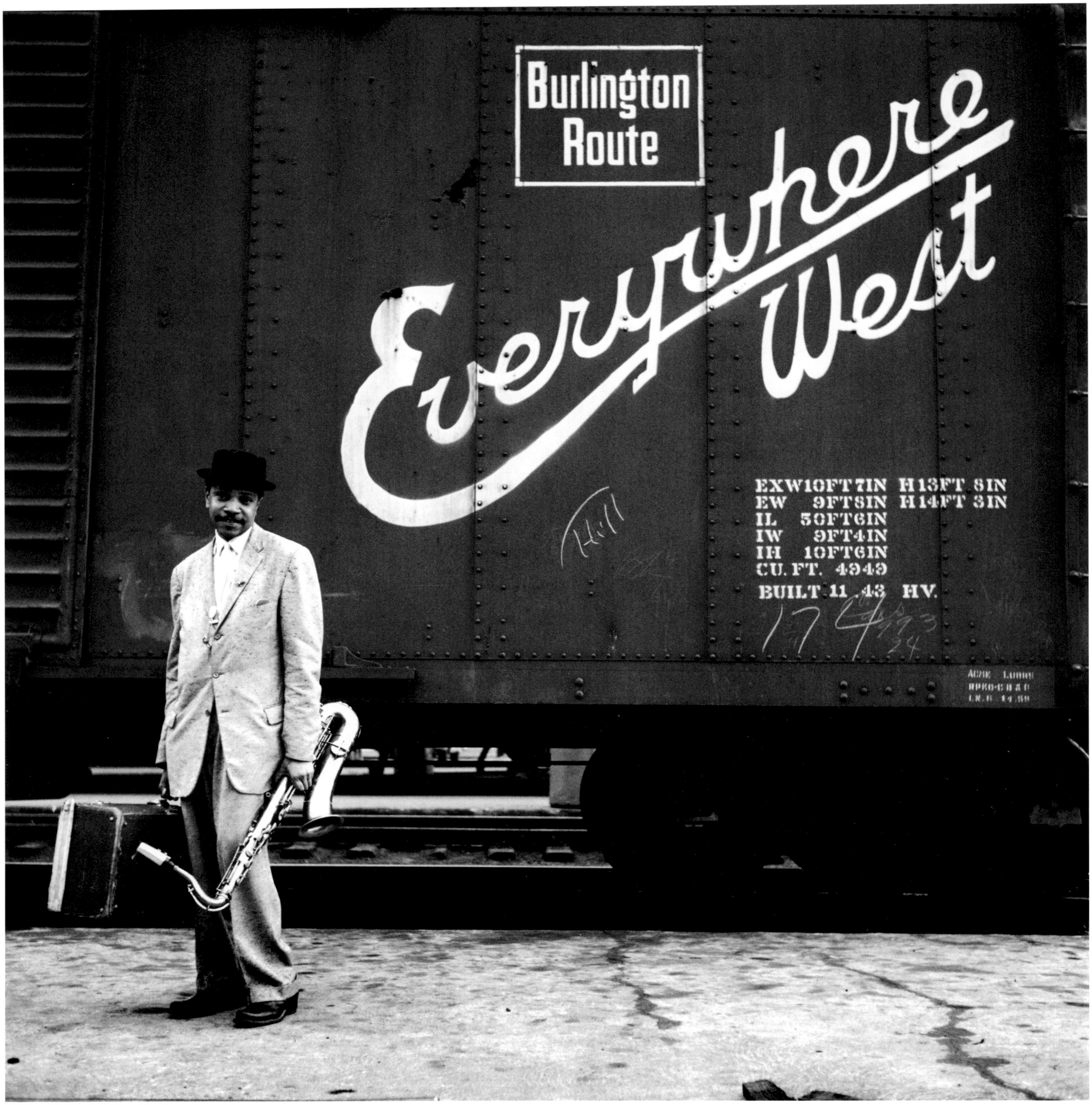

Oscar "Fats" Dennis Kansas City · 1960

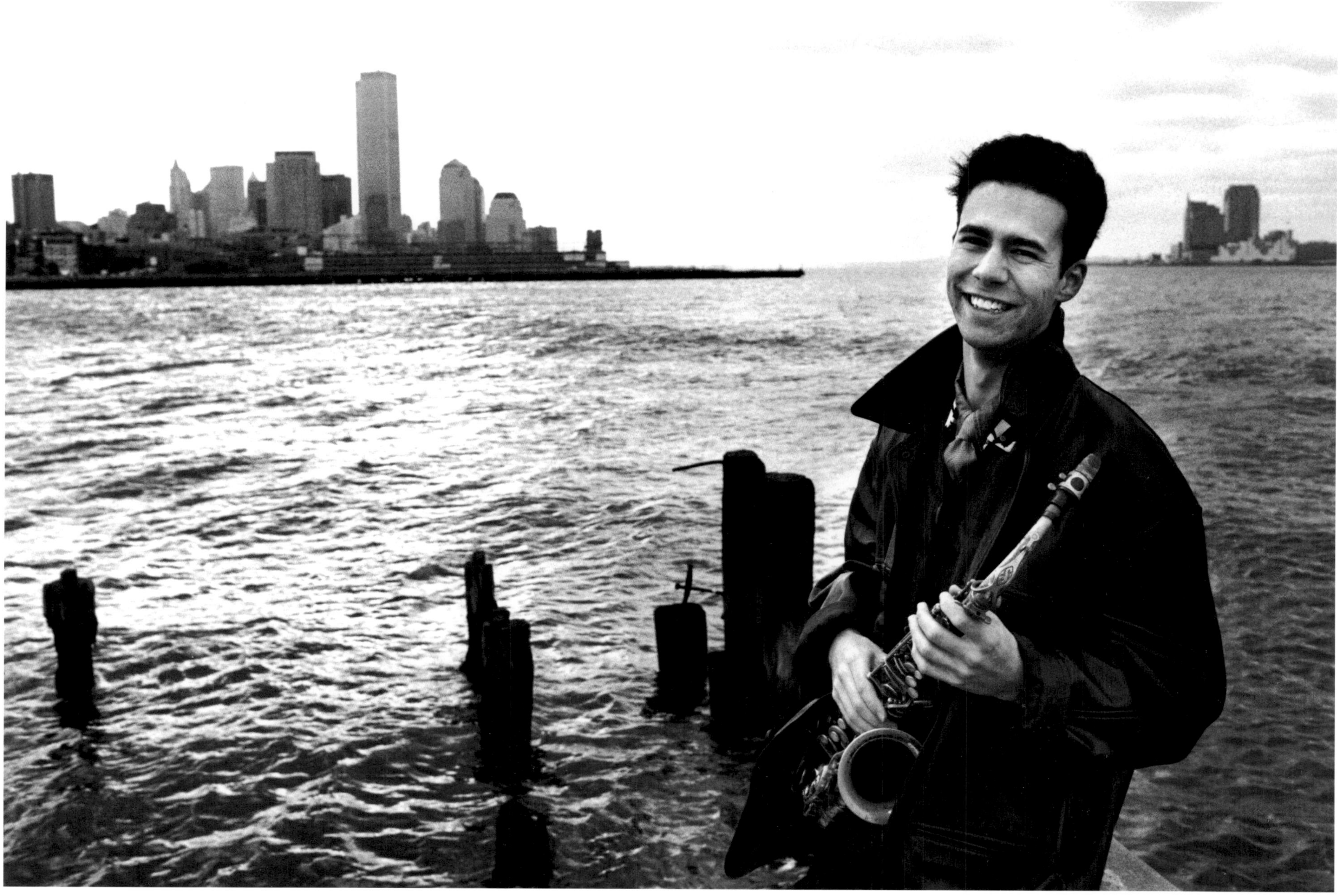

Christopher Hollyday New York City · 1993

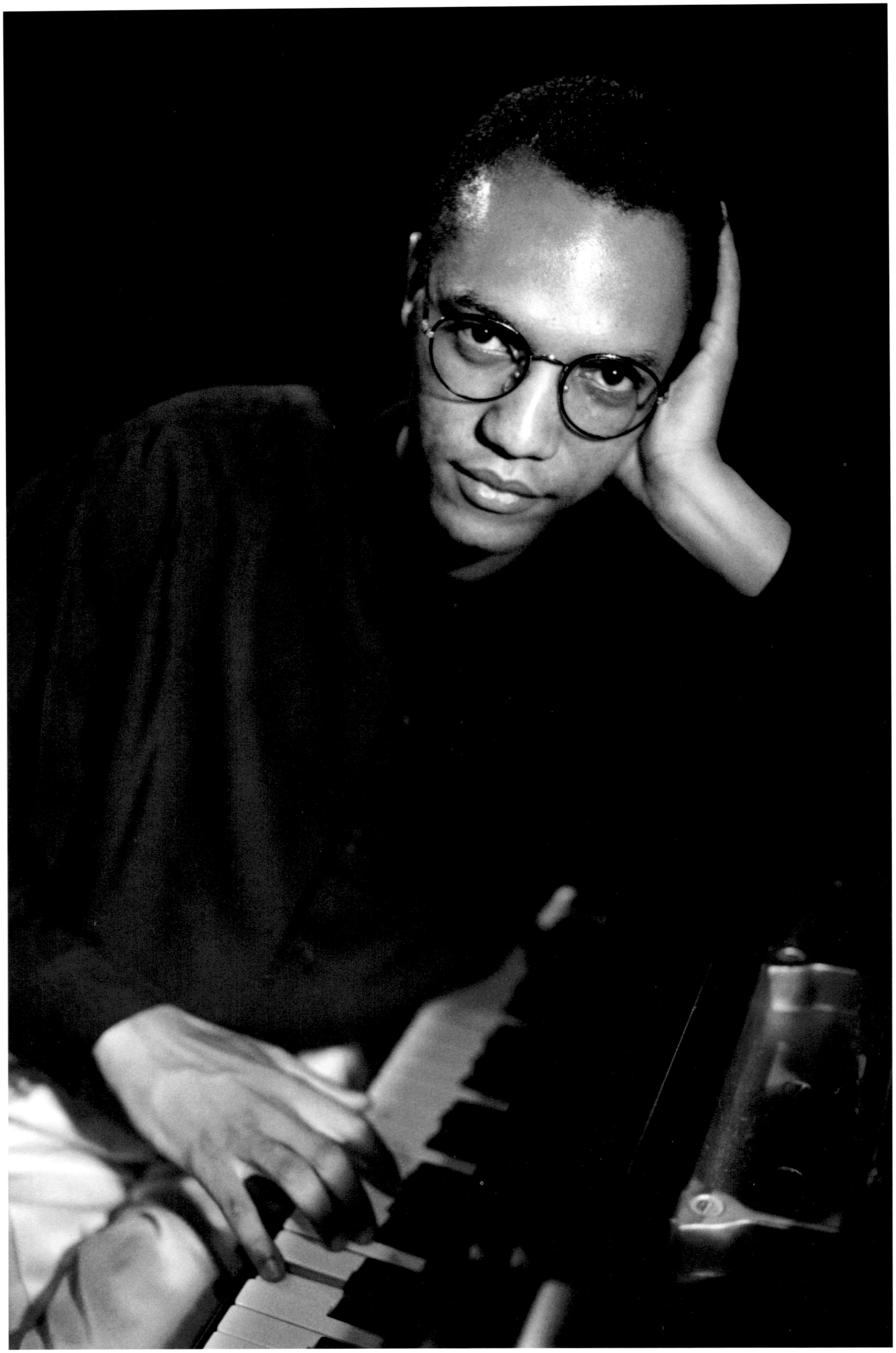

Billy Childs
Los Angeles · 1990

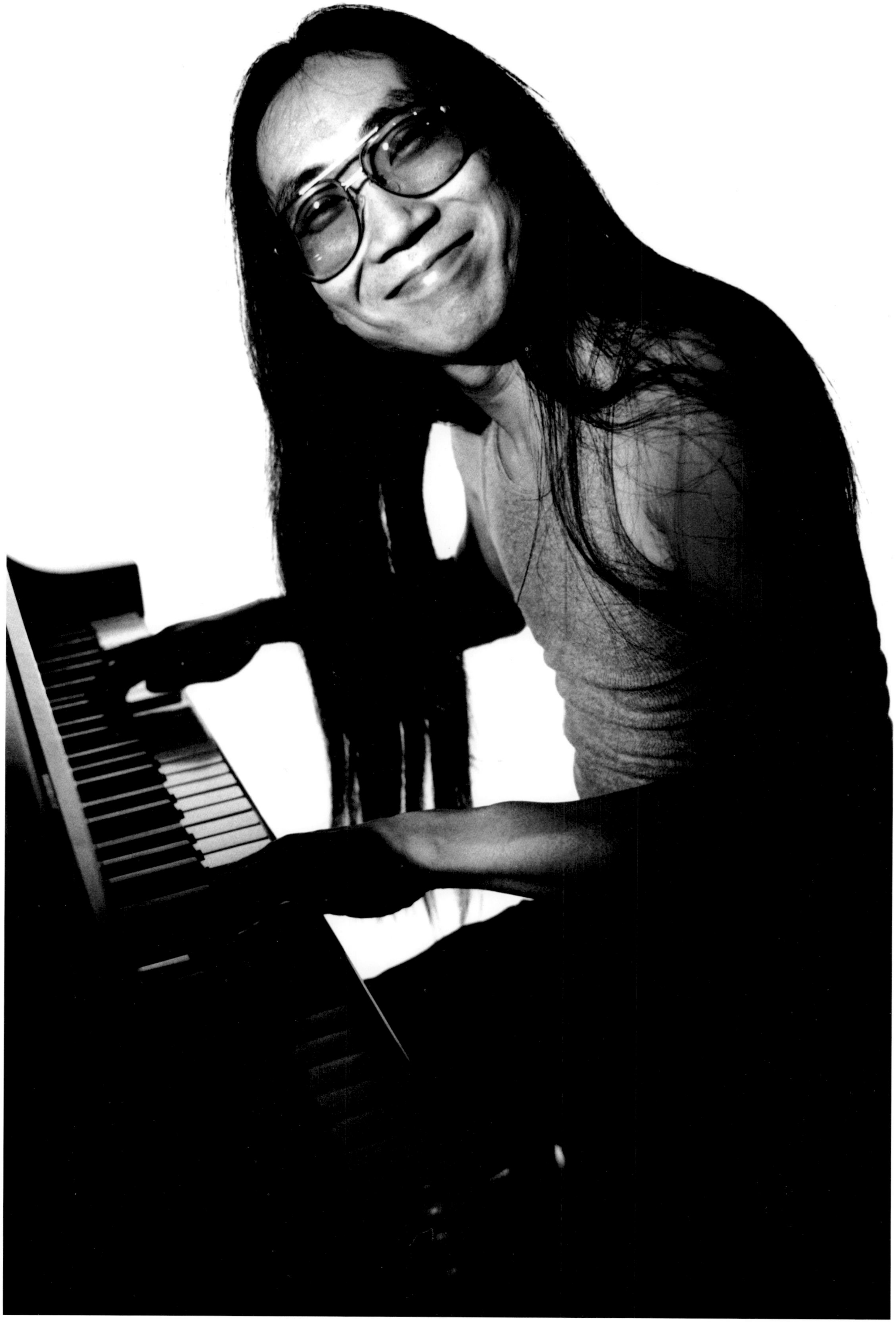

Kei Akagi
Los Angeles · 1990

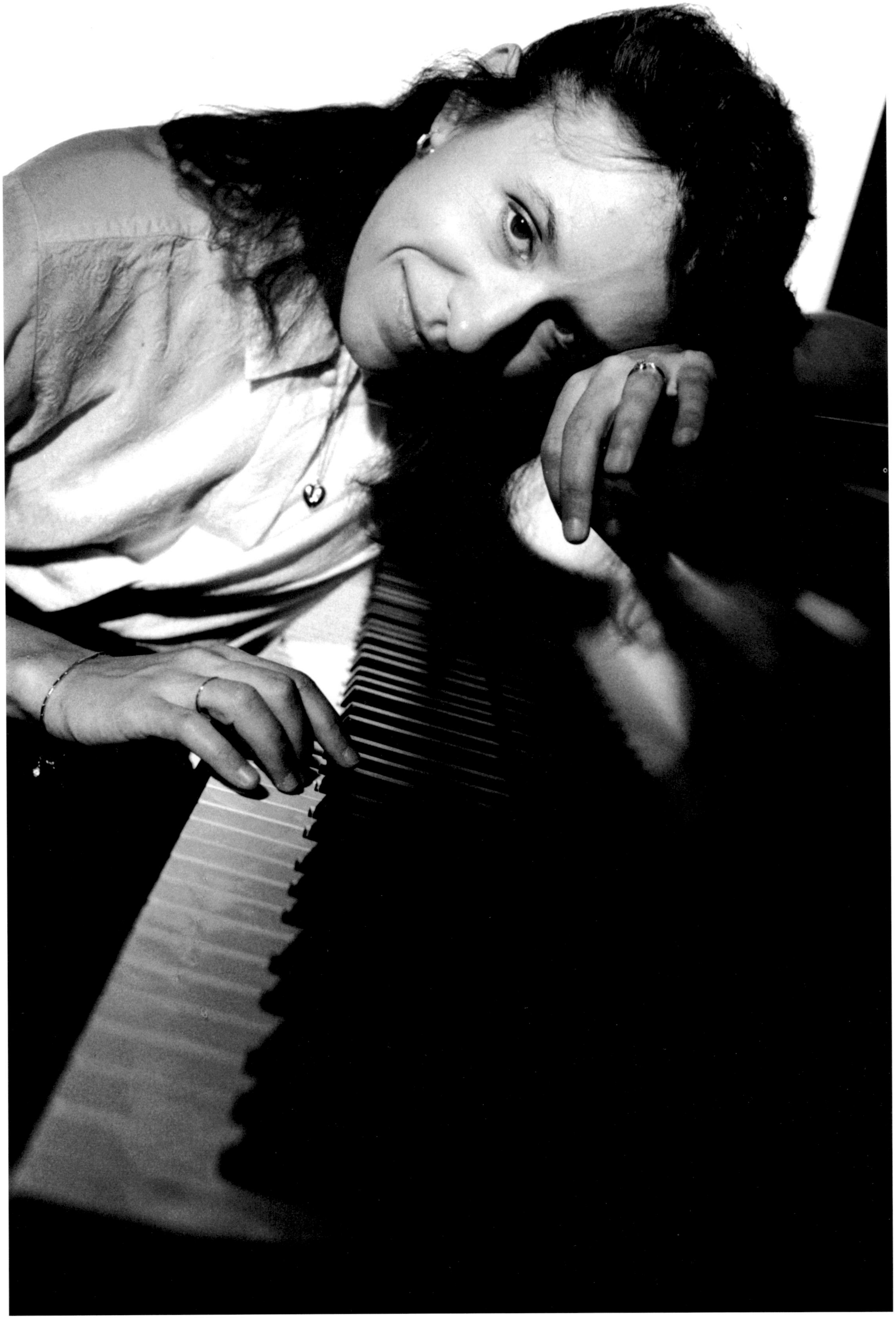

Cecilia Coleman
Los Angeles · 1990

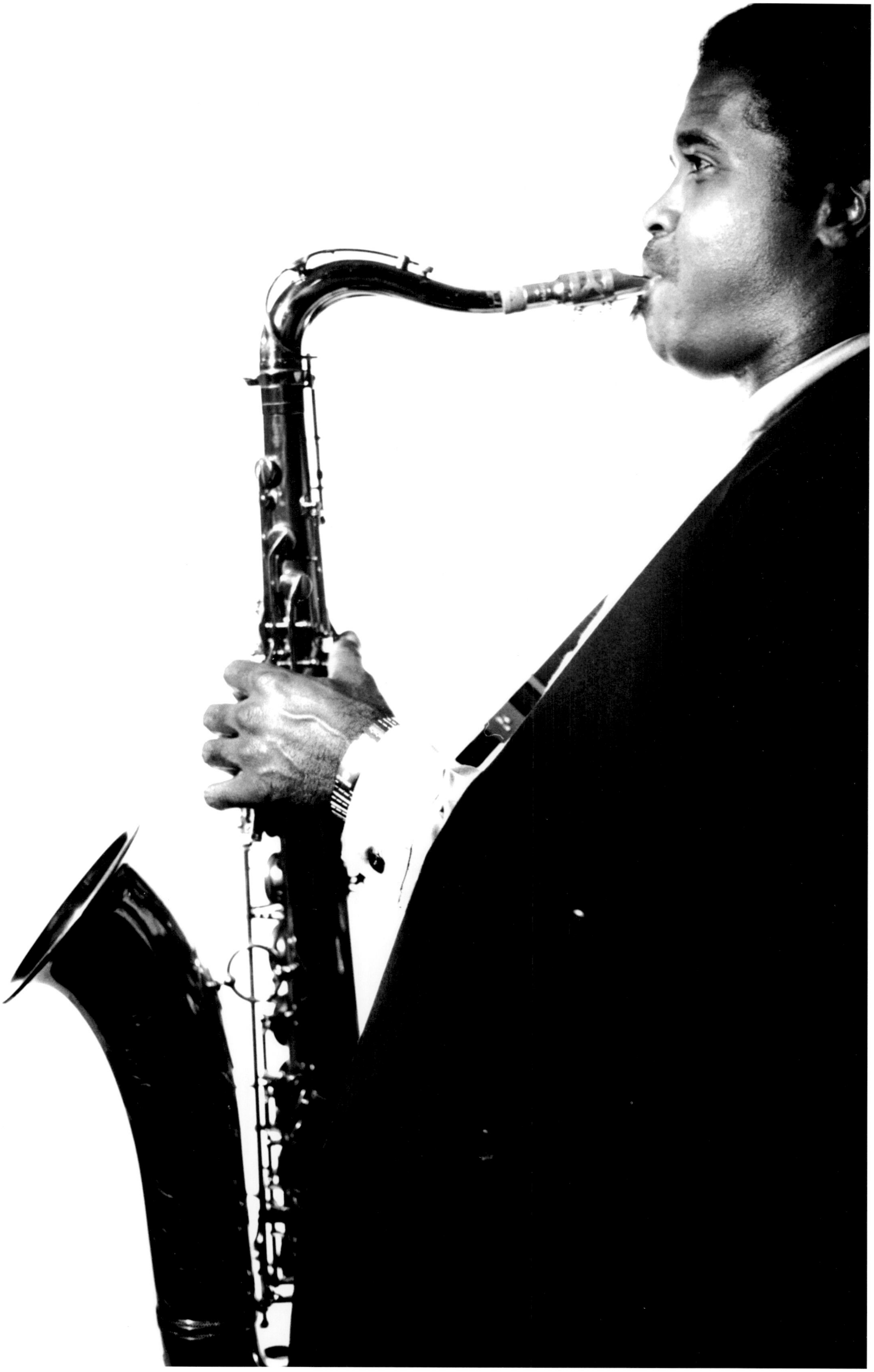

Rickey Woodard
Los Angeles · 1990

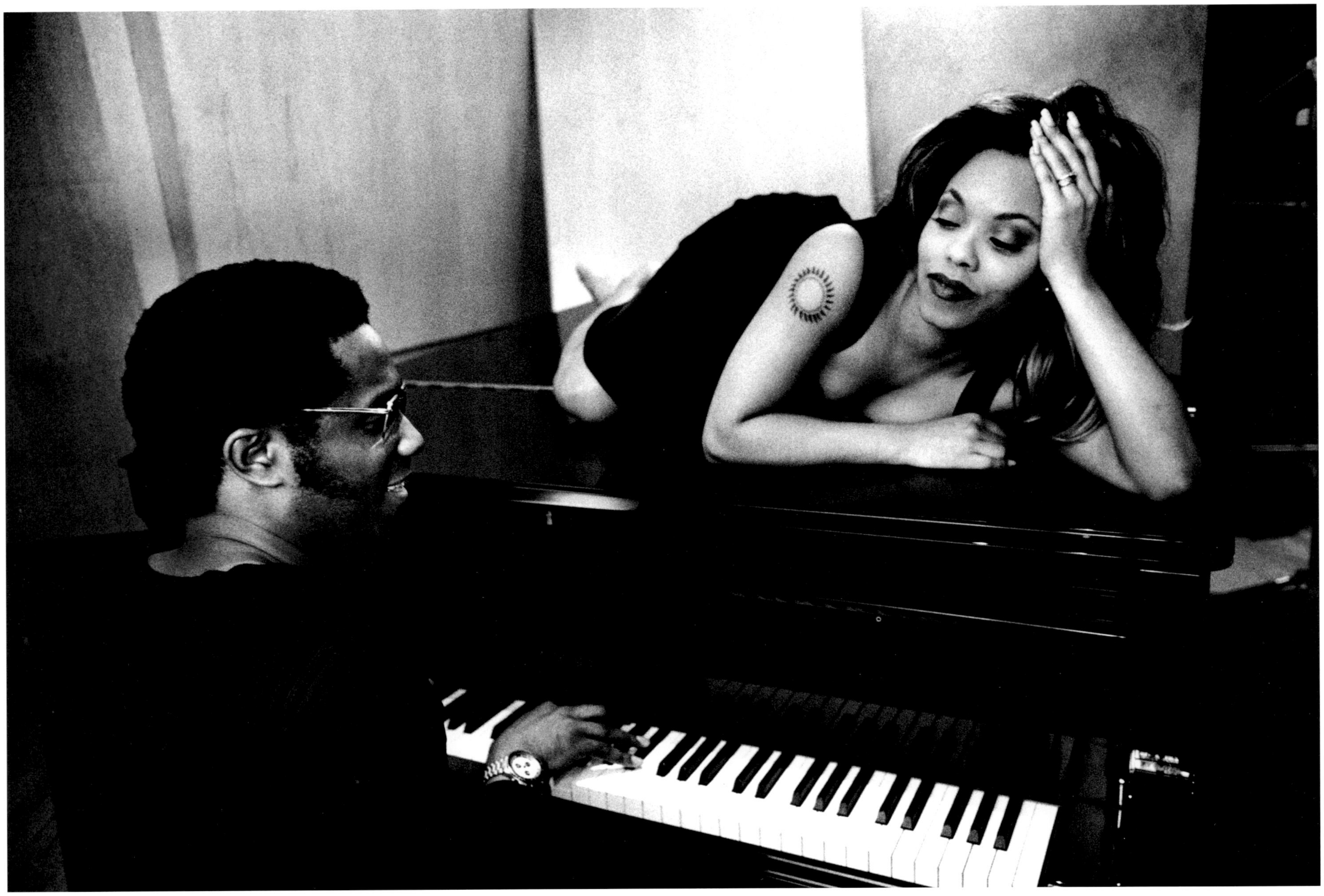

N'Dea Davenport and Andrew Levy [The Brand New Heavies] London · 1994

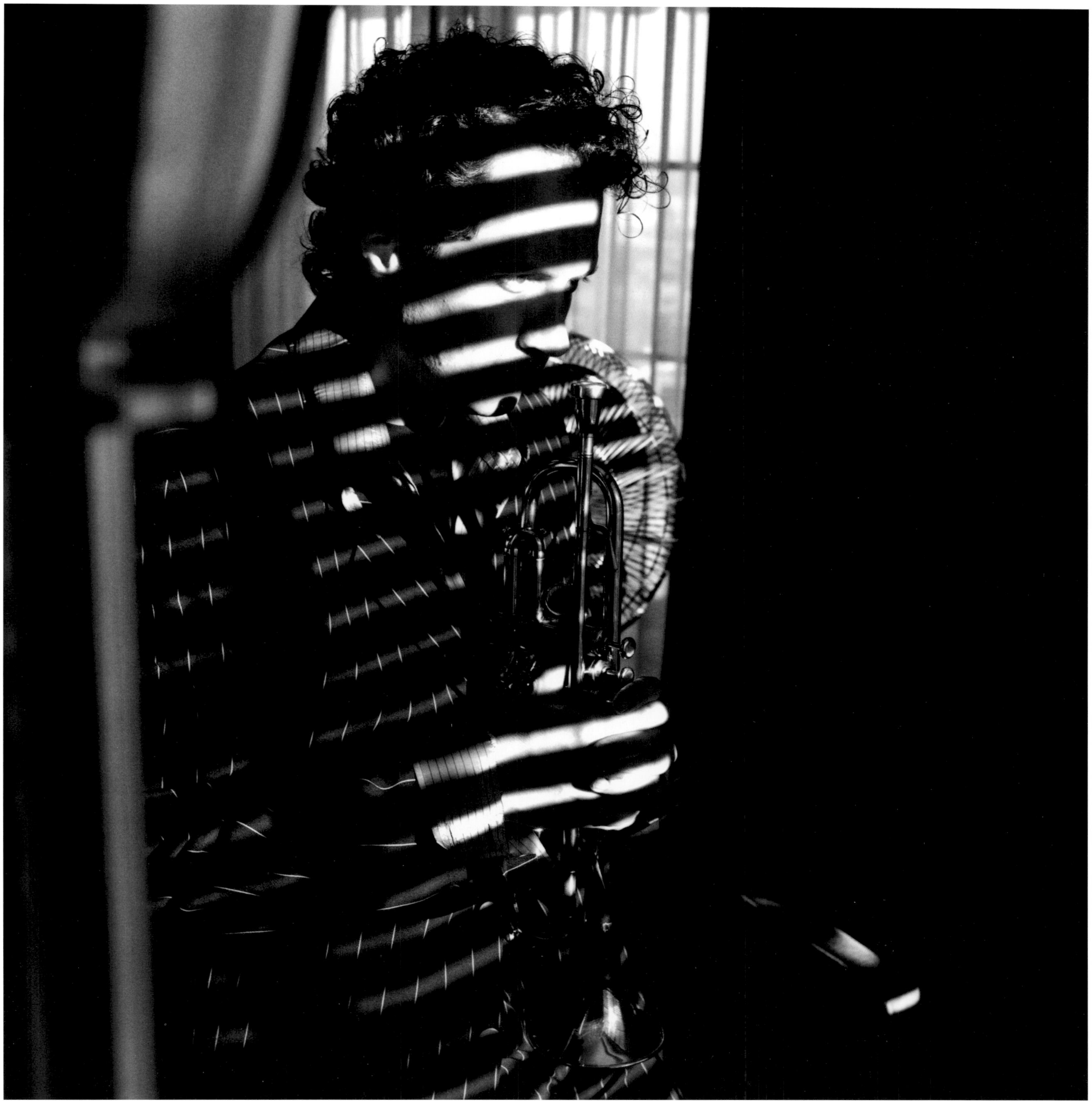

Mark Isham Los Angeles · 1995

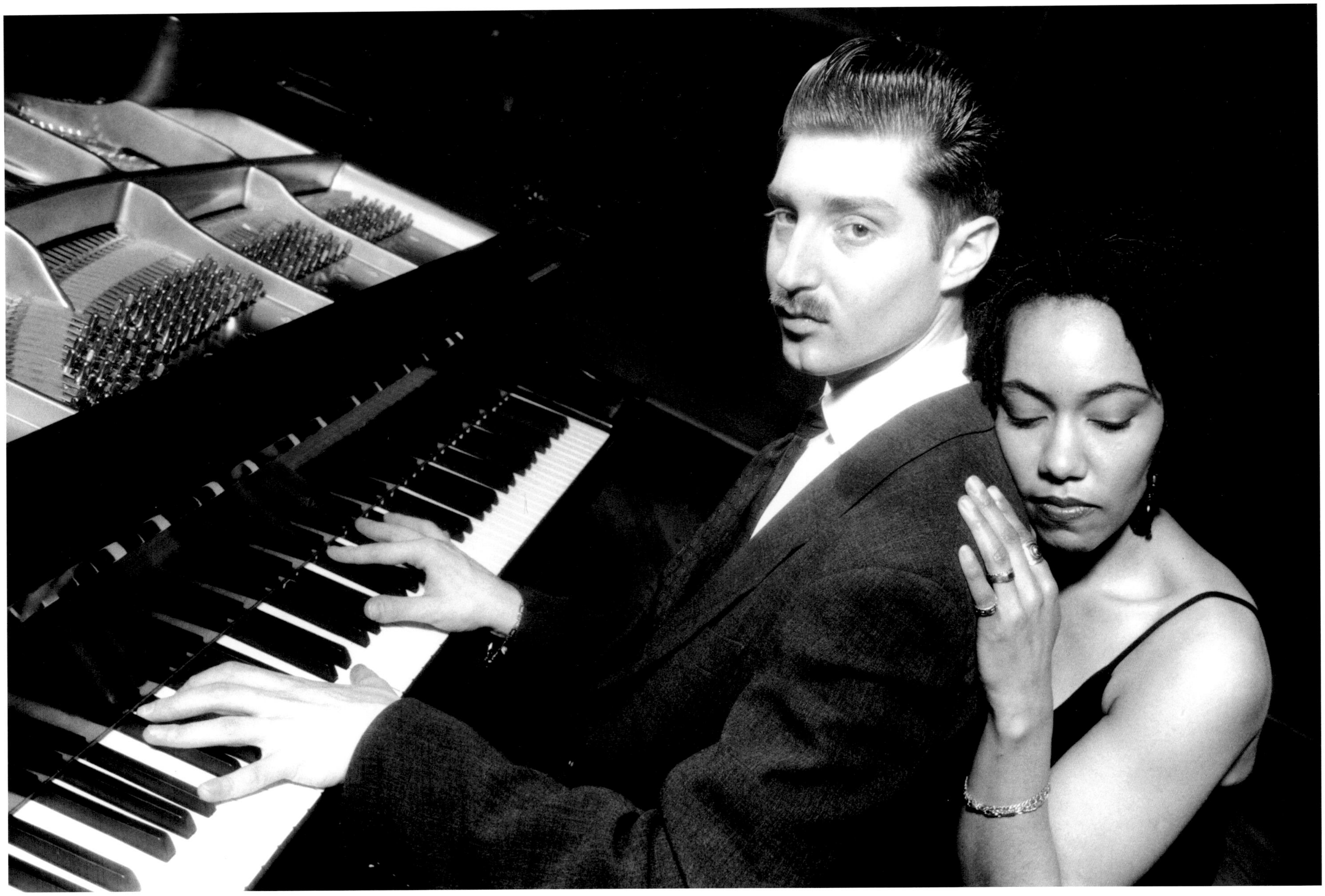

 Benny Green and Deborah Davis New York City · 1993

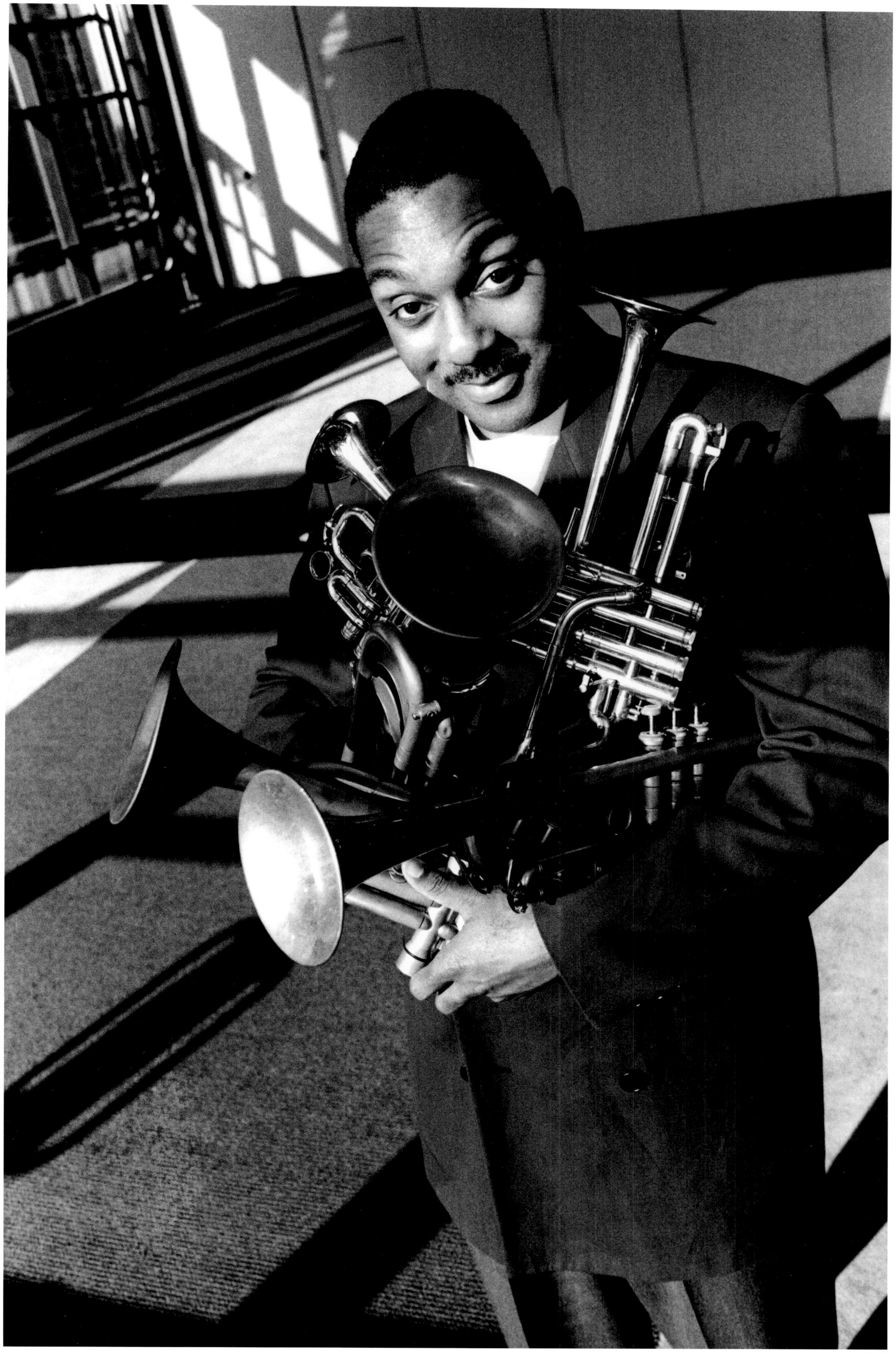

Wynton Marsalis
New York City · 1992

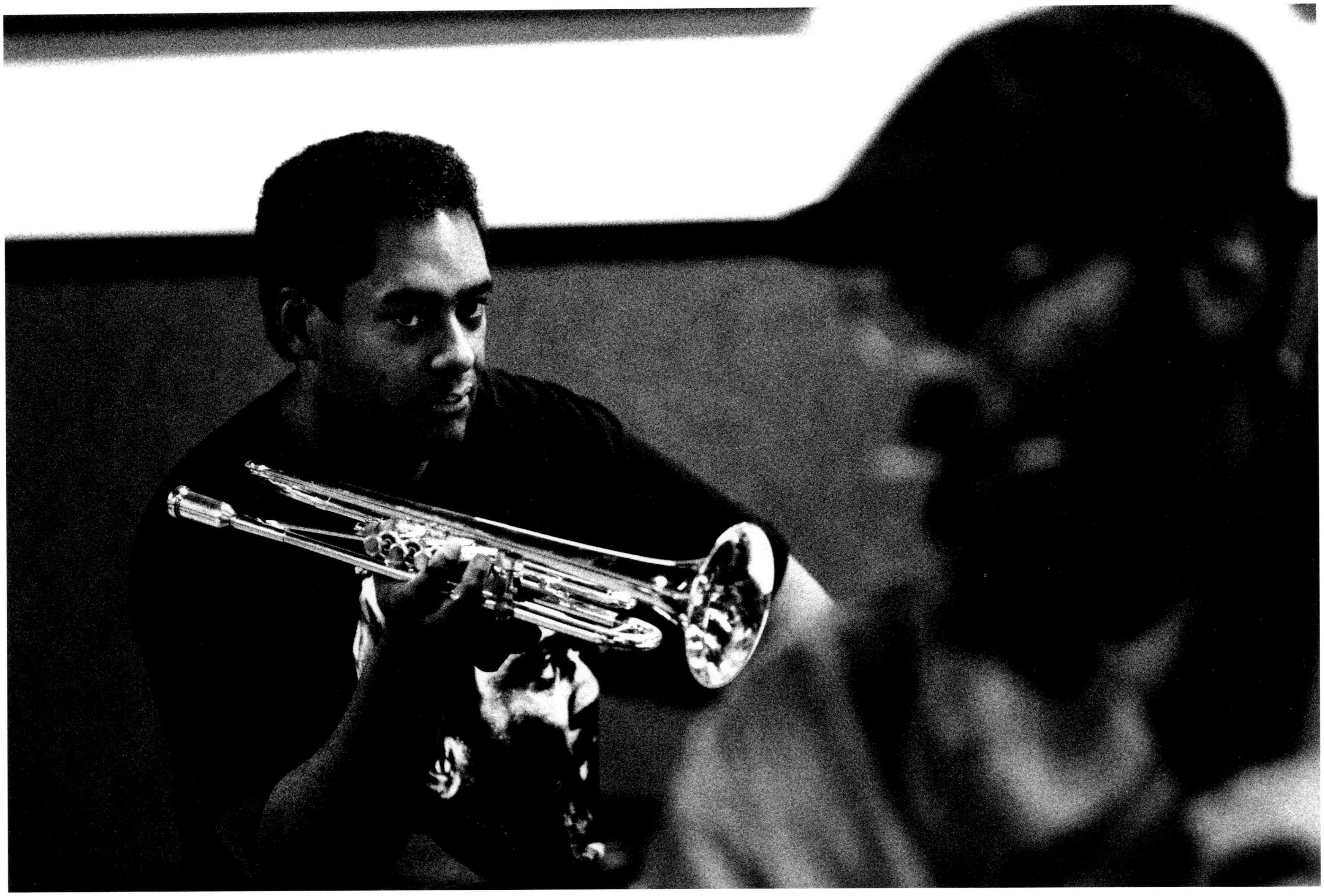

 Jon Faddis and Ron Carter New York City · 1993

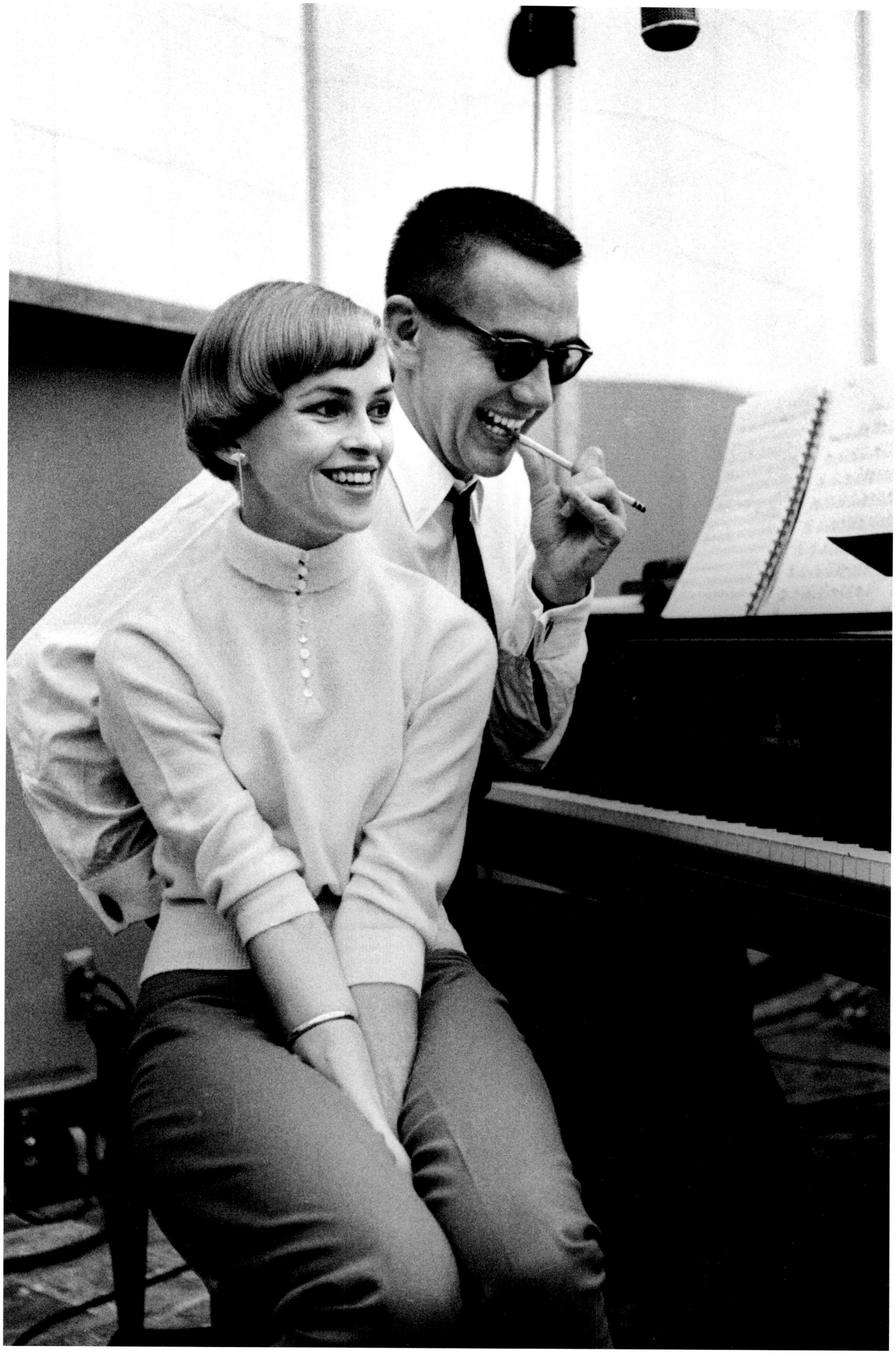

Jackie Cain and Roy Kral
Hollywood · 1958

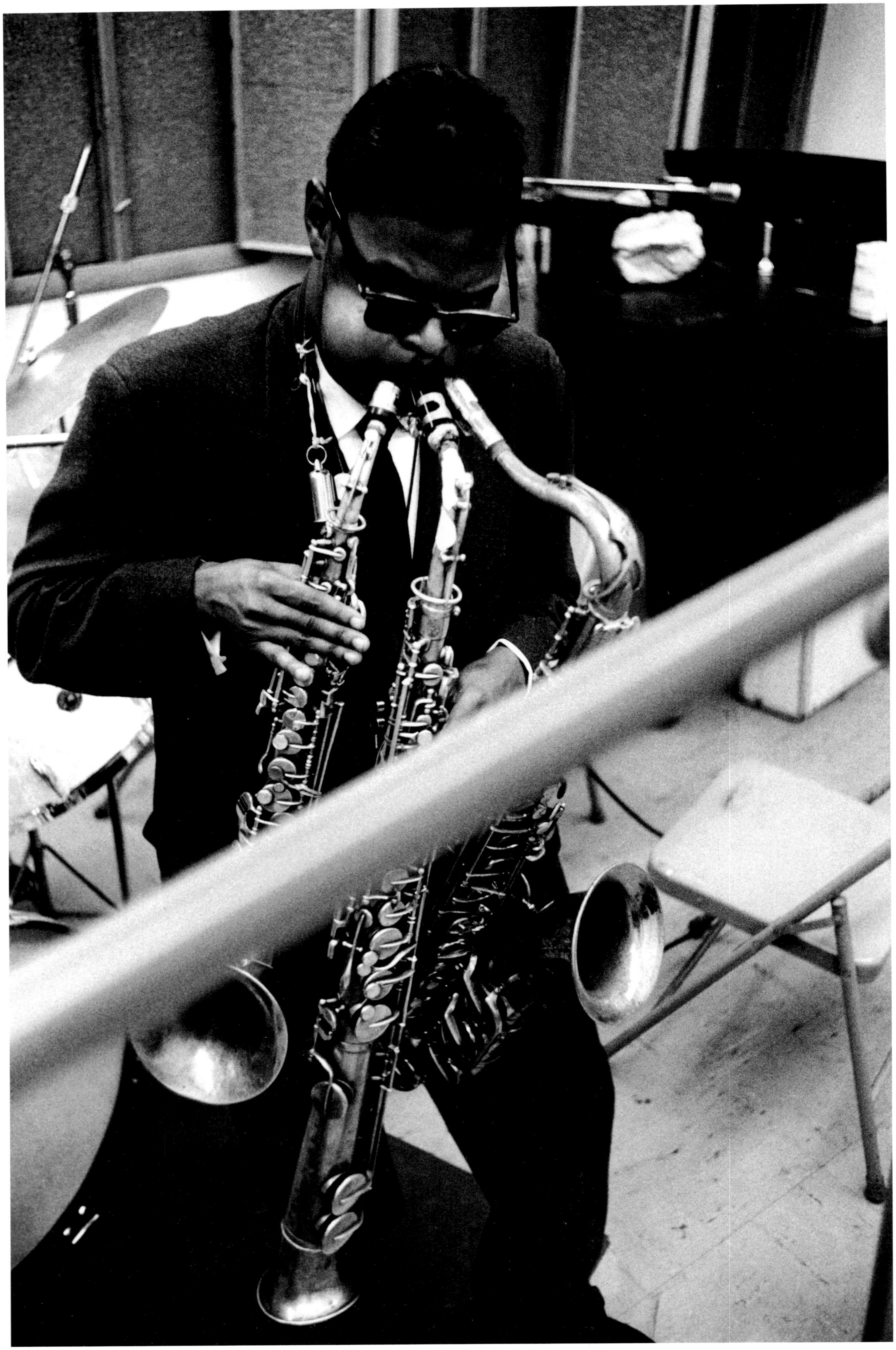

Rahsaan Roland Kirk
New York City · 1959

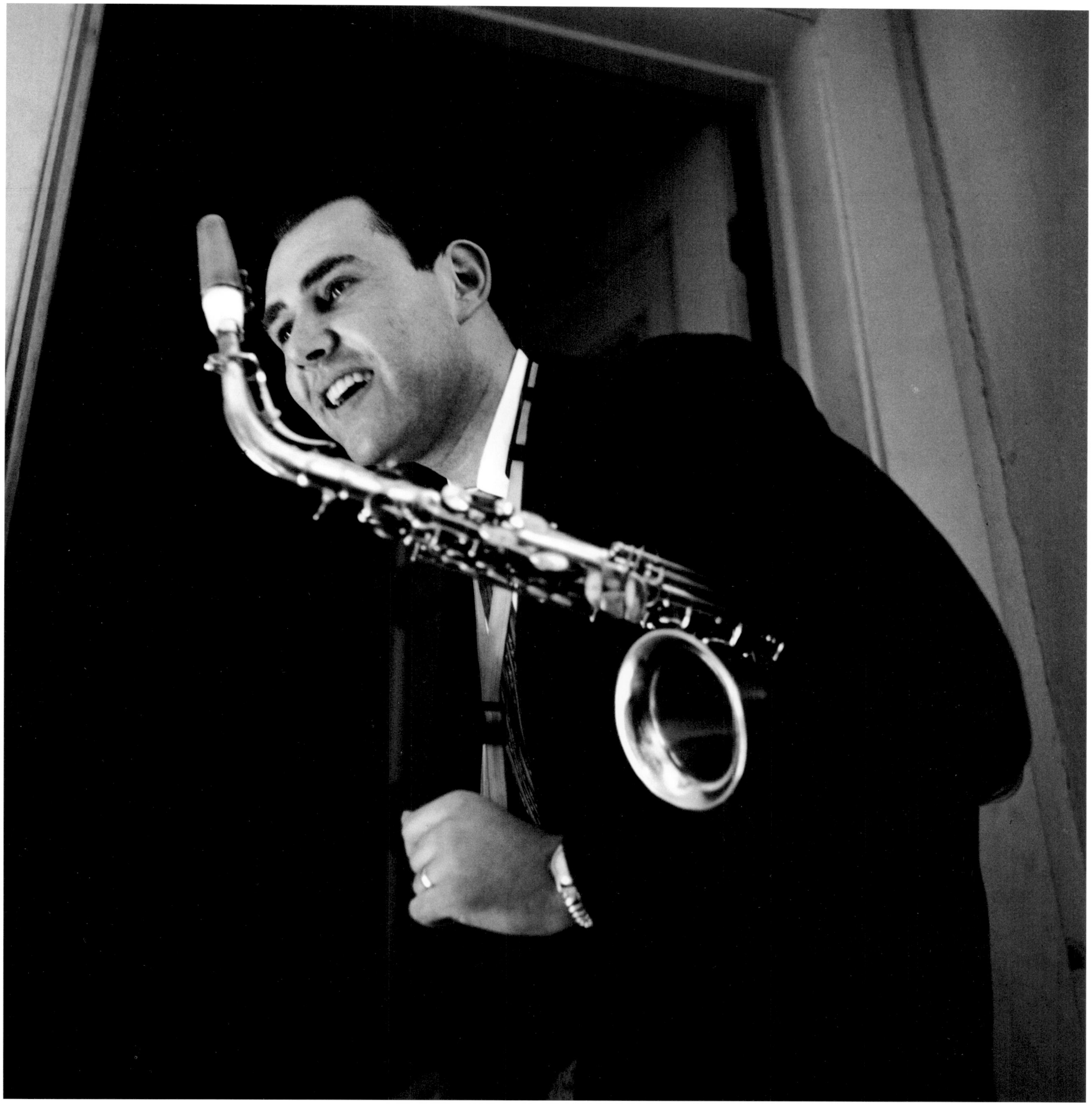

Herb Geller Hollywood · 1954

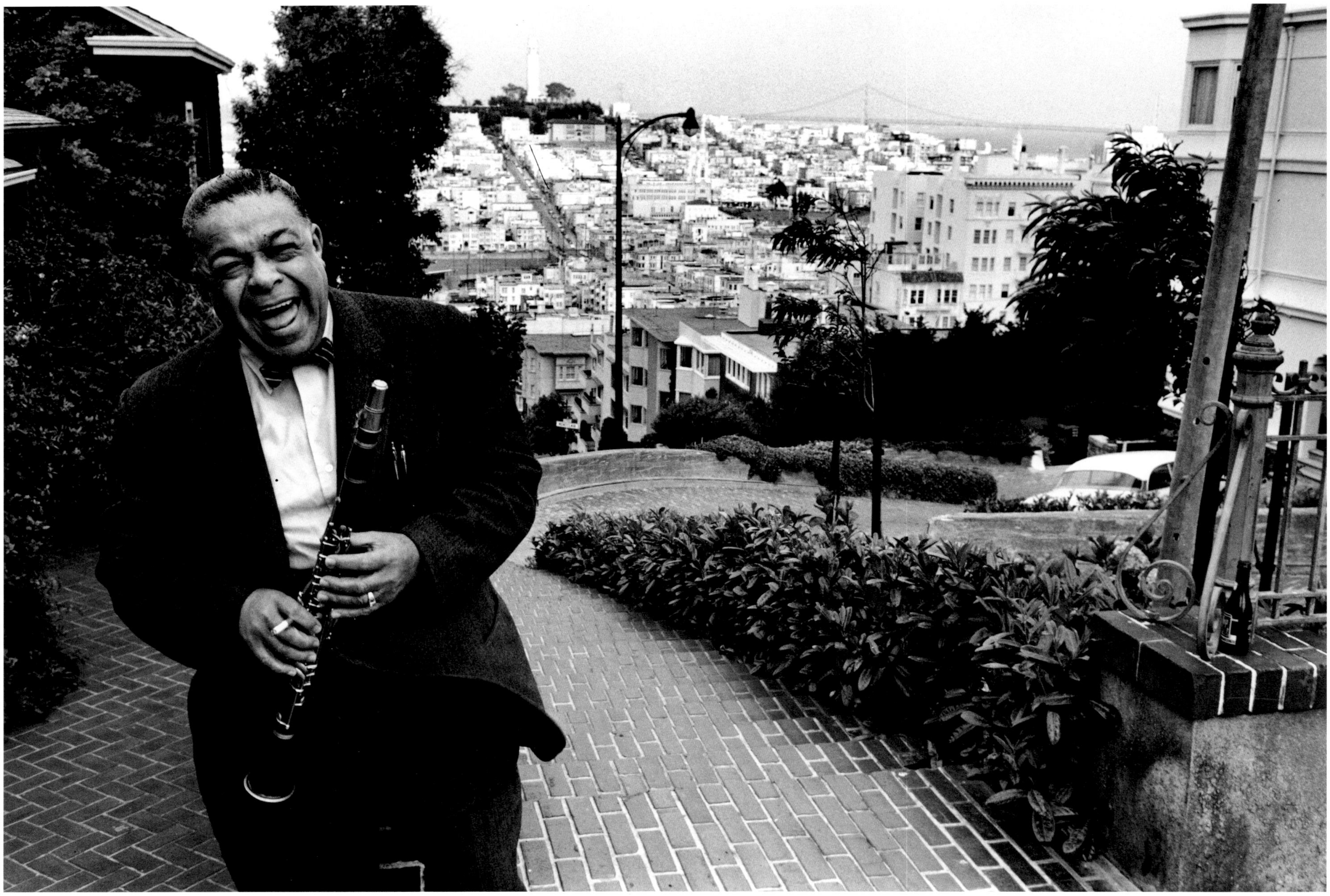

 Darnell Howard San Francisco · 1960

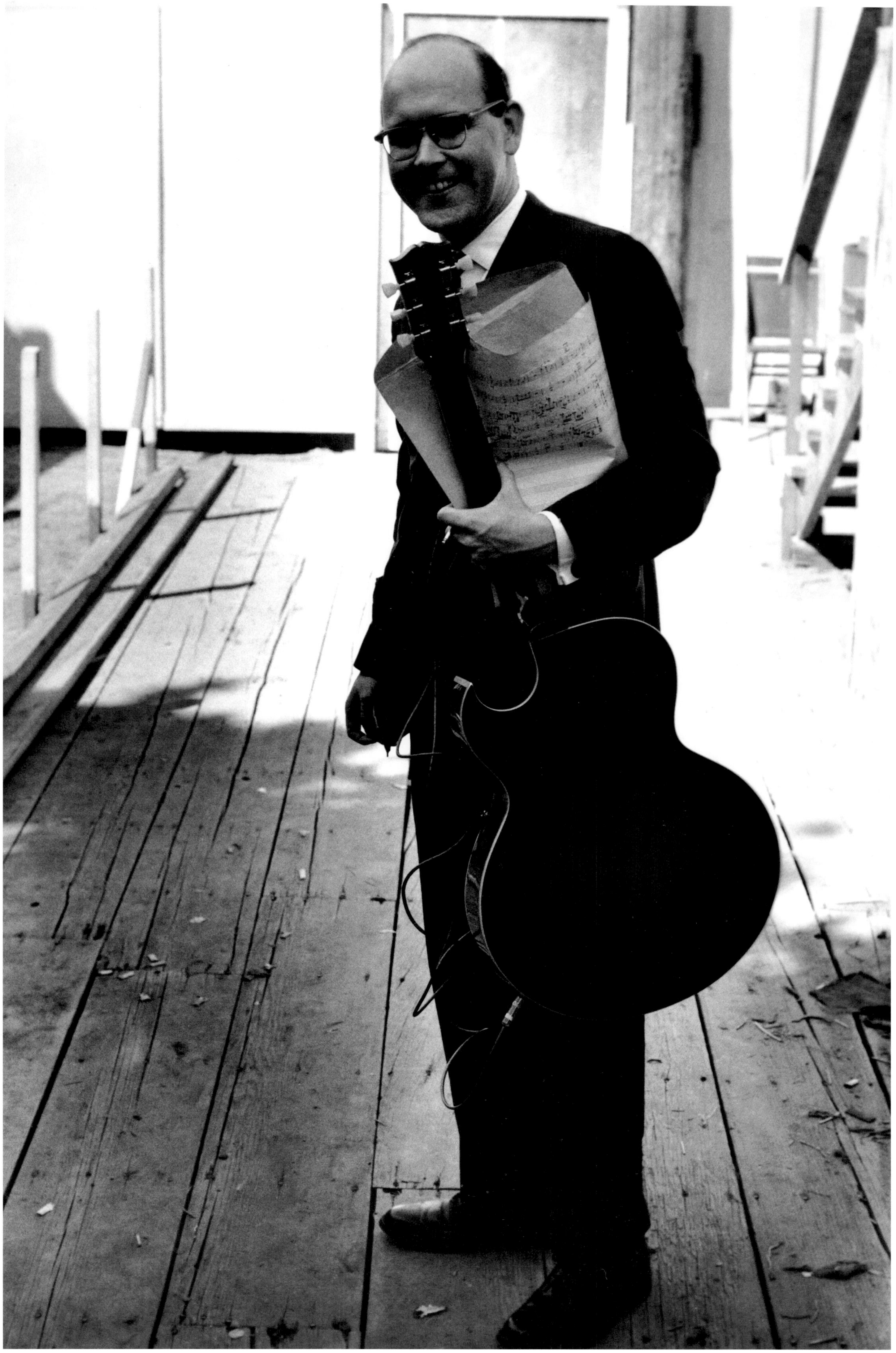

Jim Hall
Monterey · 1958

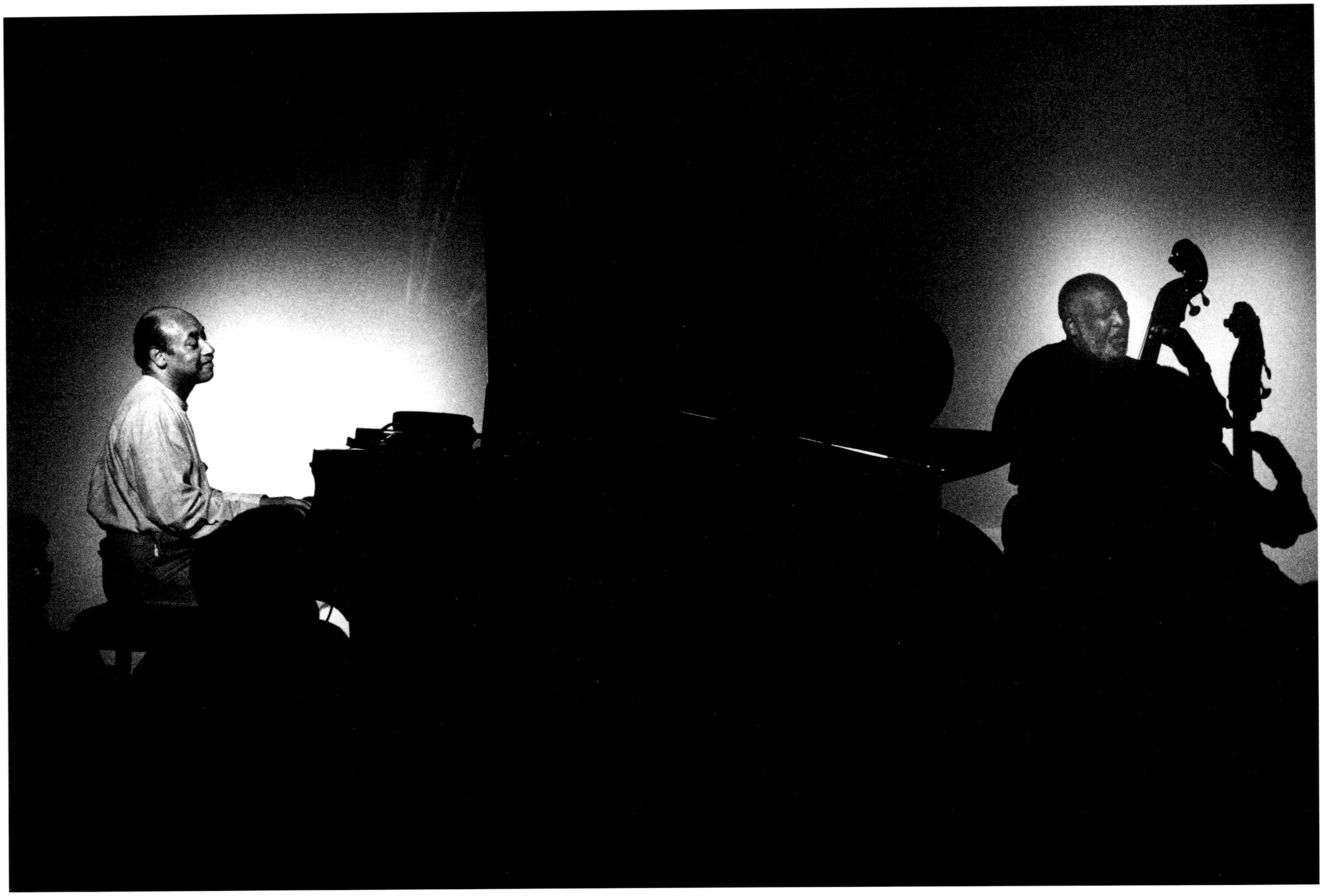

 Kenny Barron and Andy Simpkins Culver City · 1994

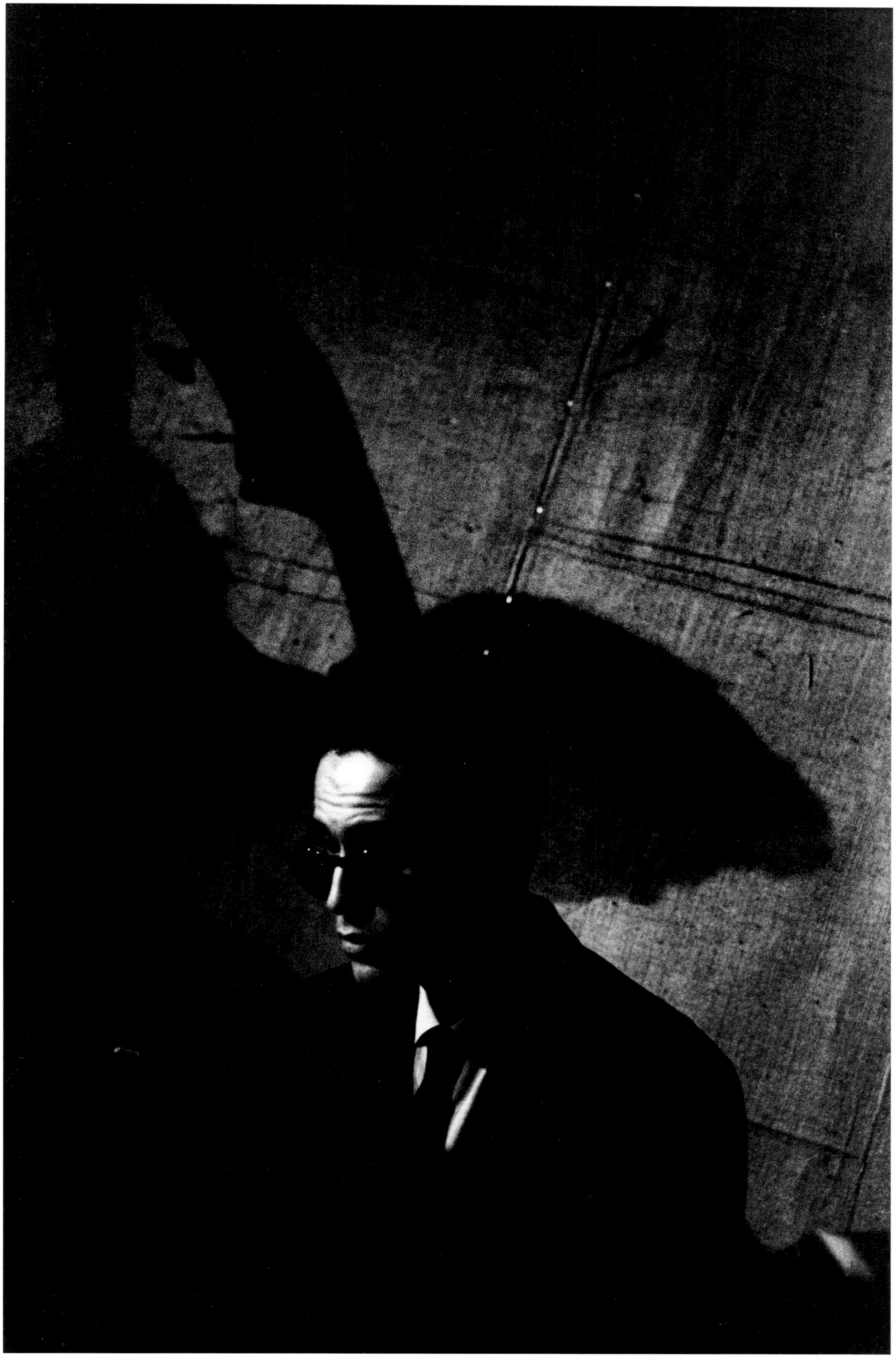

Bill Evans
Hollywood · 1962

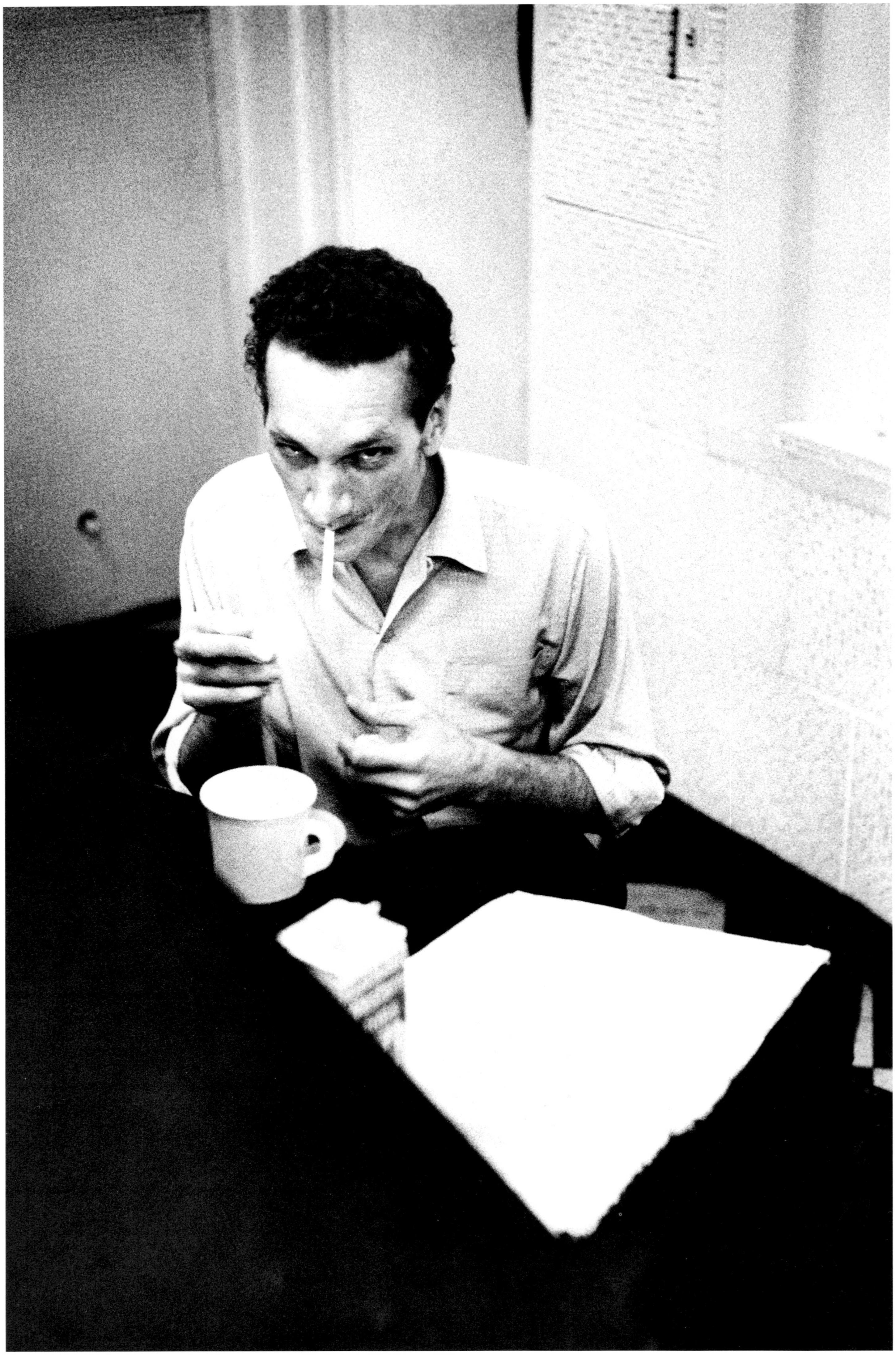

Joe Albany
Hollywood · 1954

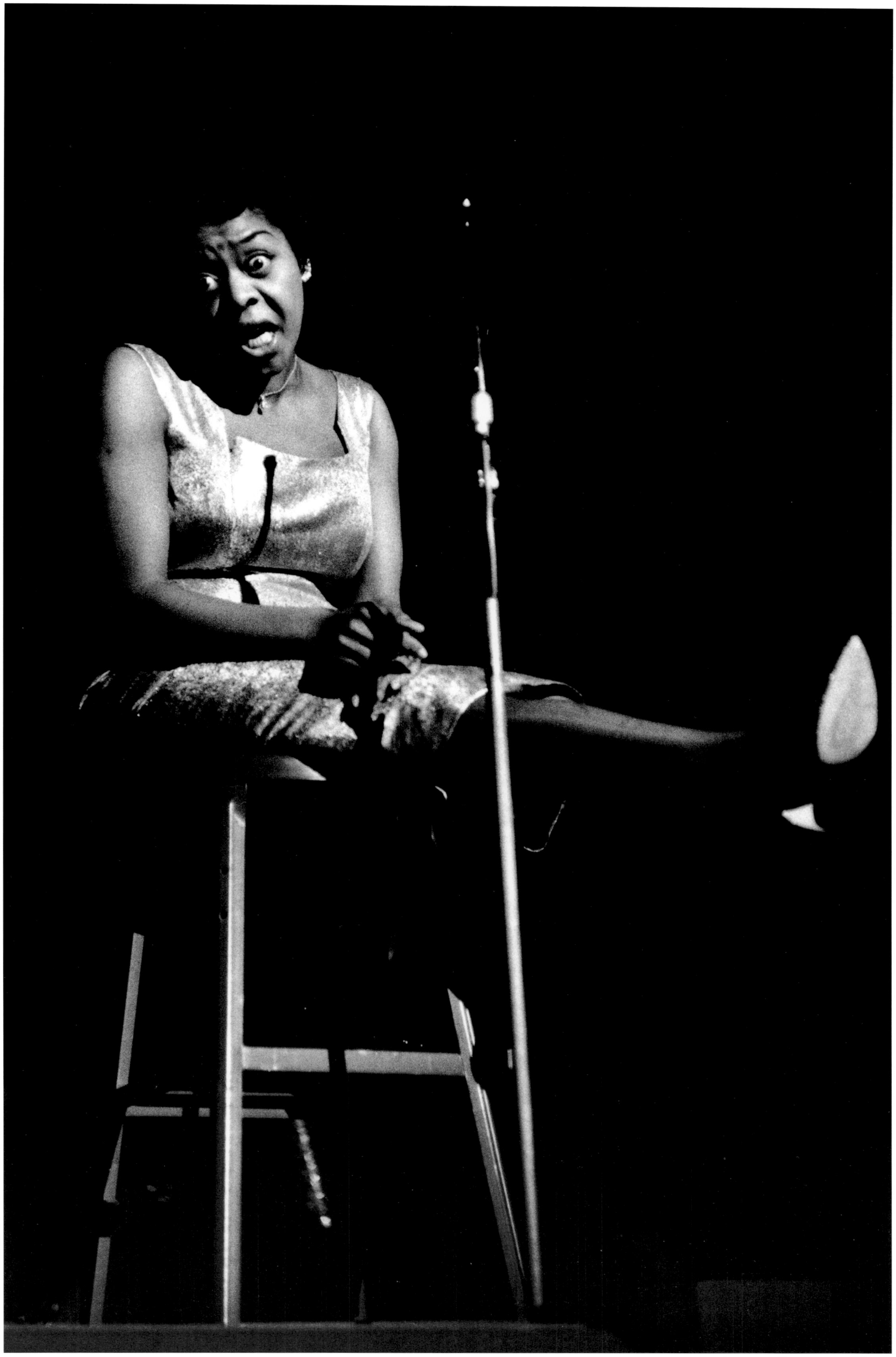

Dinah Washington
Hollywood · 1958

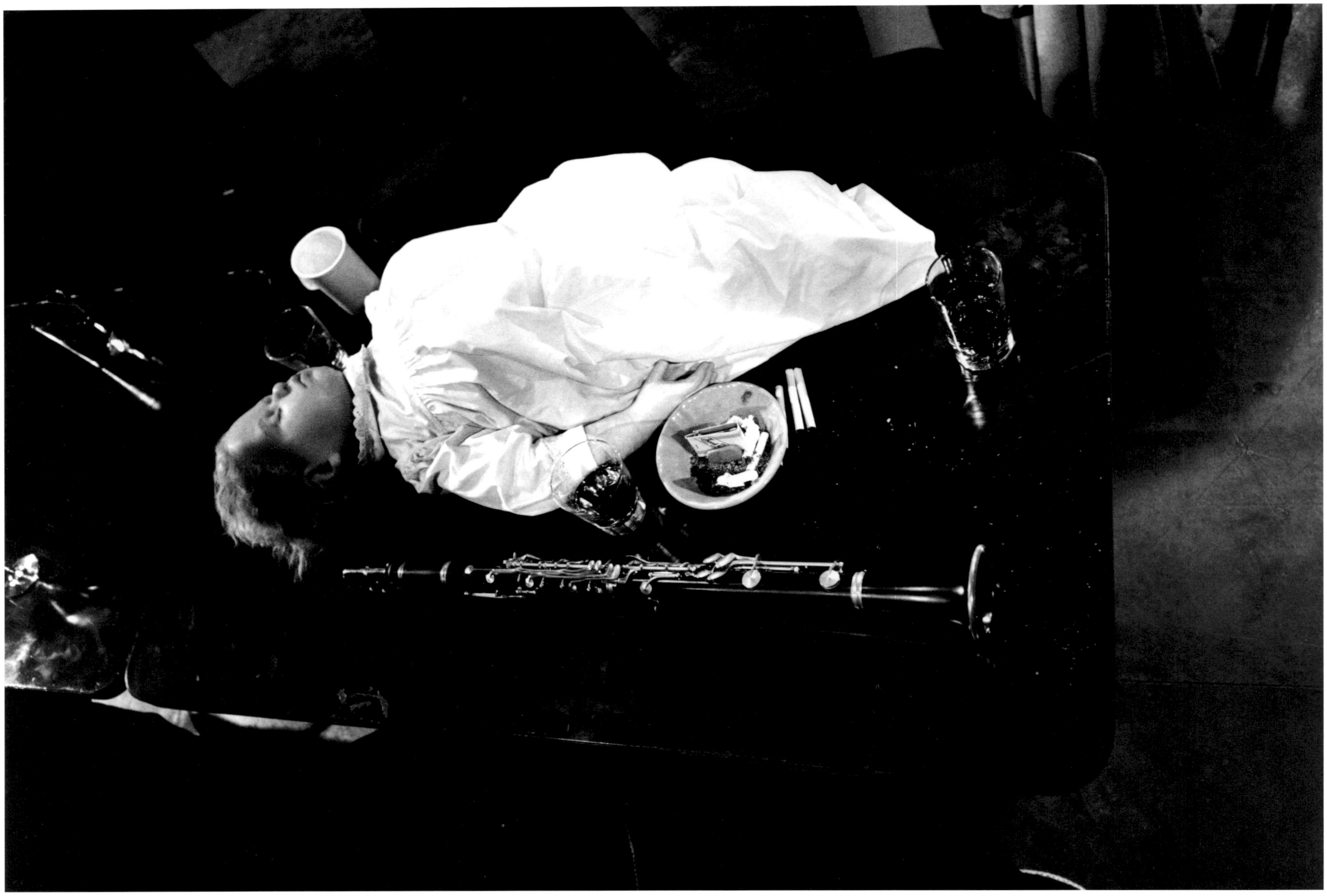

 Jazz baby, Paramount Studios Hollywood · 1956

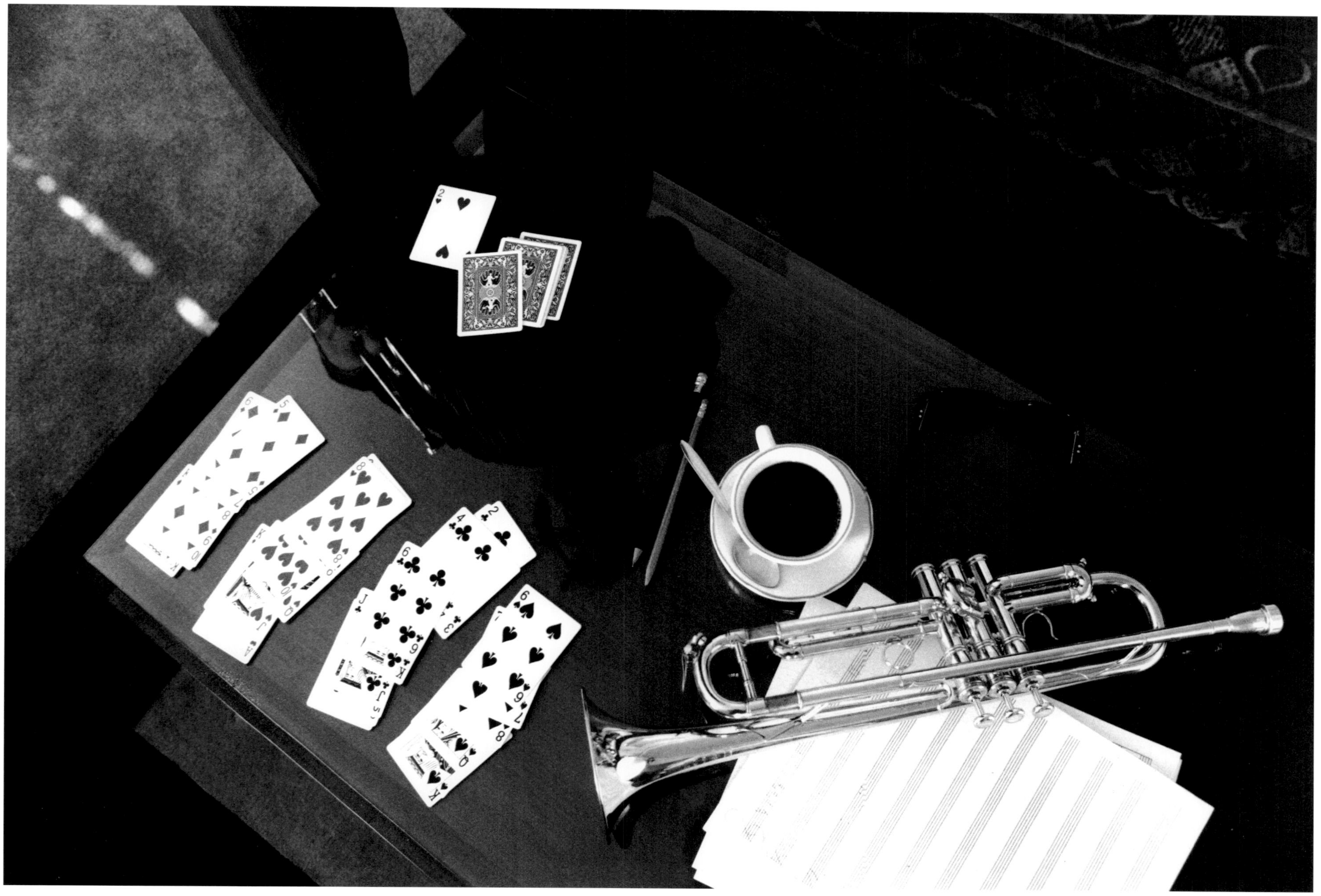

Reflection of Mark Isham Los Angeles · 1995

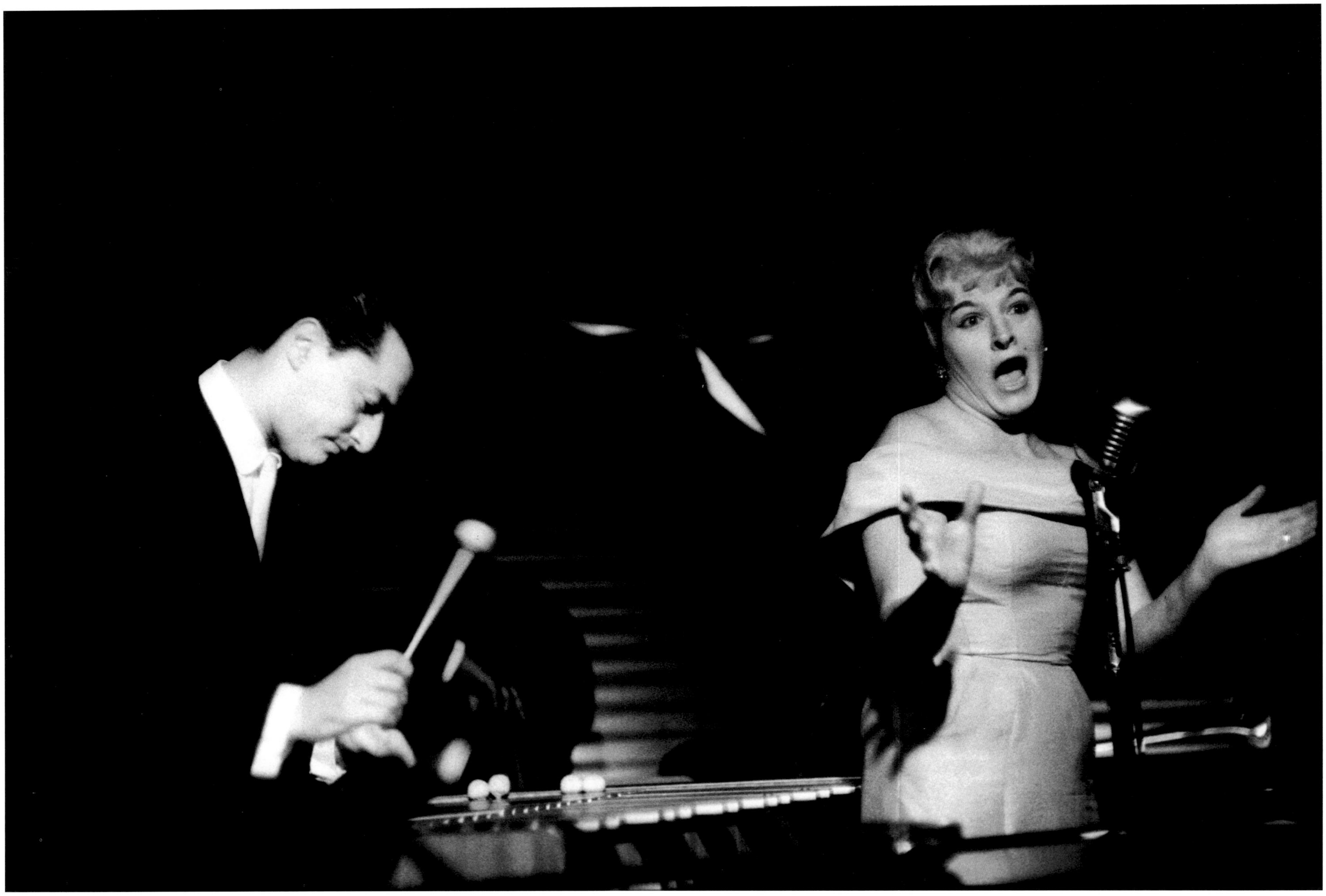

 Terry Gibbs and Mary Ann McCall Hollywood · 1962

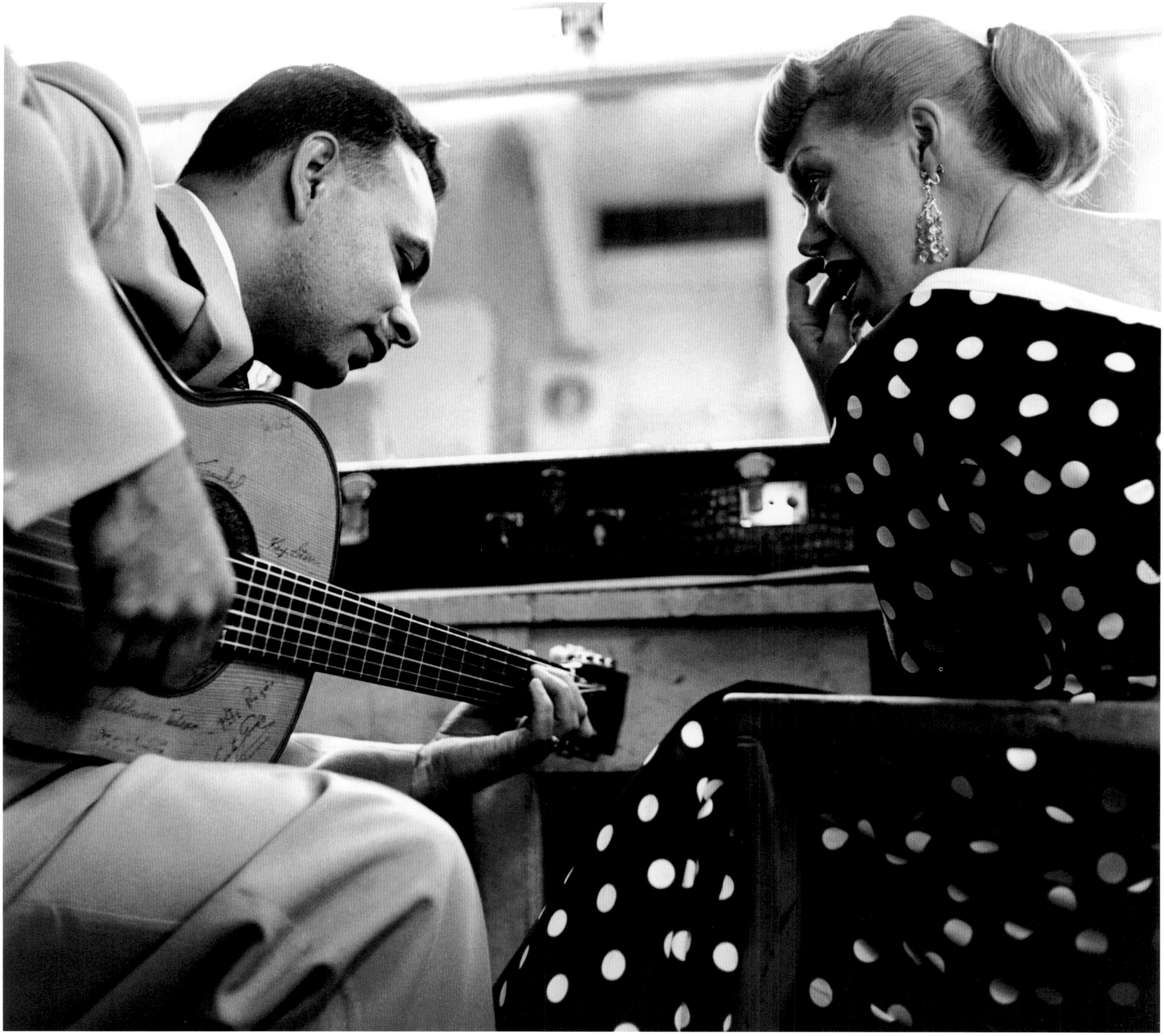

Laurindo Almeida and June Christy Hollywood · 1954

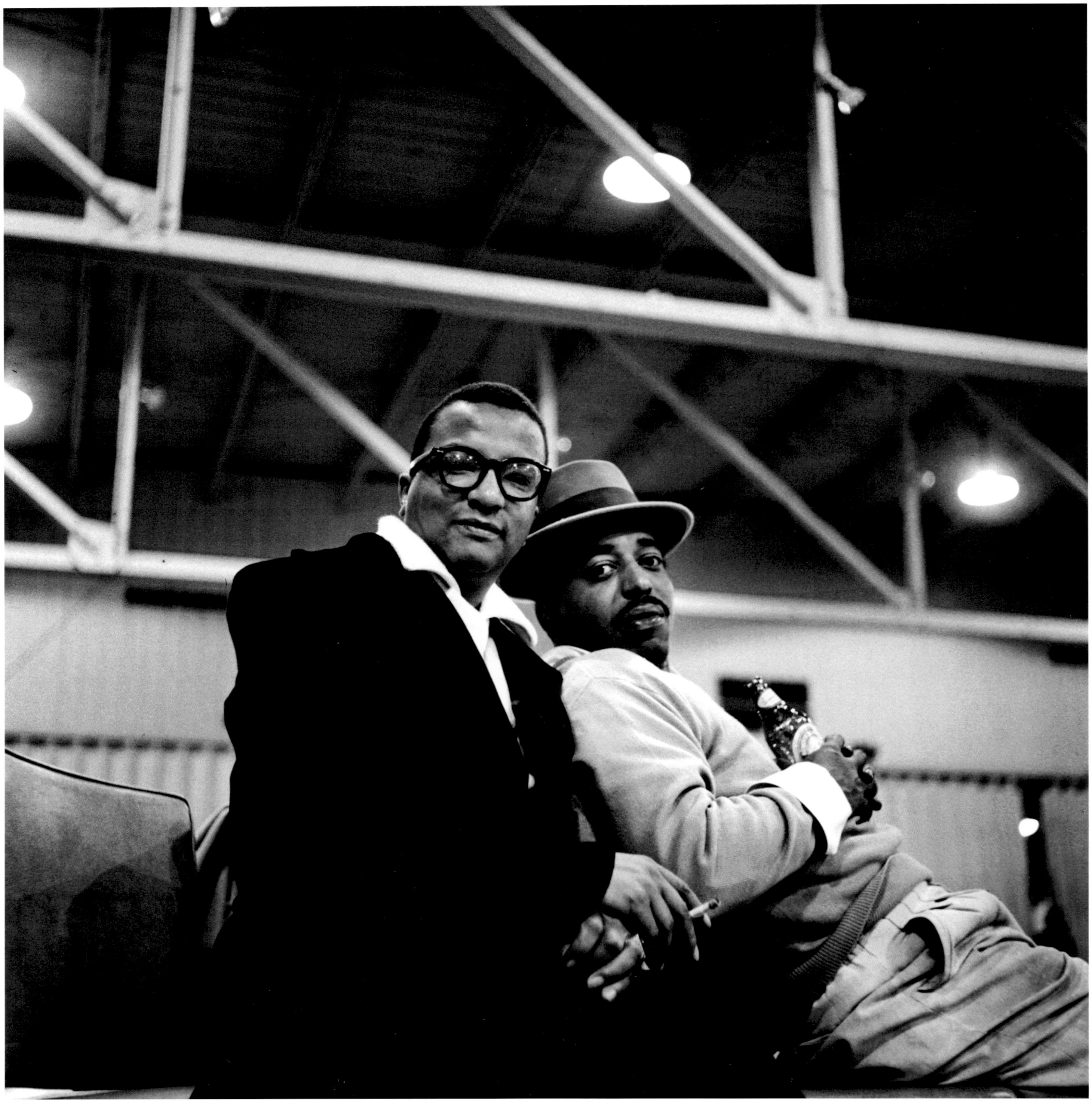

 Billy Strayhorn and Chico Hamilton Las Vegas · 1955

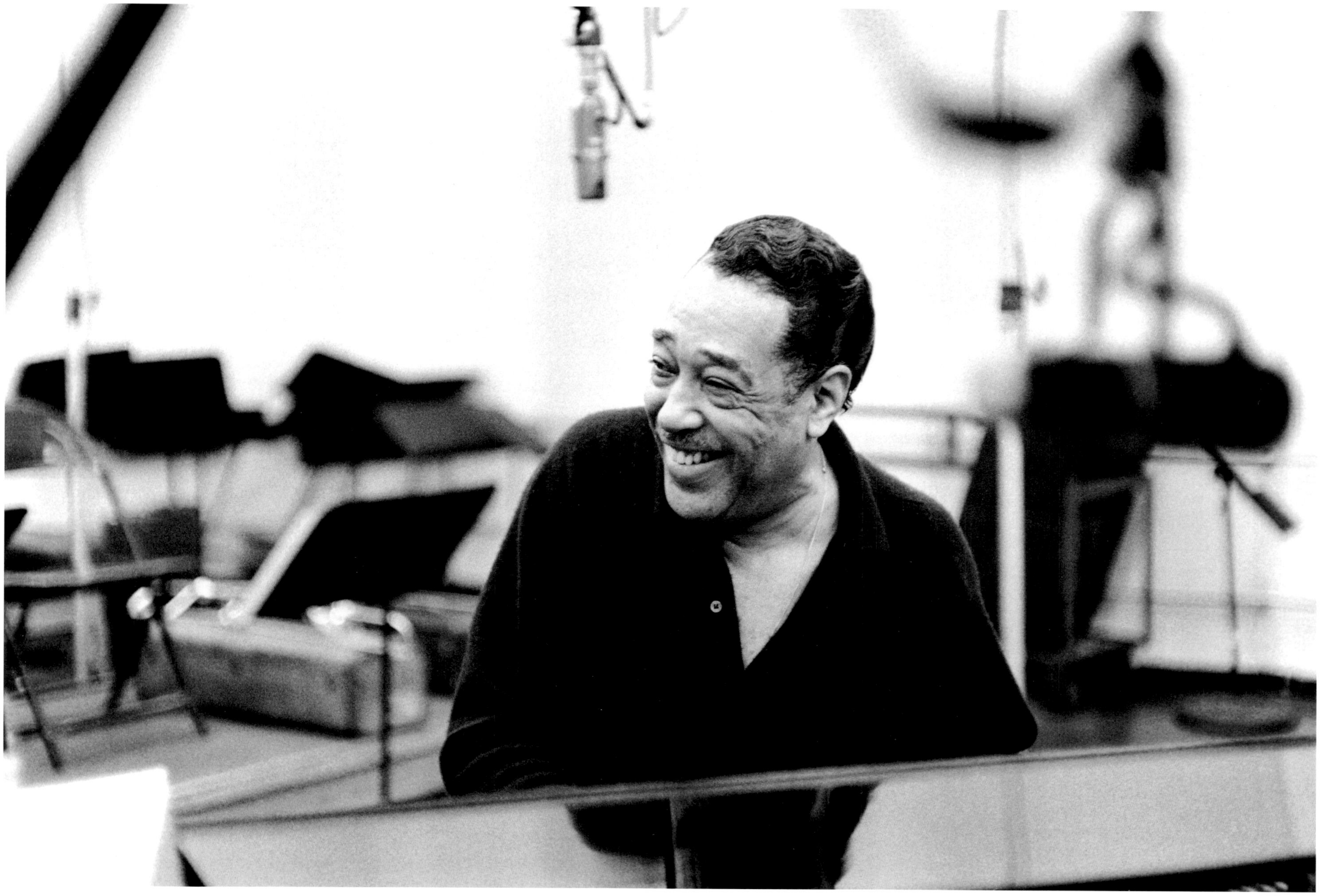

Duke Ellington Hollywood · 1960

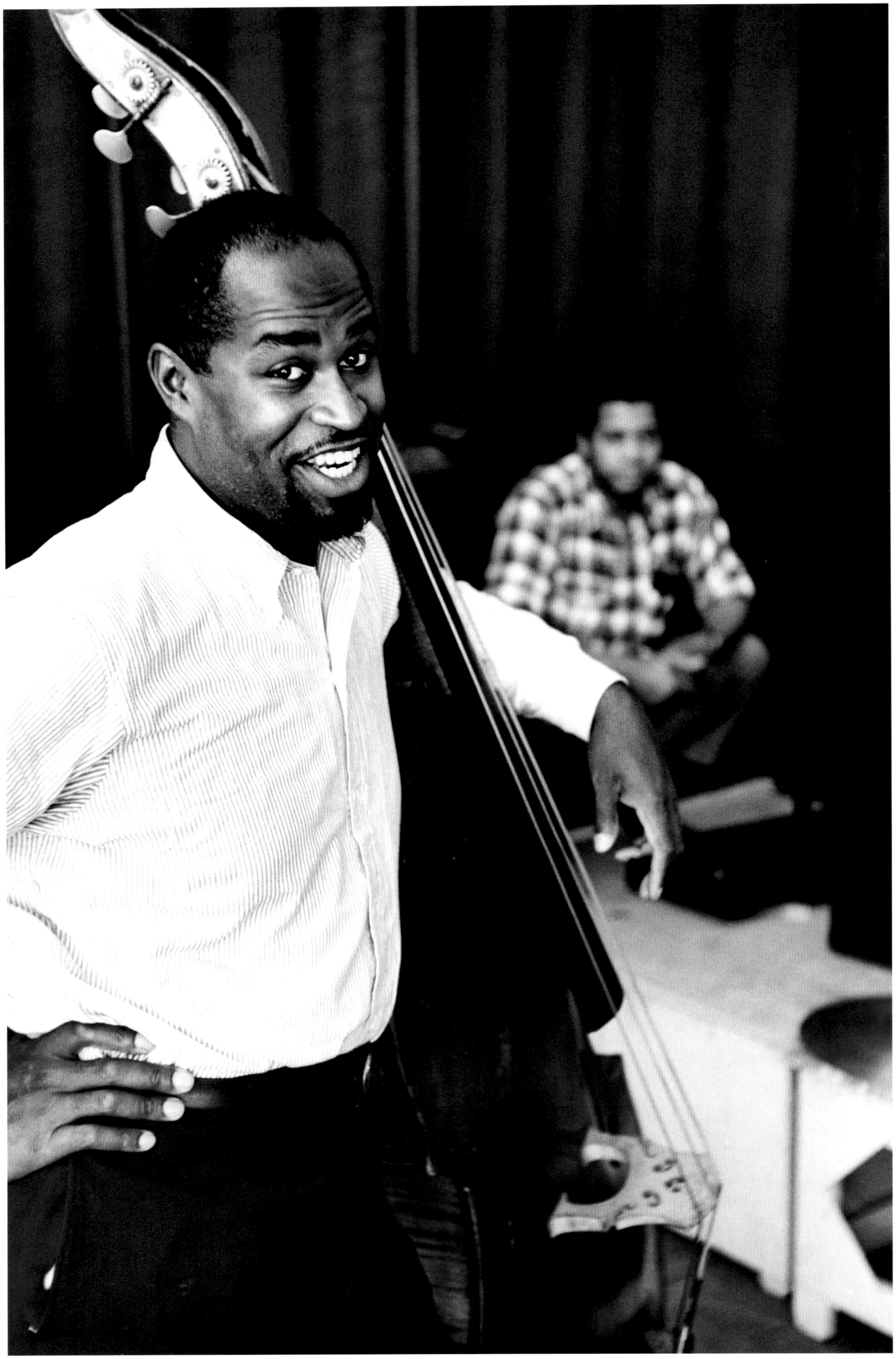

Eddie Jones
Hollywood · 1960

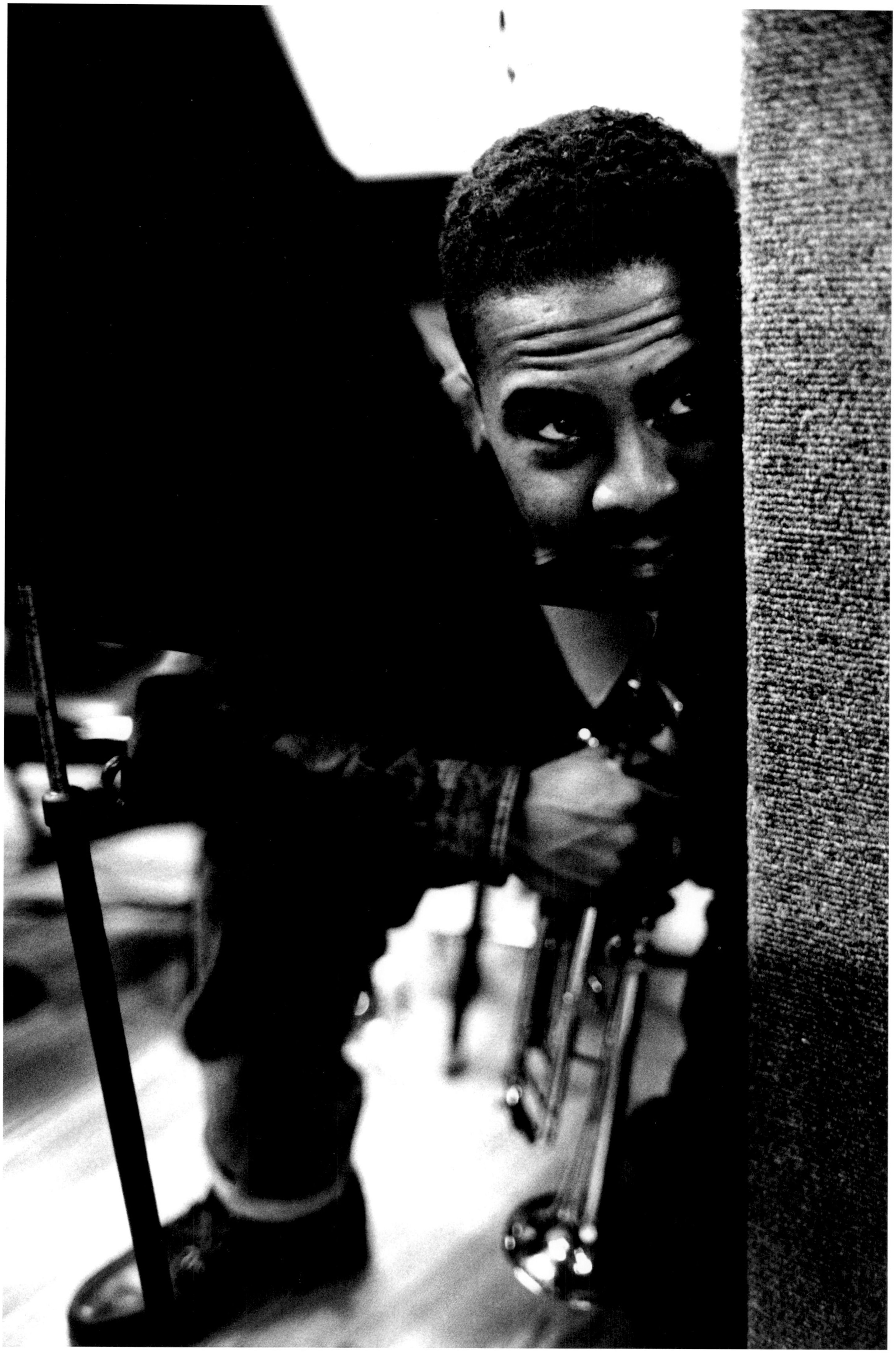

Roy Hargrove
New York City · 1993

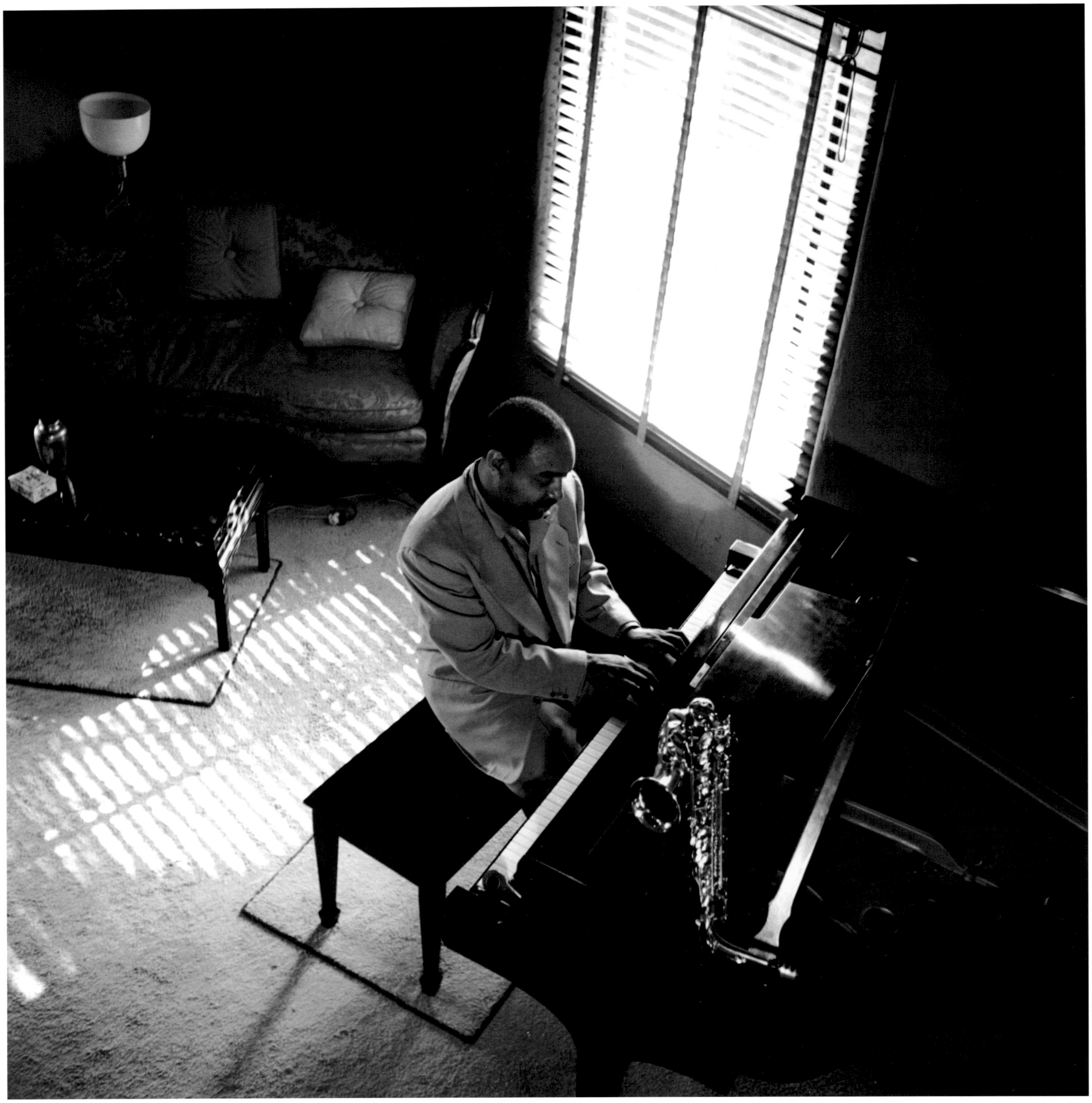

 Benny Carter Hollywood · 1955

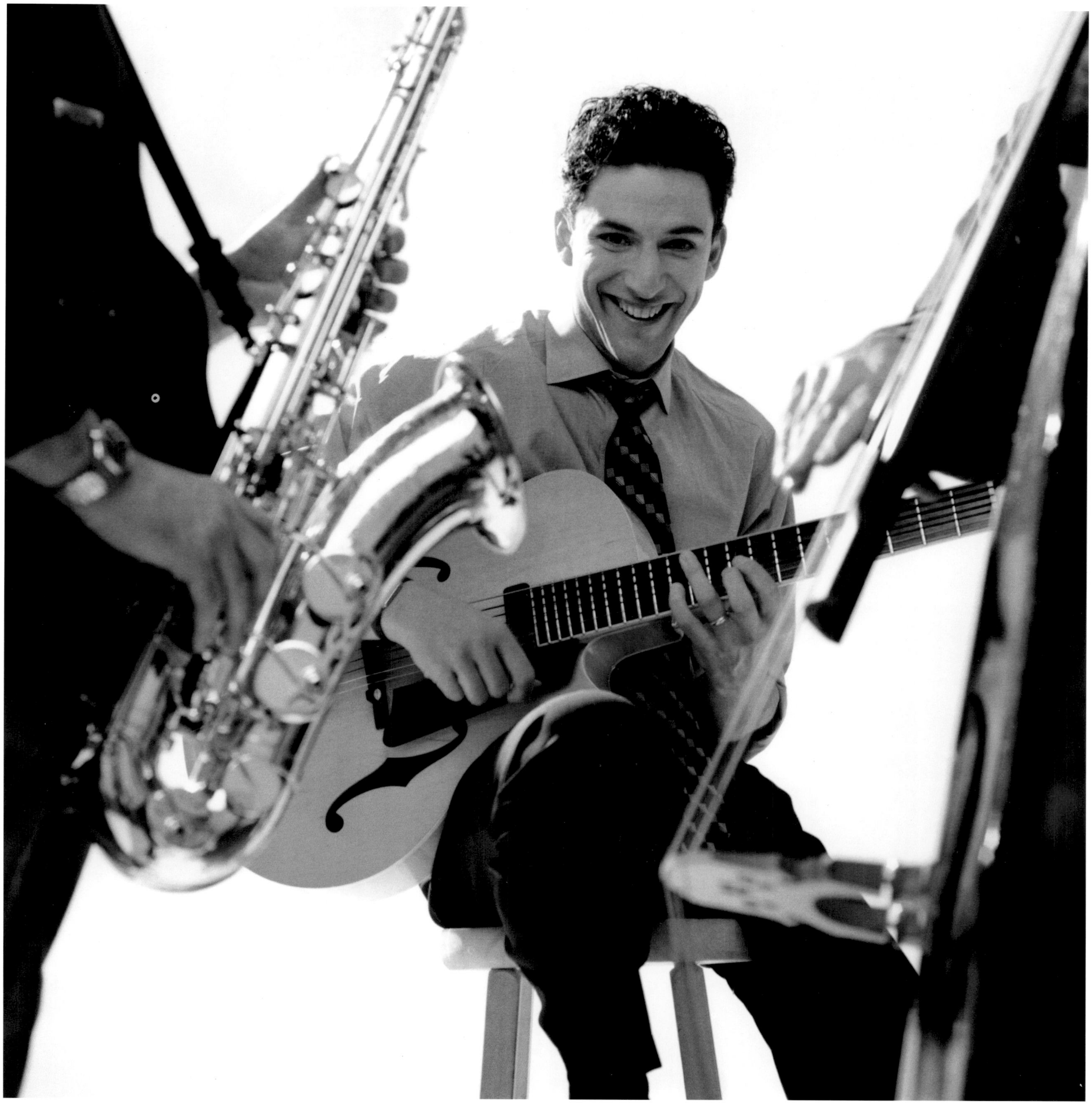

John Pizzarelli Hollywood · 1994

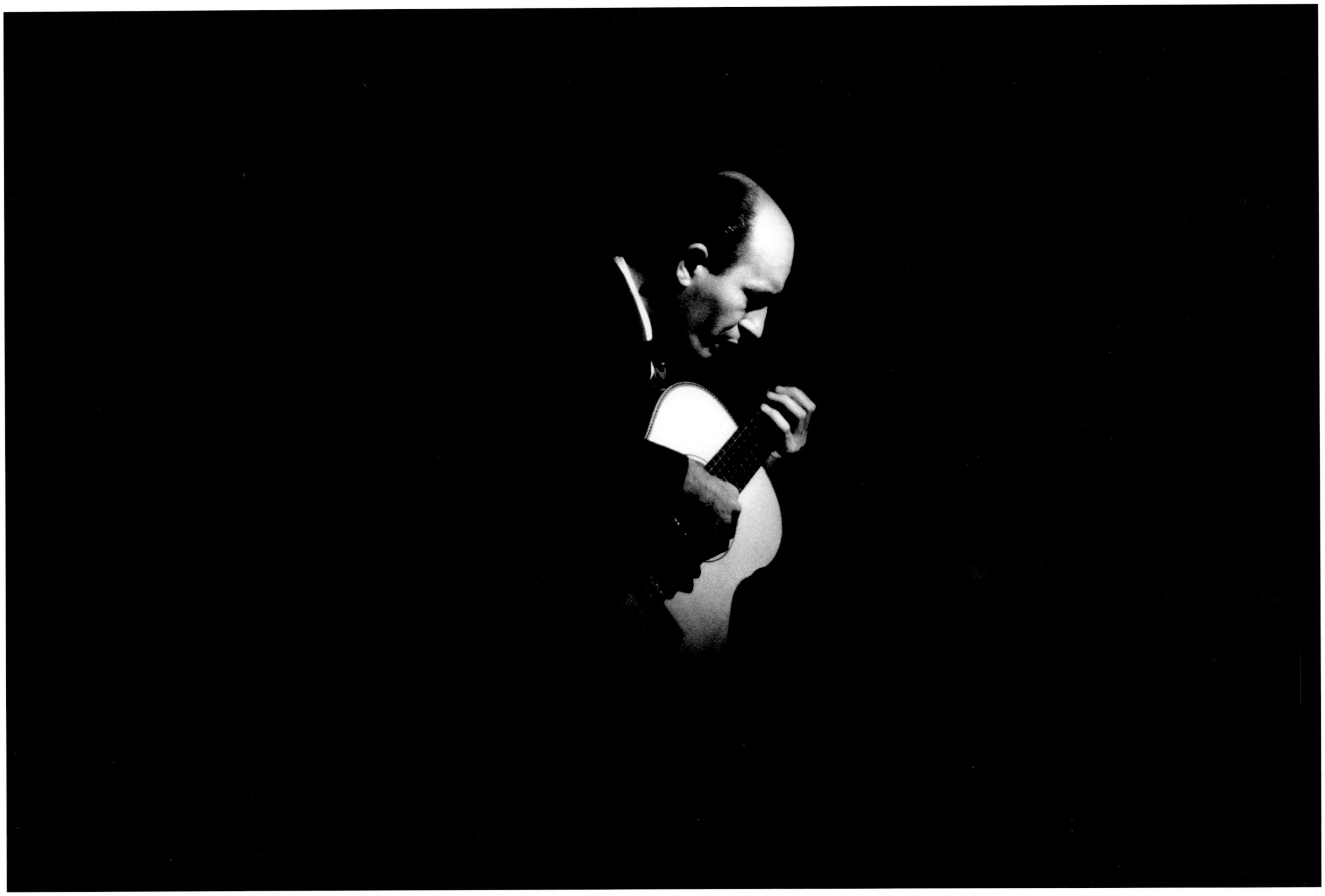

 Charlie Byrd Washington D.C. · 1960

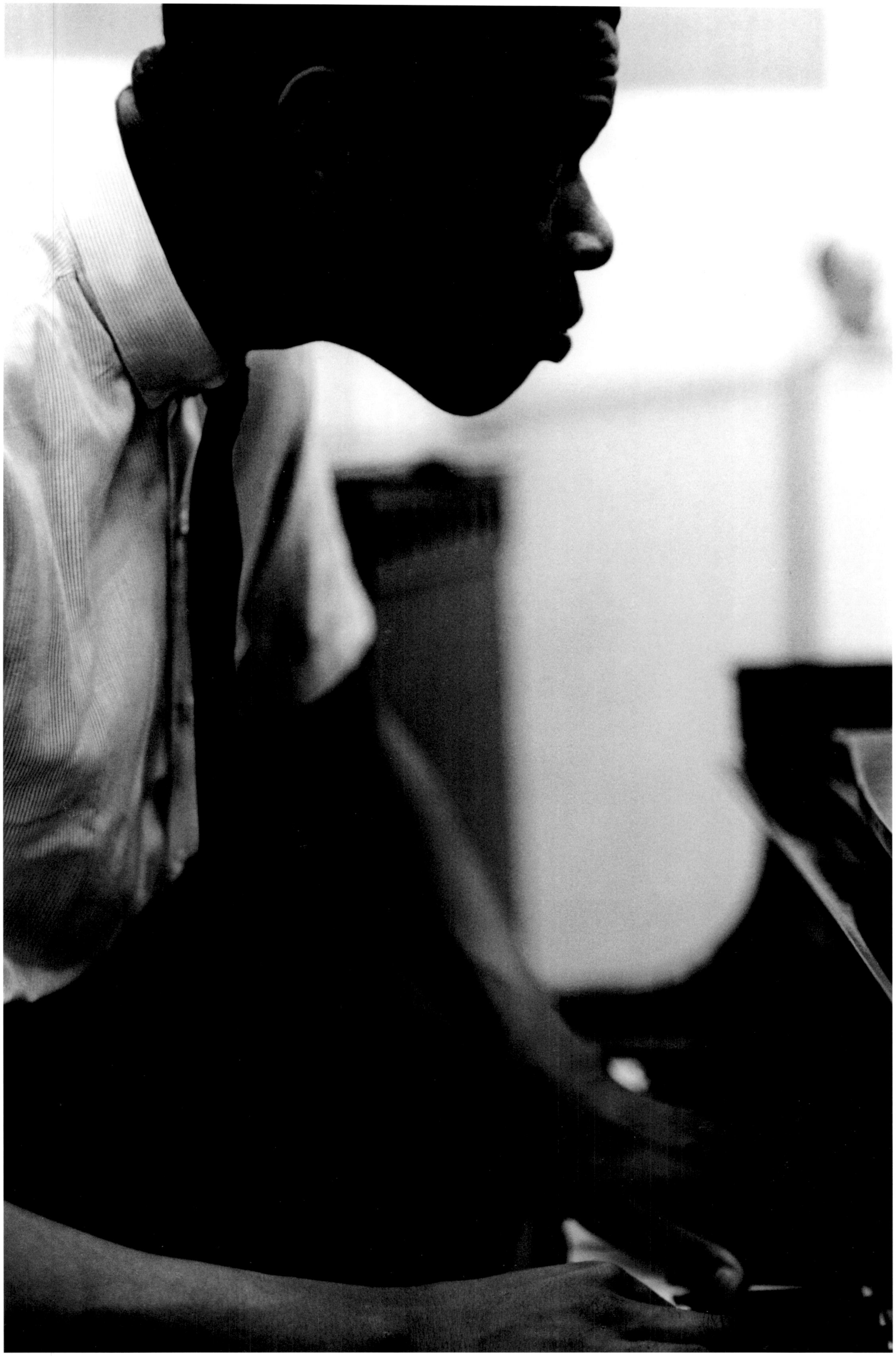

Billy Preston
Hollywood · 1956

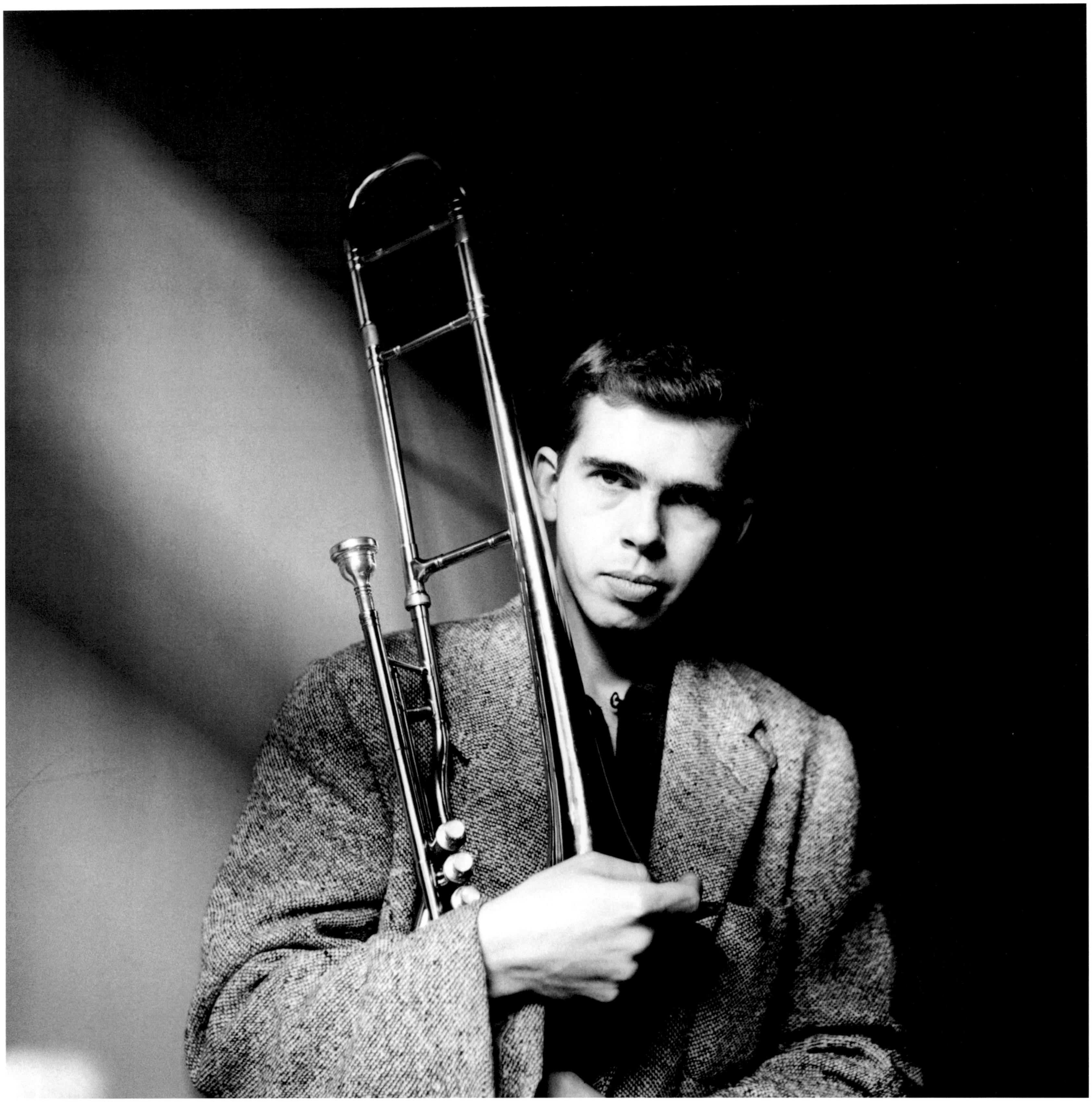

 Bob Brookmeyer Hollywood · 1955

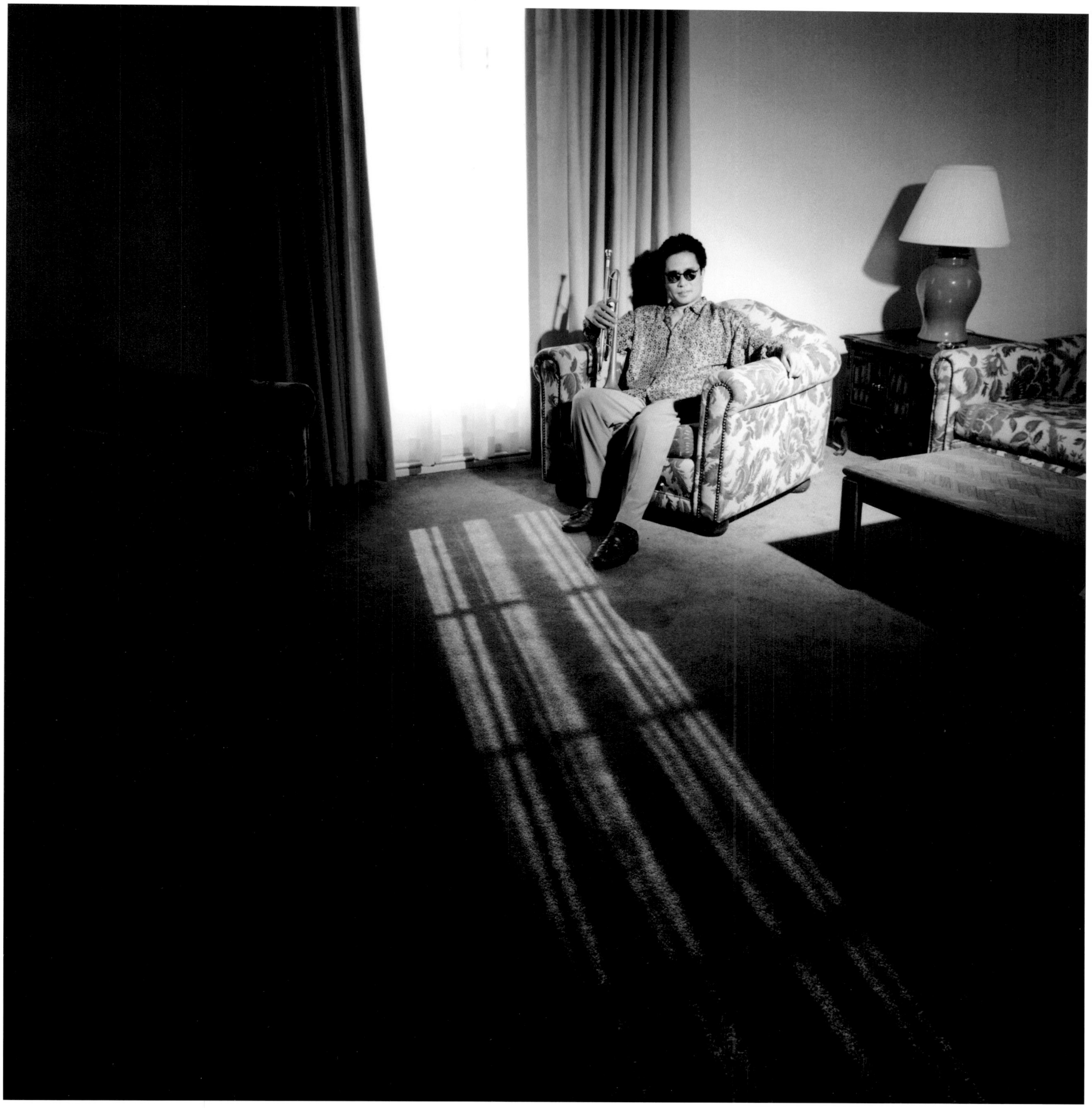

Tiger Okoshi Los Angeles · 1994

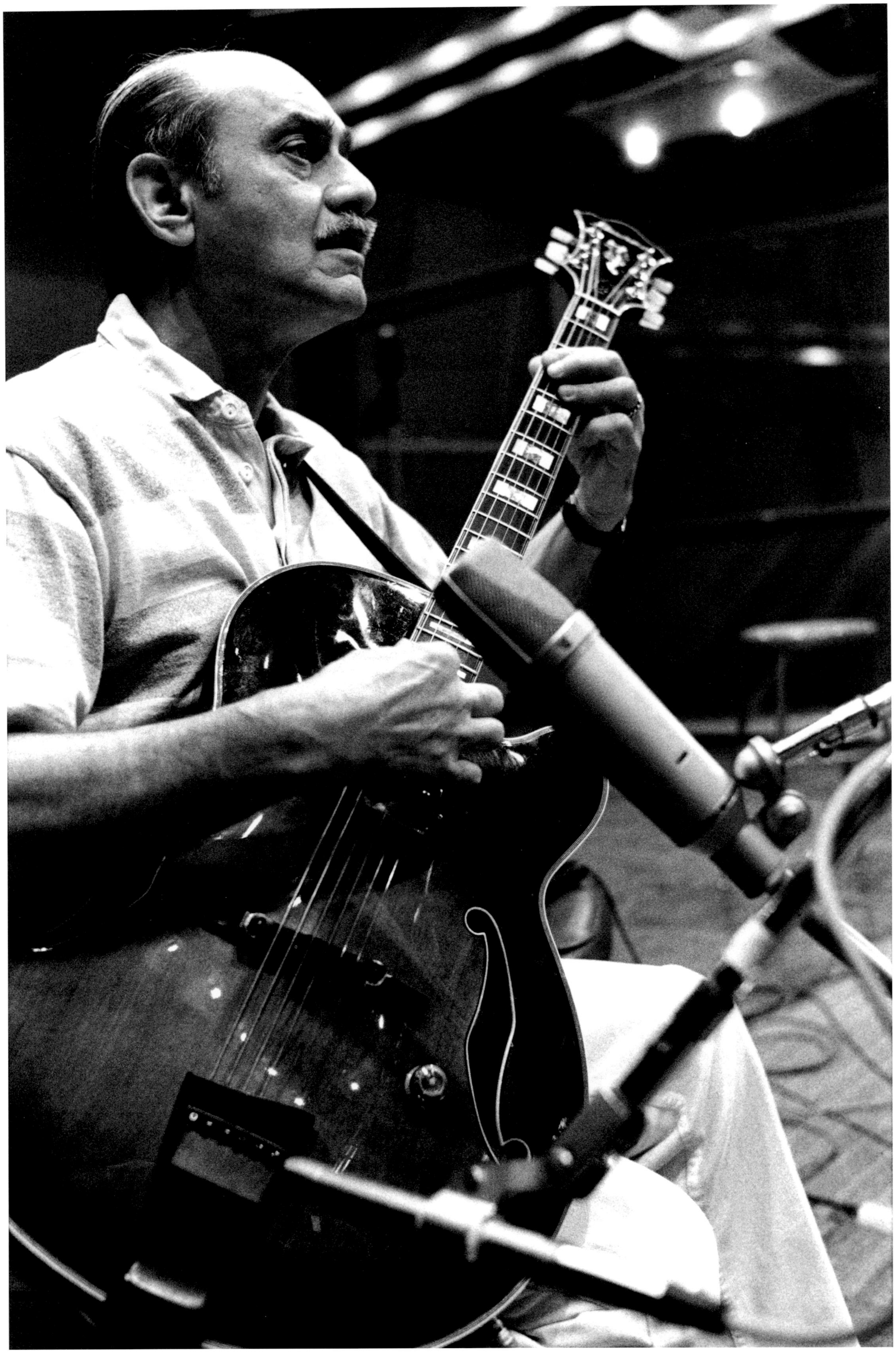

Joe Pass
Hollywood · 1991

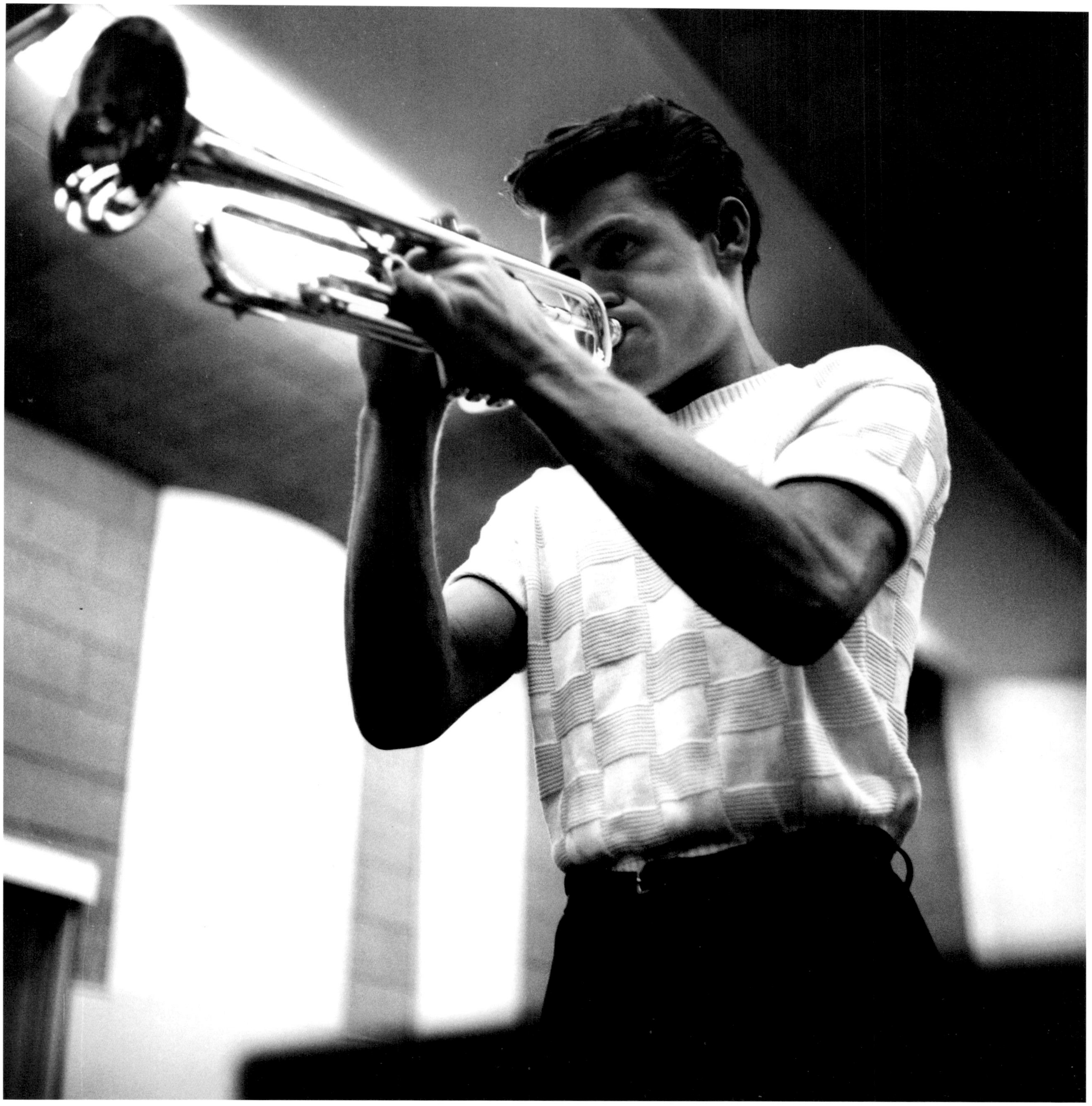

Chet Baker Hollywood · 1954

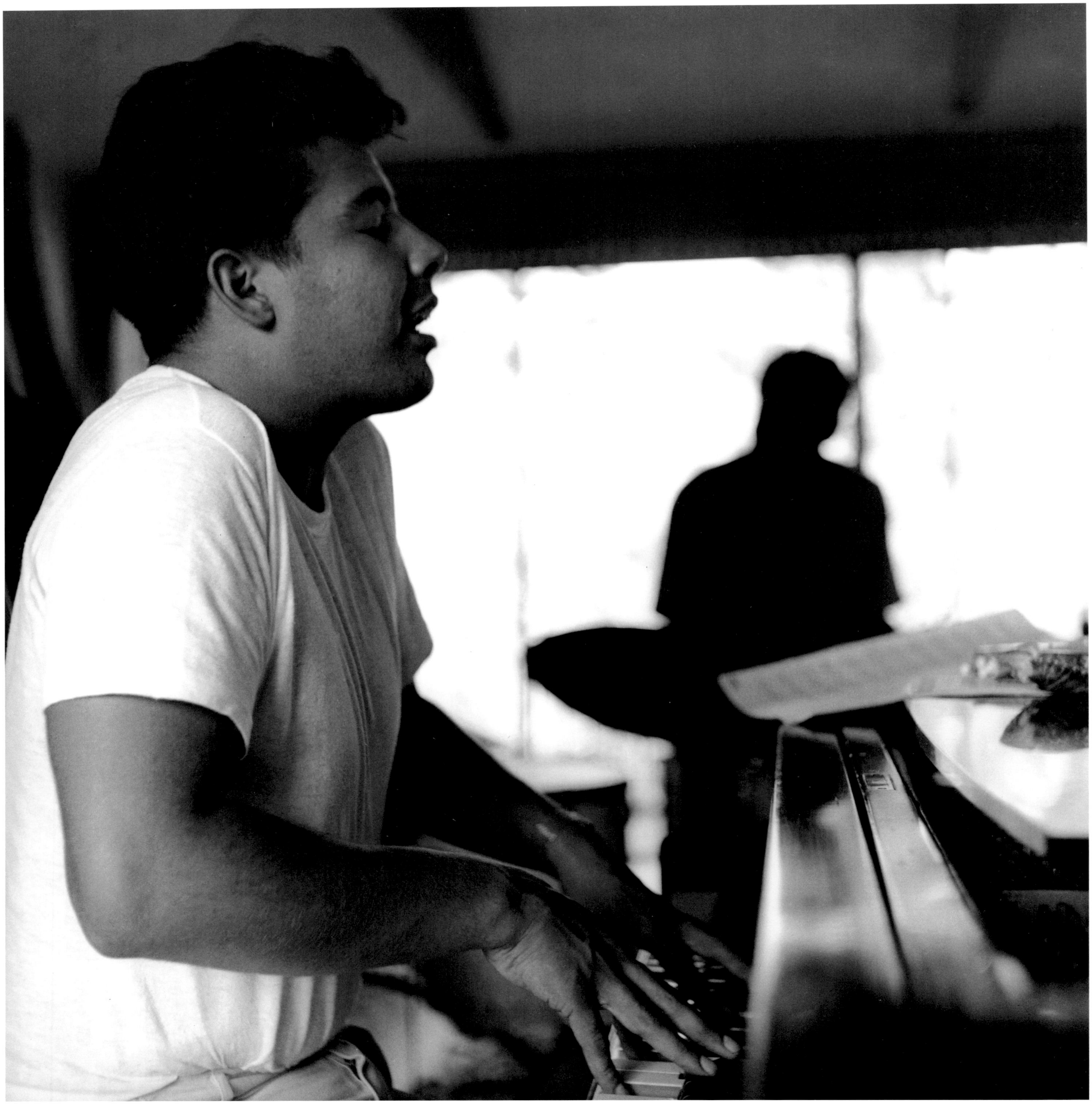

 Joe Castro and Chico Hamilton ***(drums)*** Beverly Hills · 1959

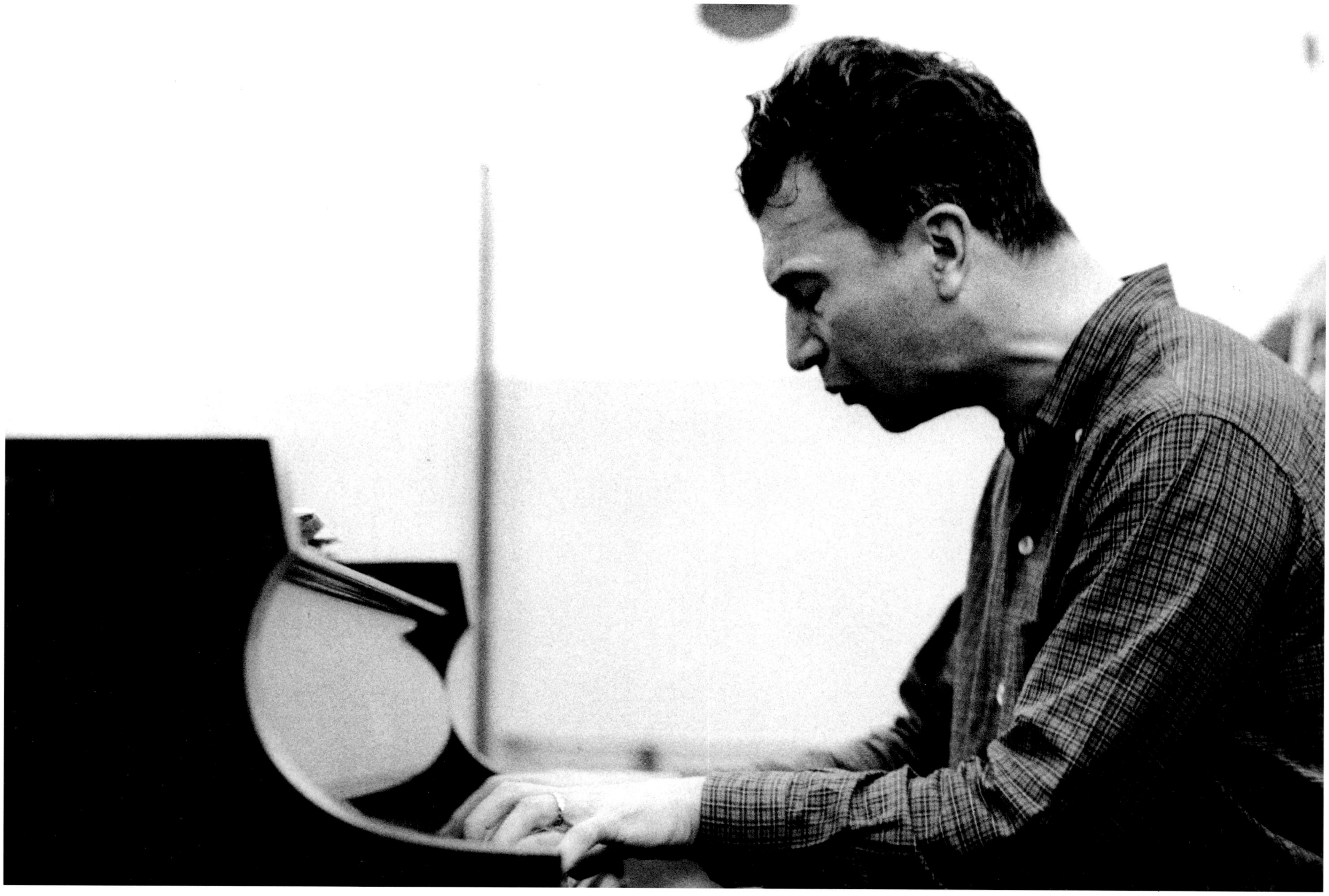

Dave Brubeck Hollywood · 1955

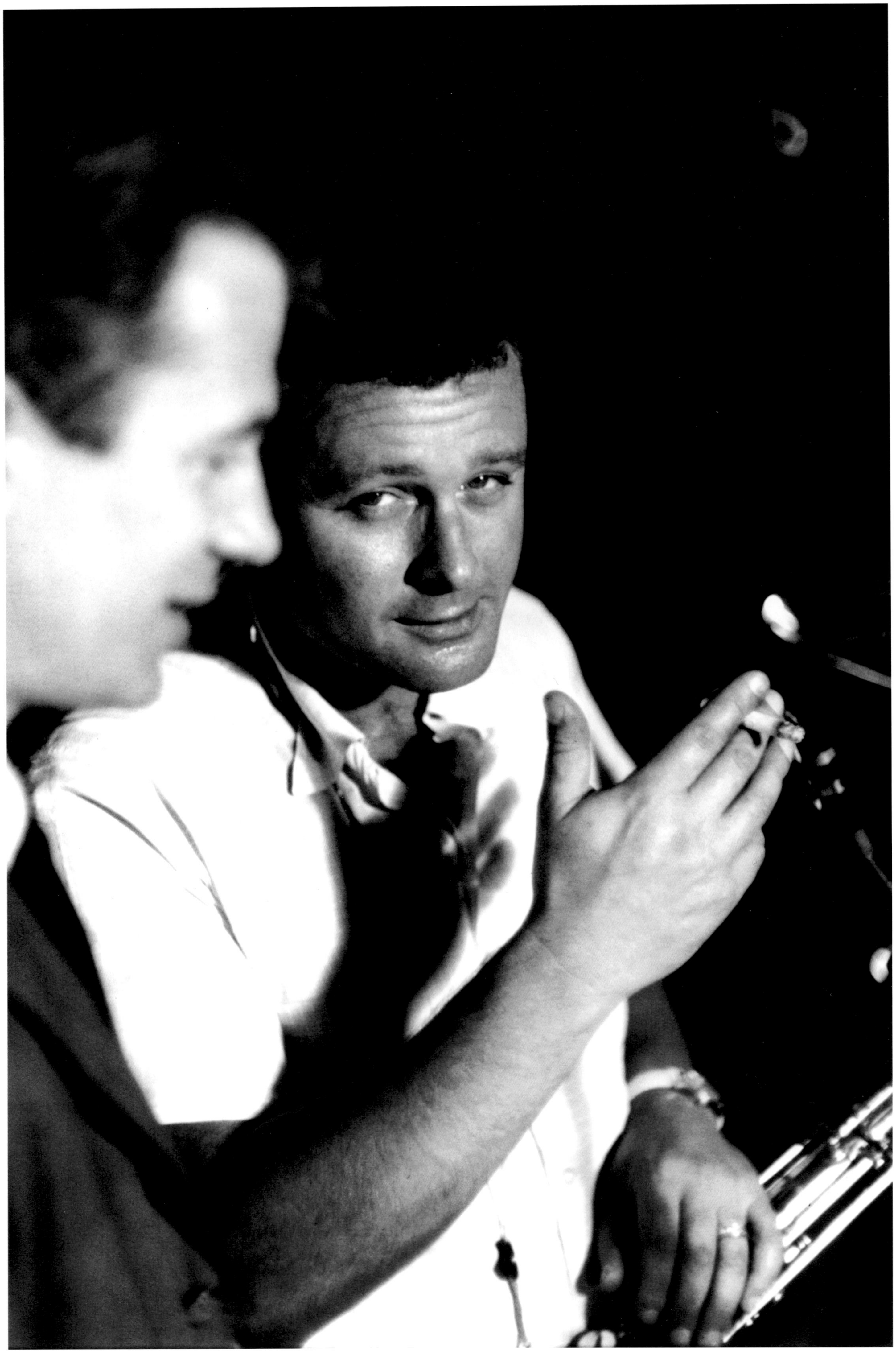

Stan Getz
and Gary McFarland
Englewood Cliffs · 1962

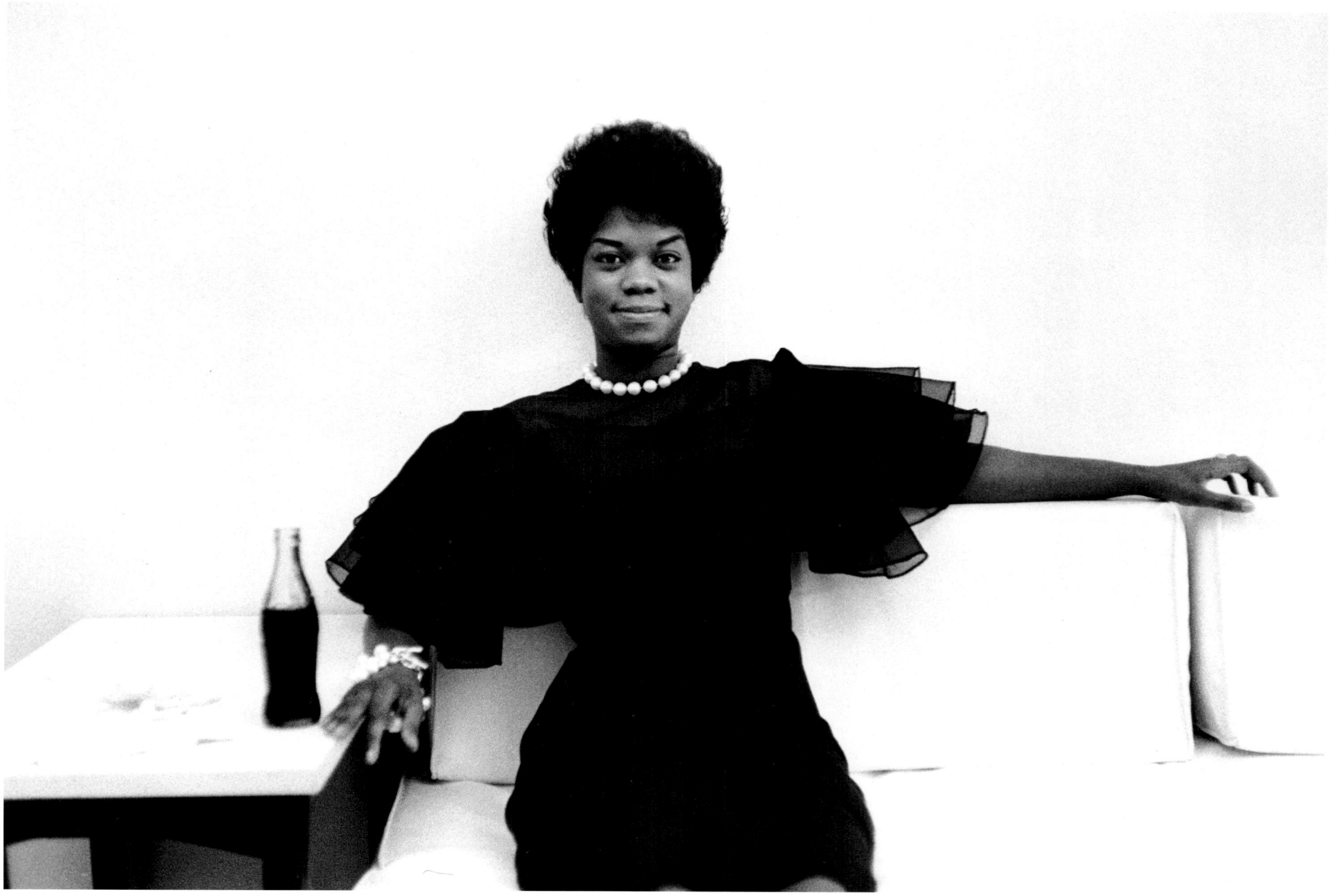

Ernestine Anderson Hollywood · 1960

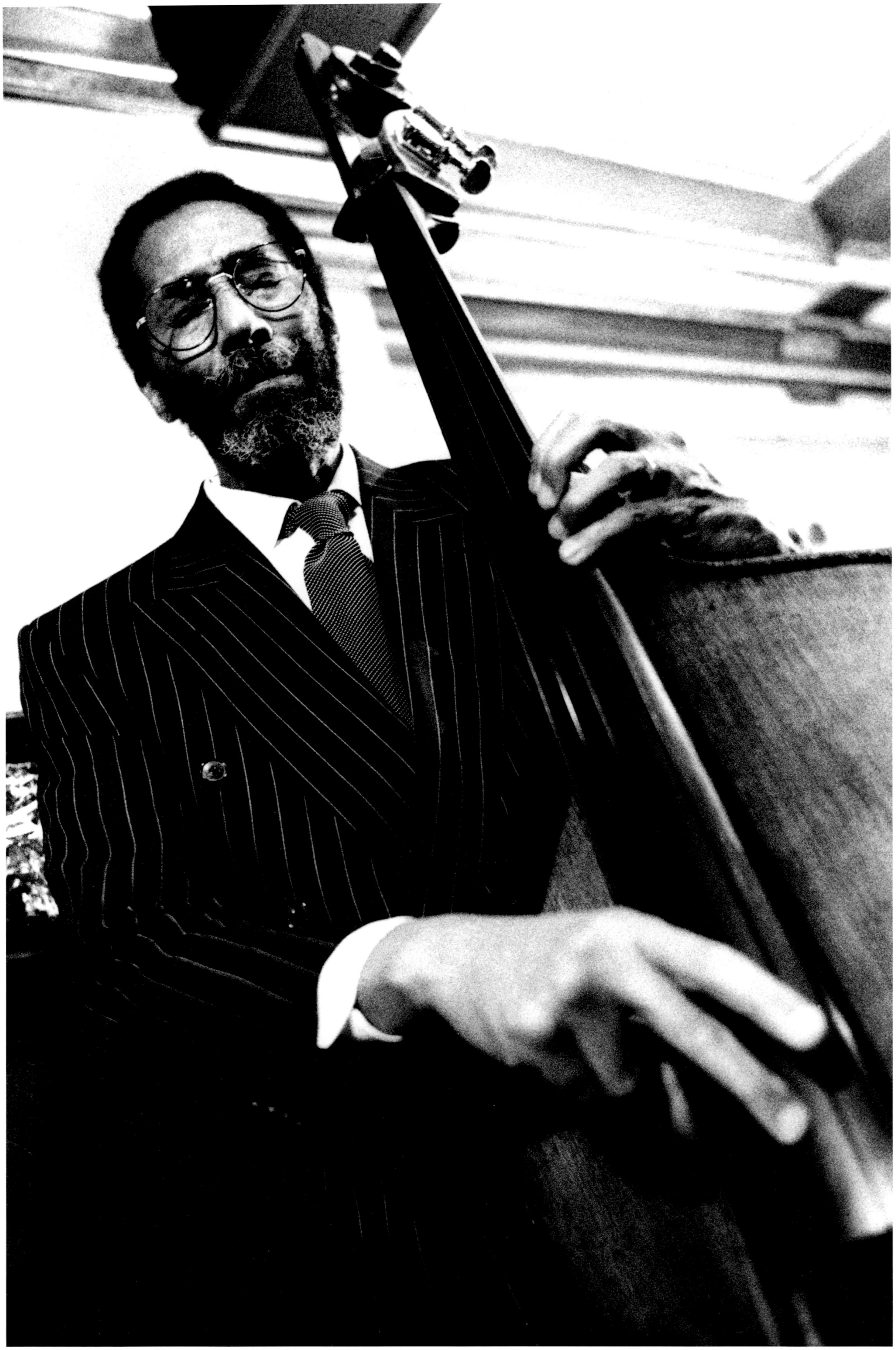

Ron Carter
New York City · 1992

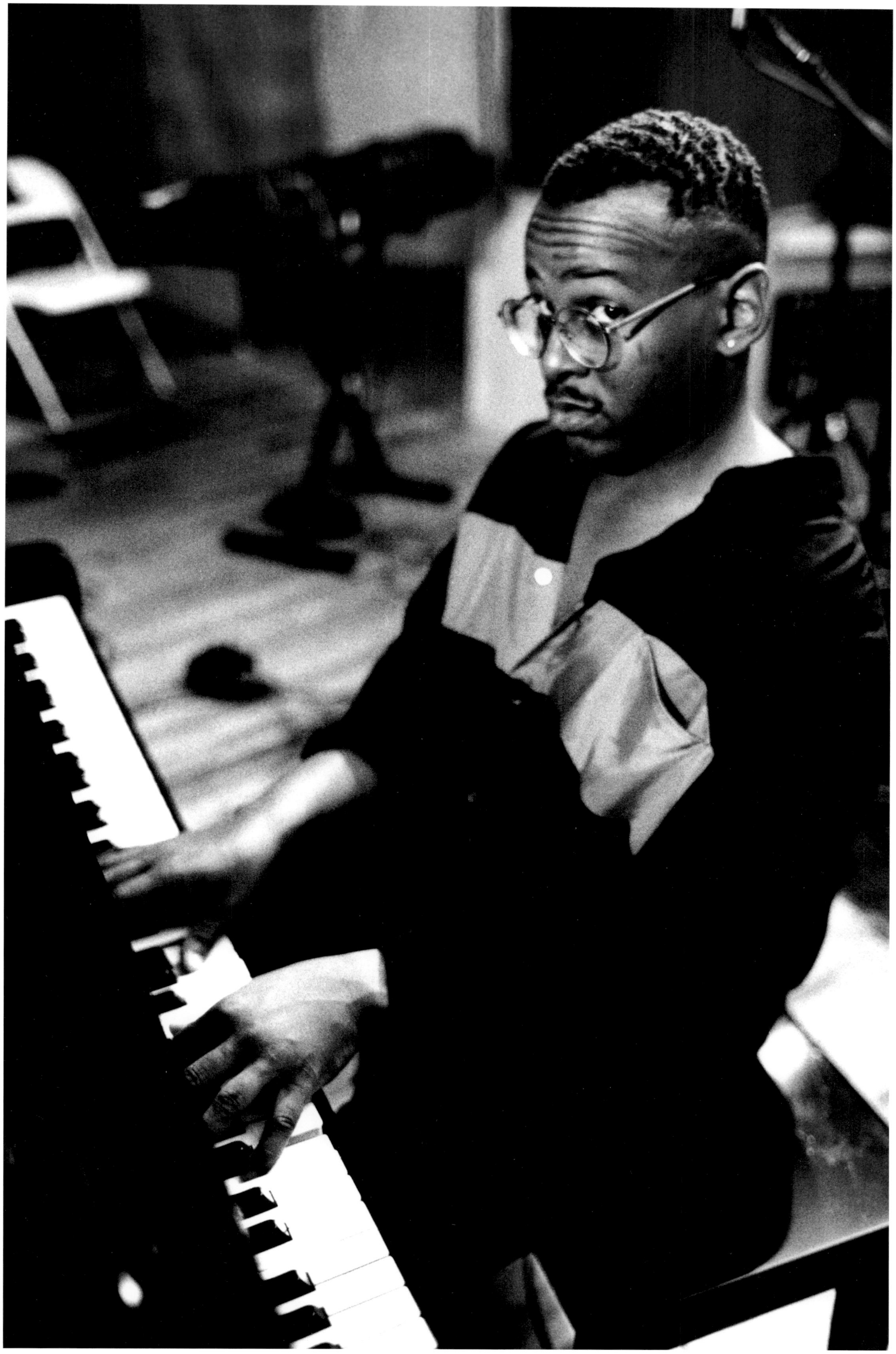

Stephen Scott
New York City · 1992

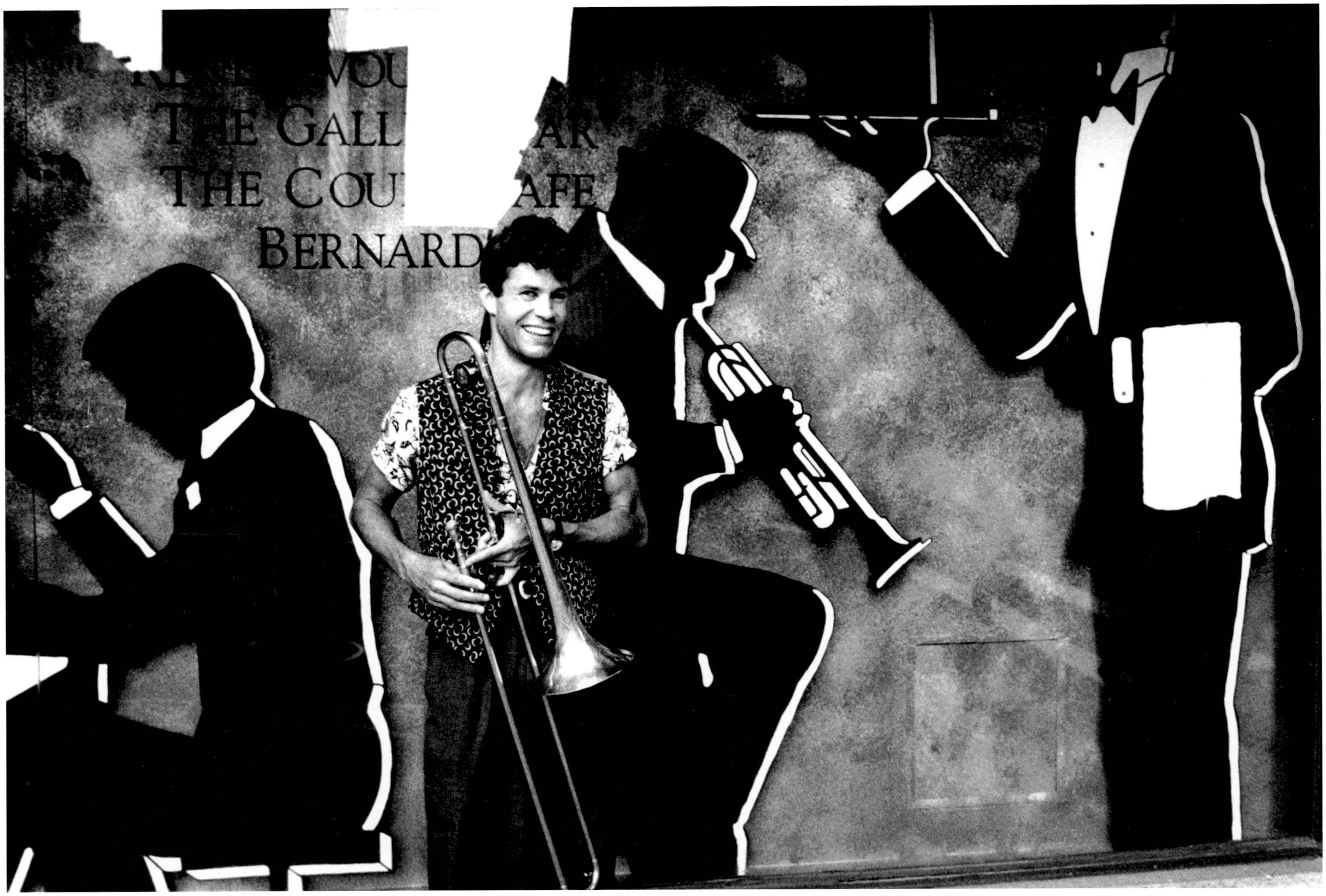

 Ray Anderson Los Angeles · 1990

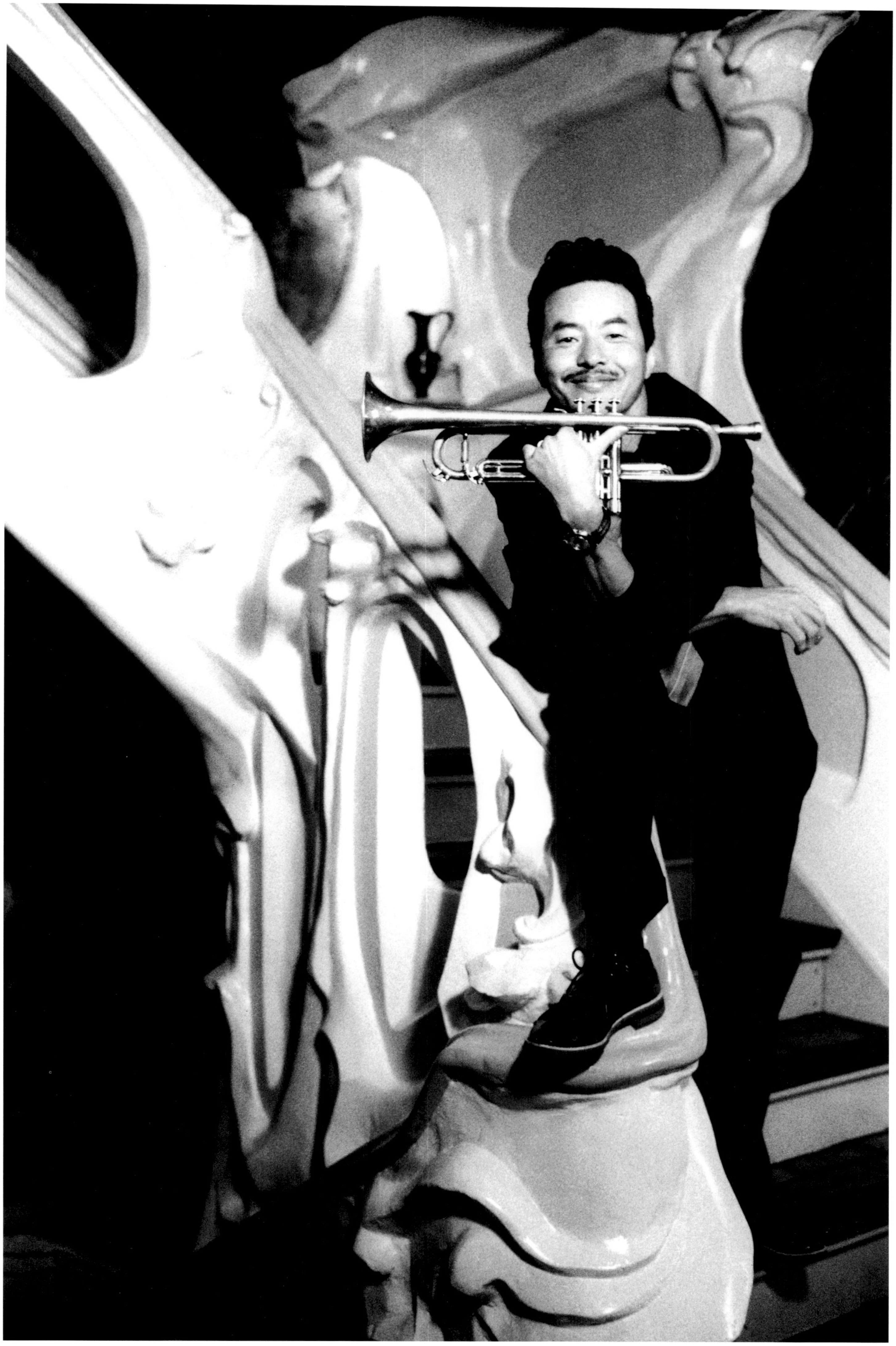

Terumasa Hino
New York City · 1992

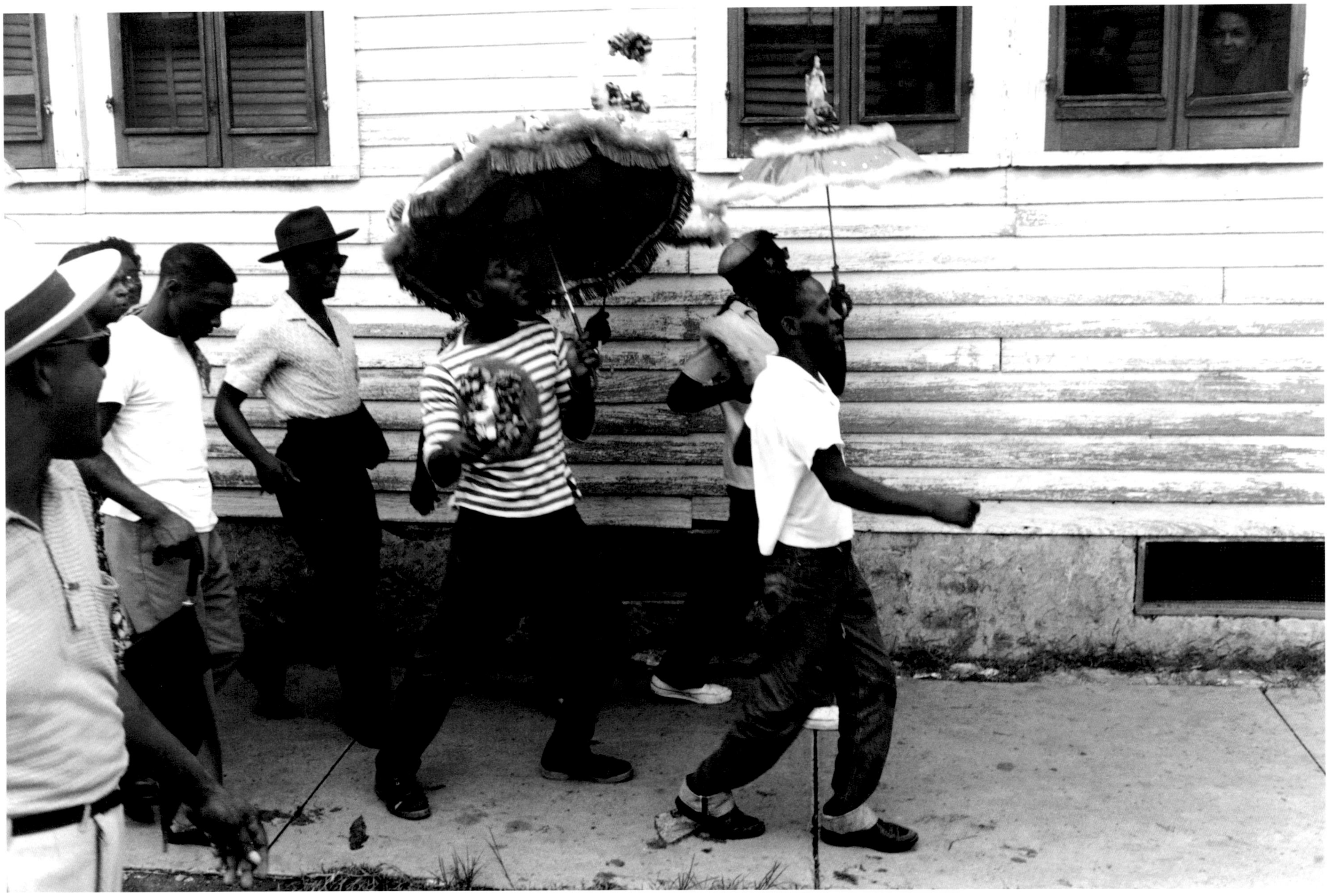

Second Liners New Orleans · 1960

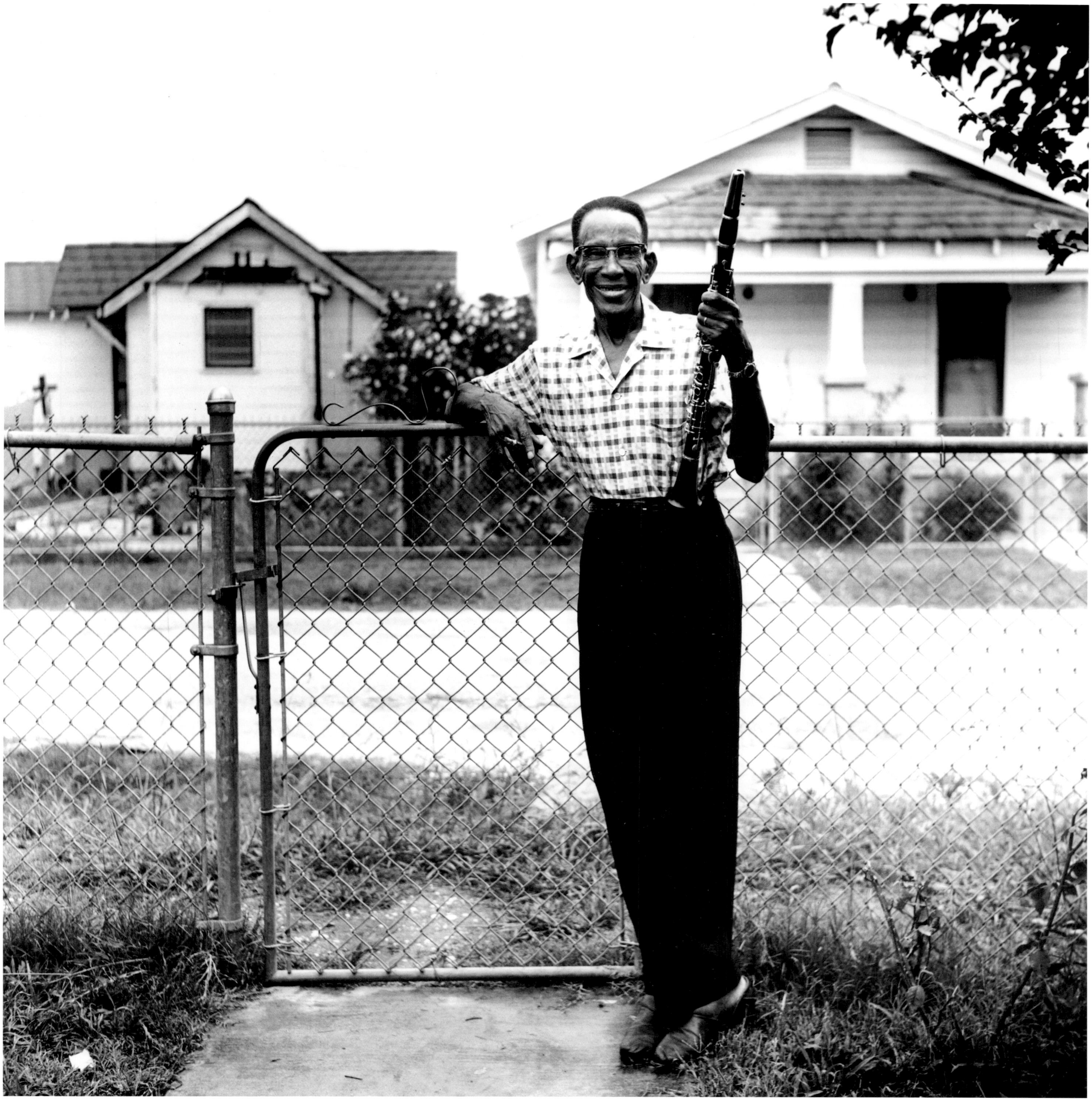

George Lewis Algiers, Louisiana · 1960

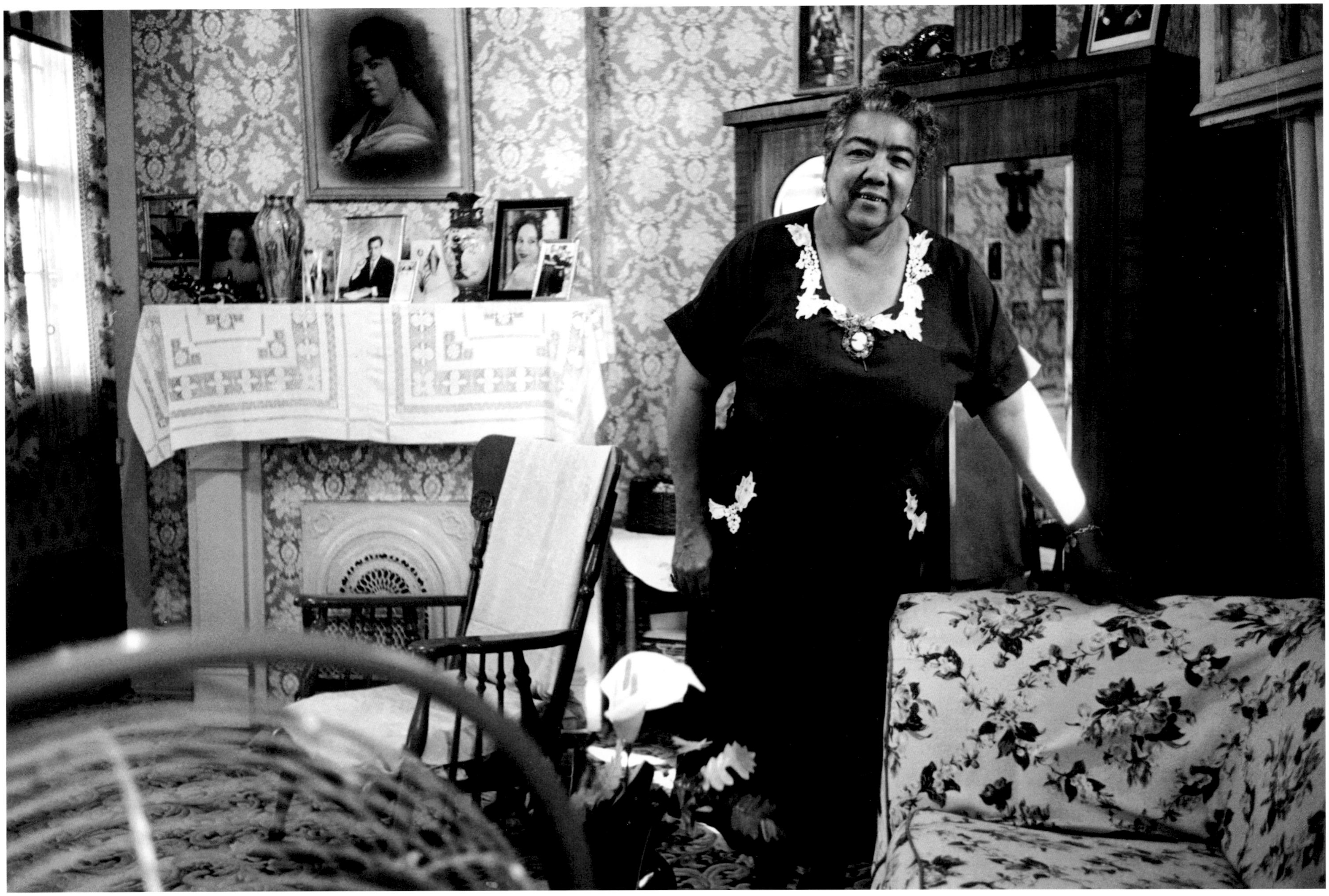

 Lizzie Miles New Orleans · 1960

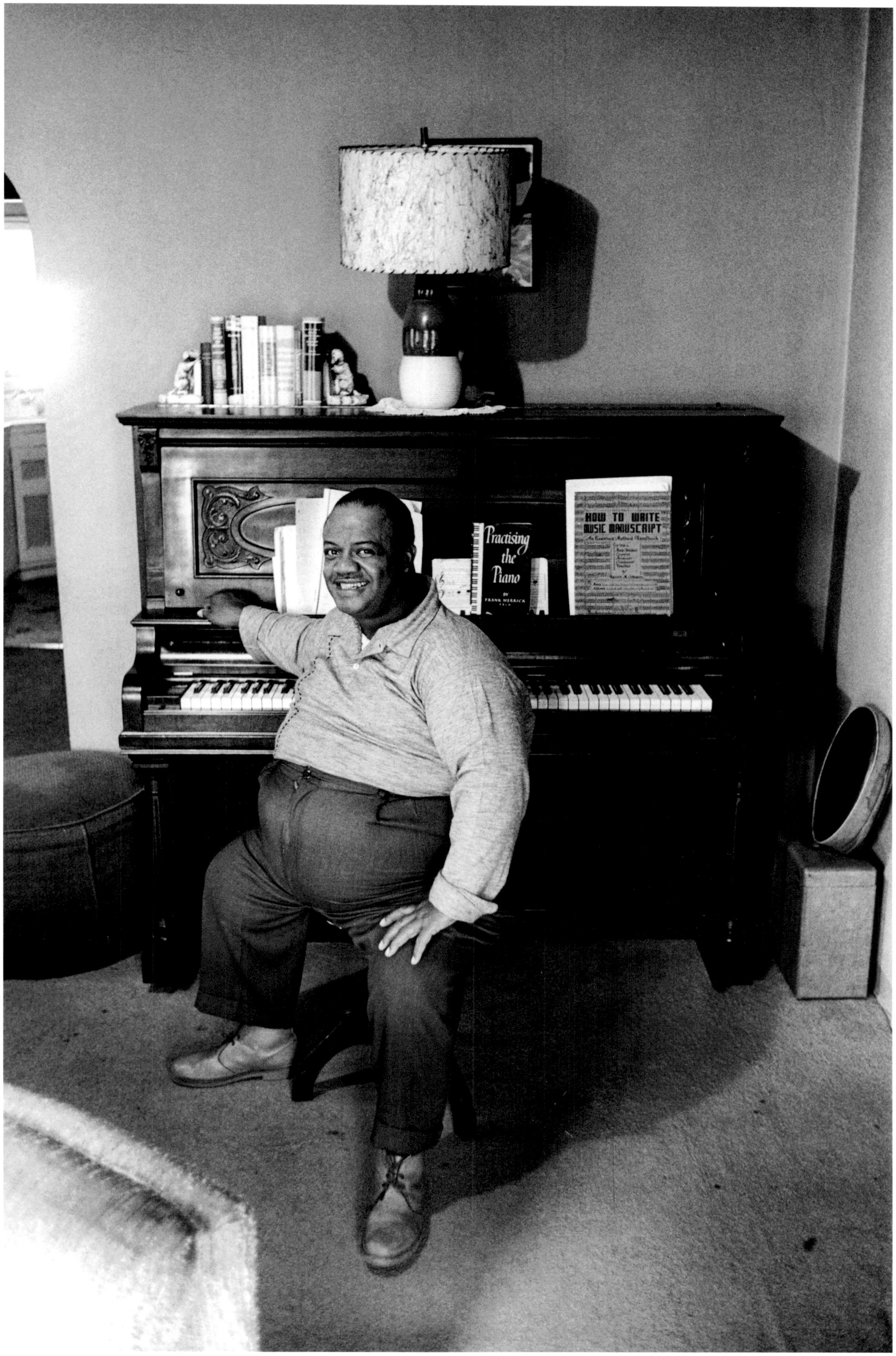

Meade Lux Lewis
Los Angeles · 1960

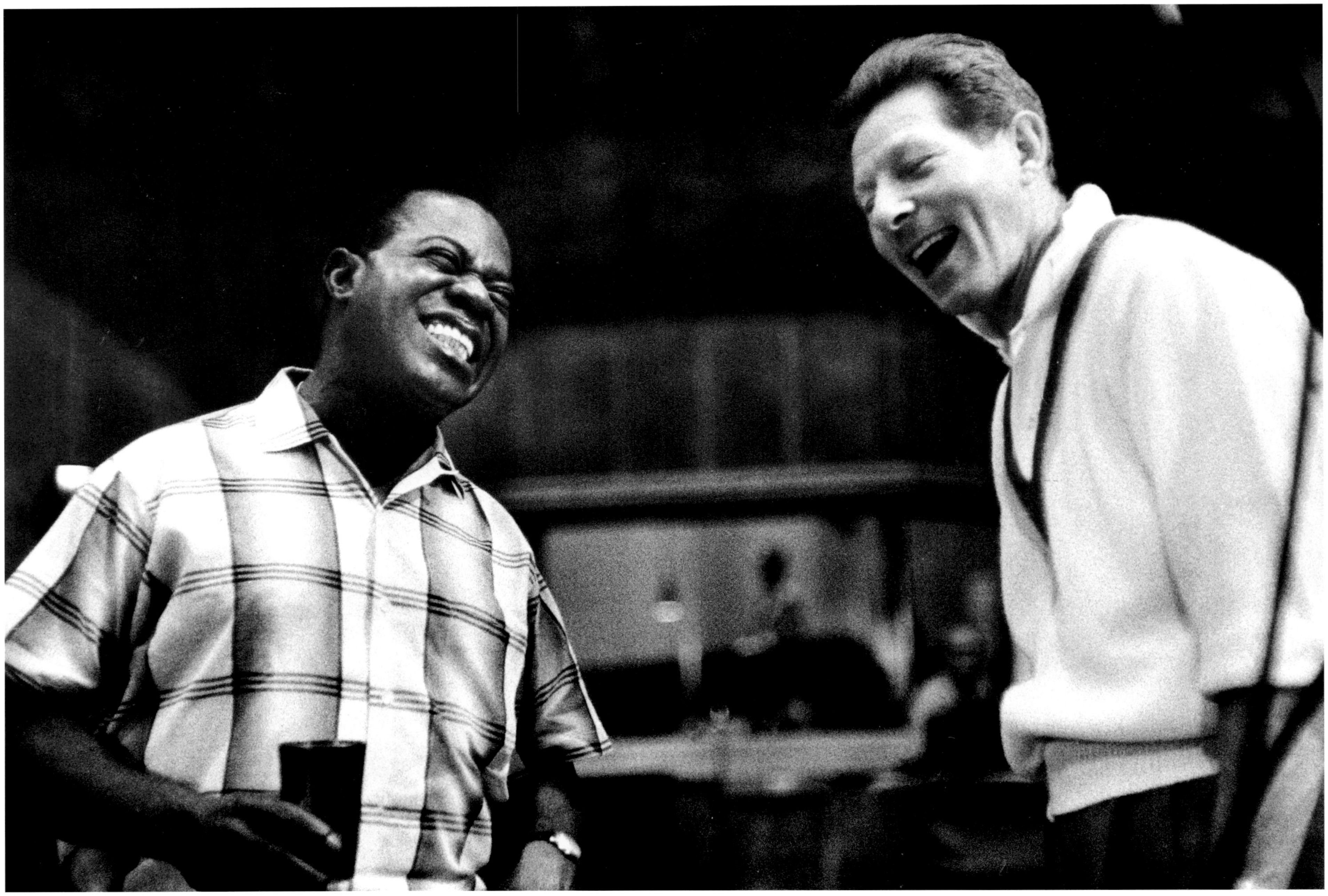

 Louis Armstrong and Danny Kaye Hollywood · 1958

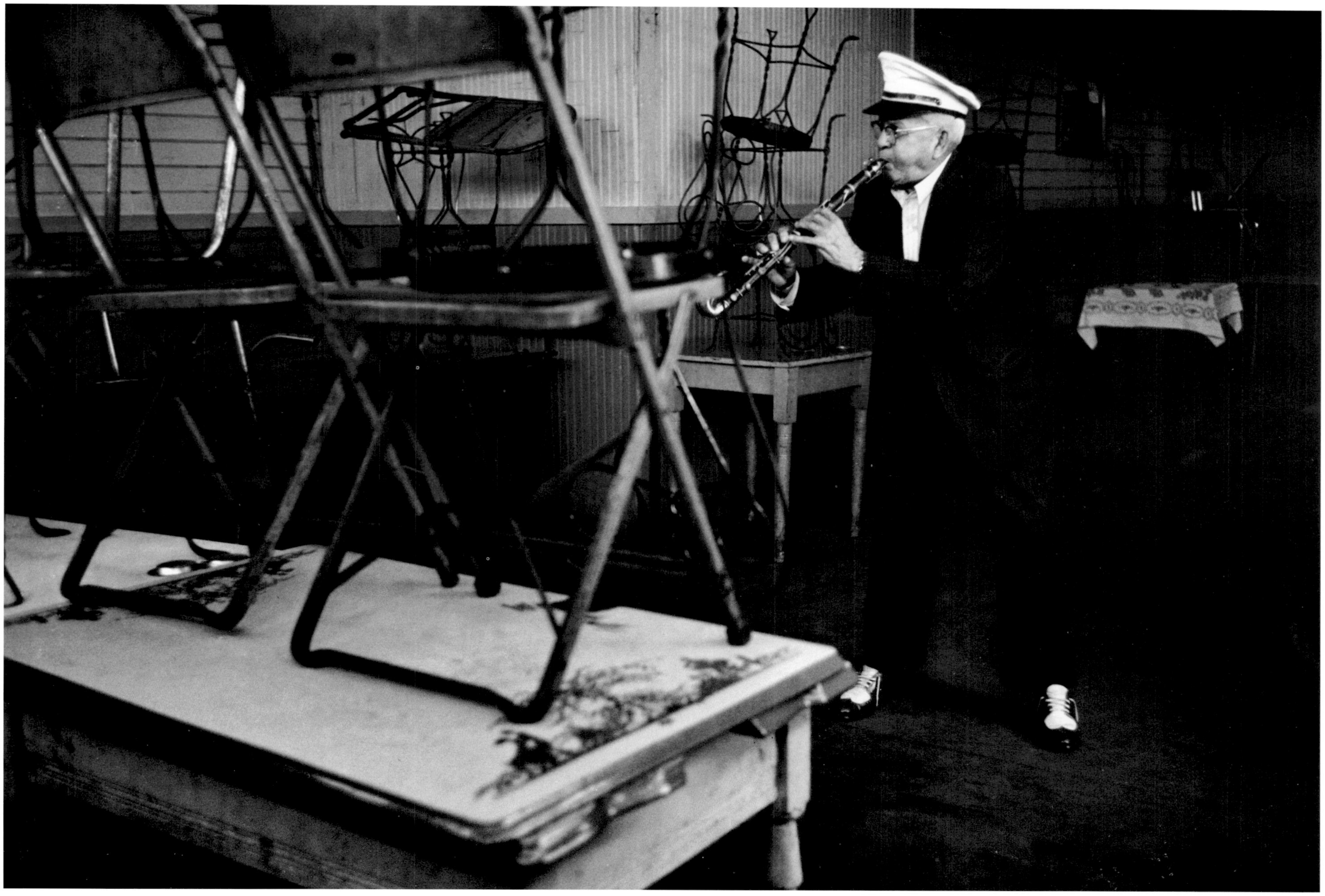

Alphonse Picou New Orleans · 1960

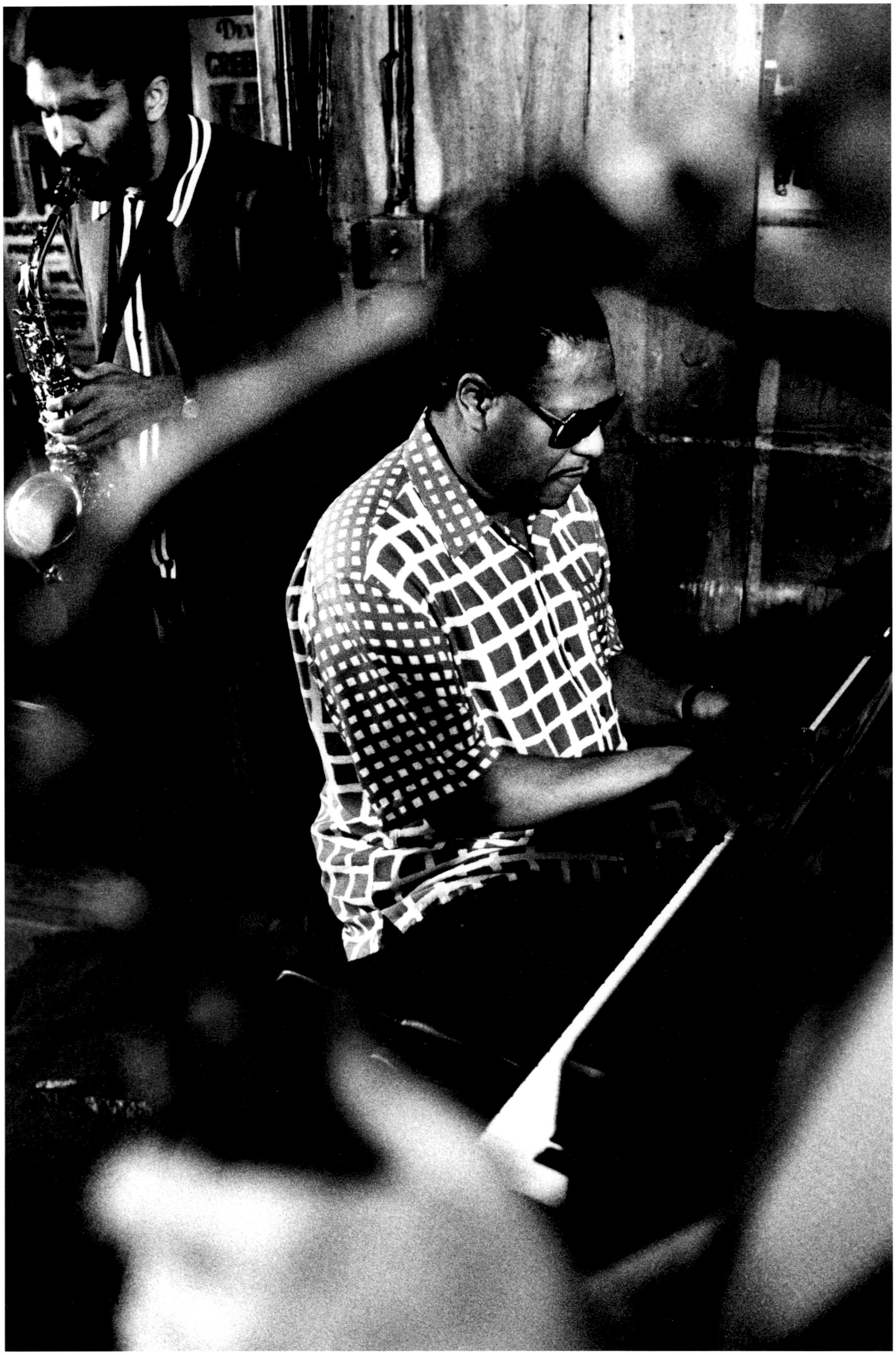

McCoy Tyner
and Art Porter
New York City · 1992

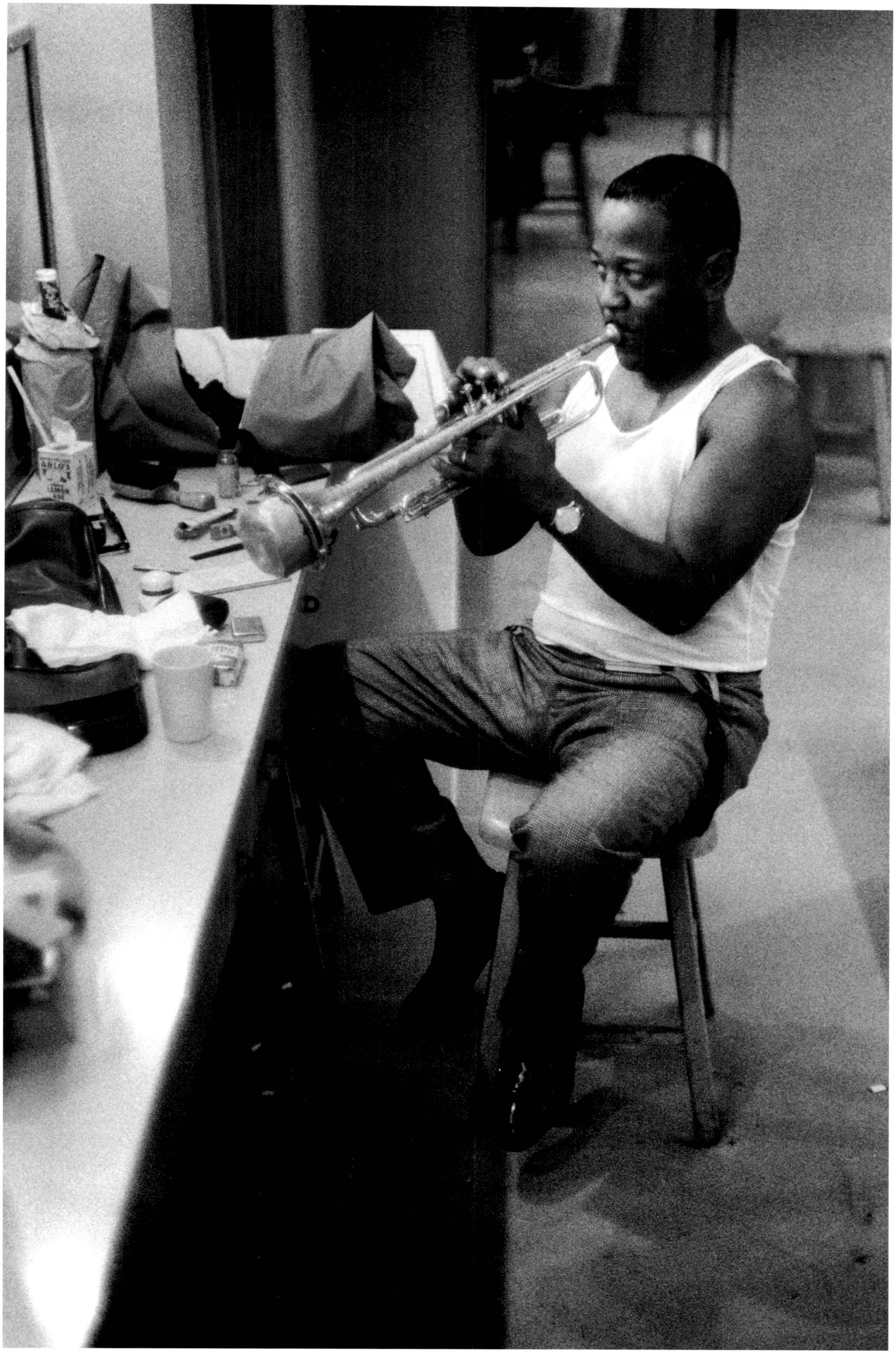

Roy "Little Jazz" Eldridge
Hollywood · 1960

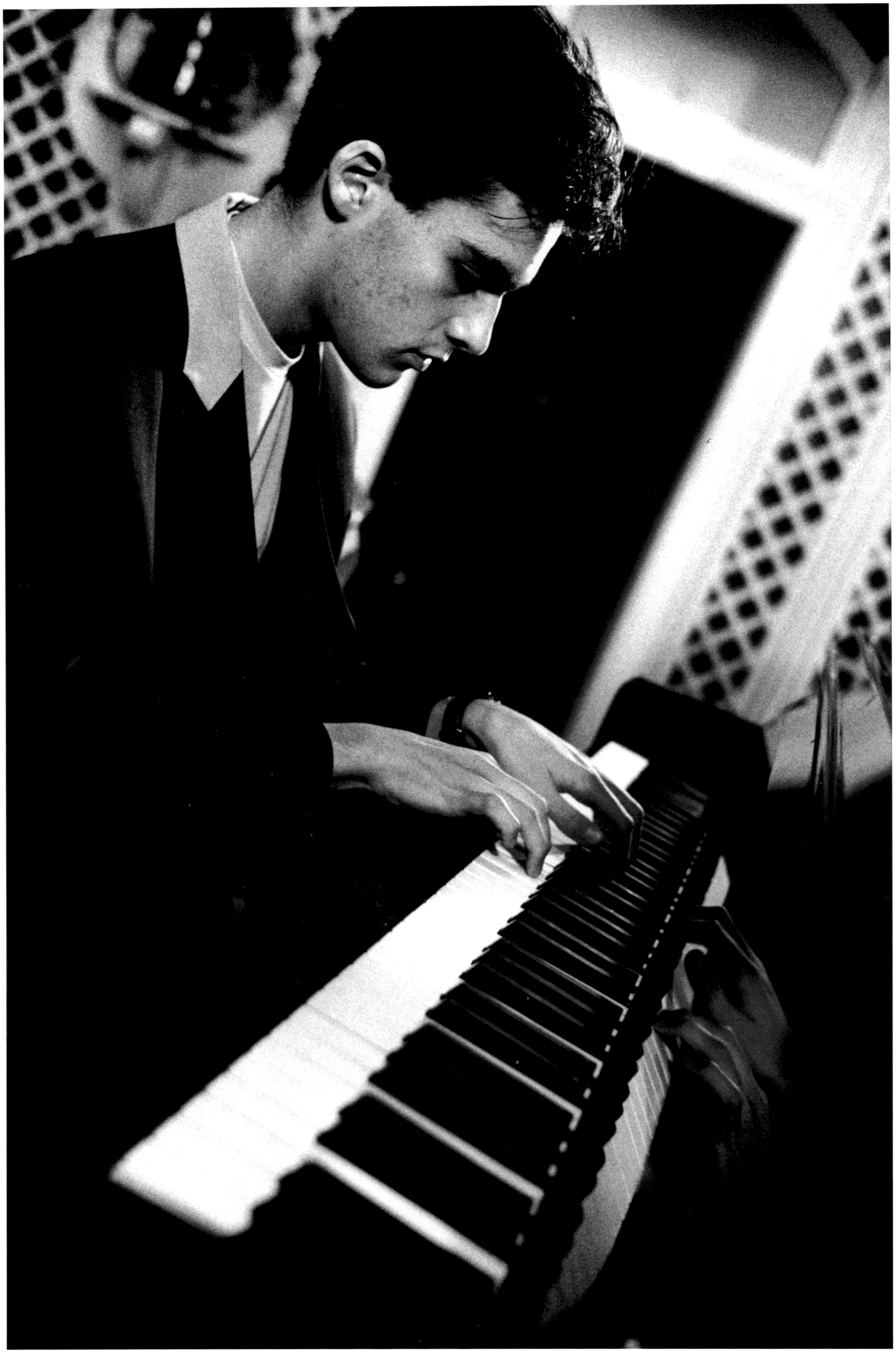

Peter Delano
New York City · 1992

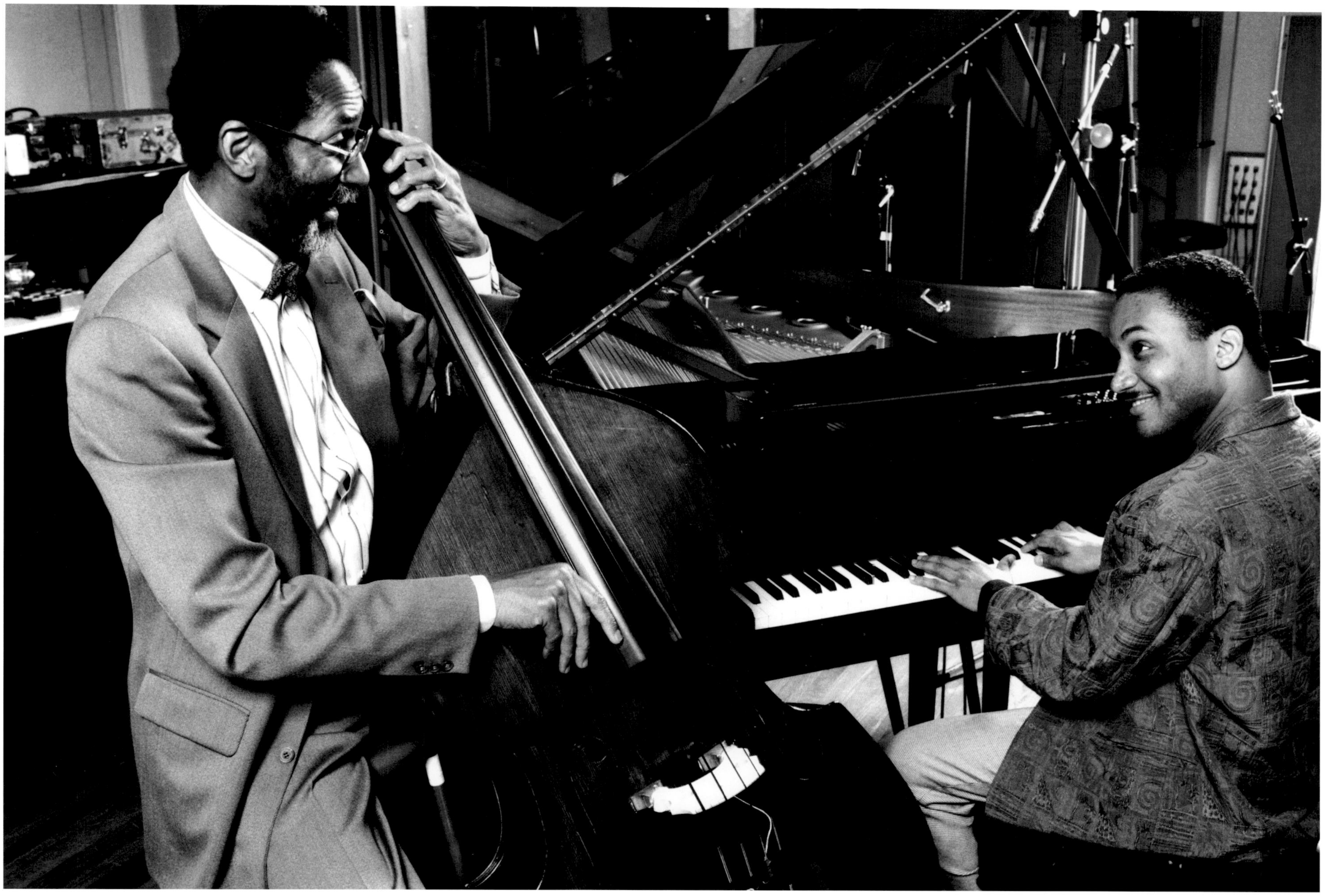

Gonzalo Rubalcaba and Ron Carter New York City · 1994

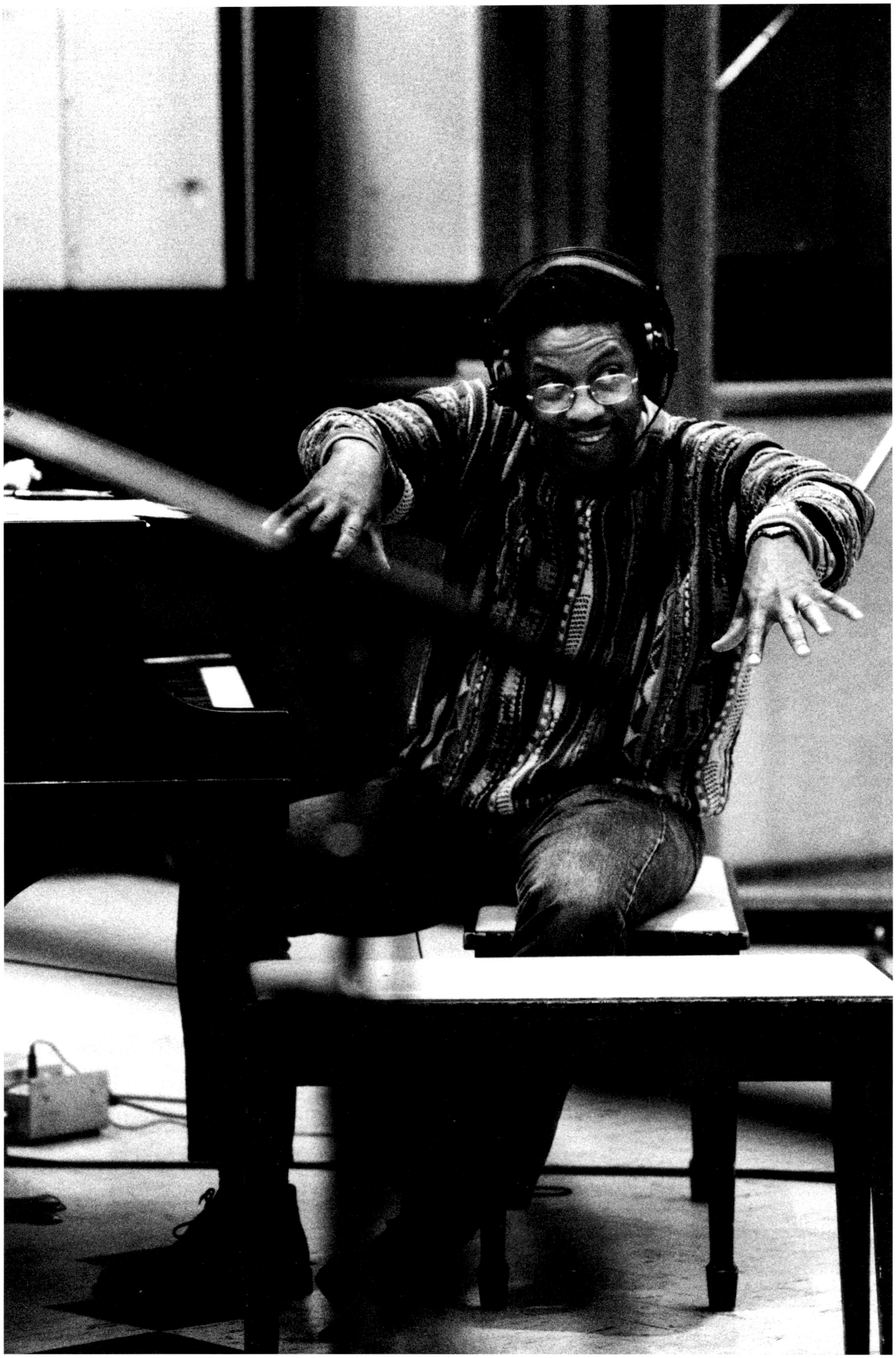

Herbie Hancock
Hollywood · 1995

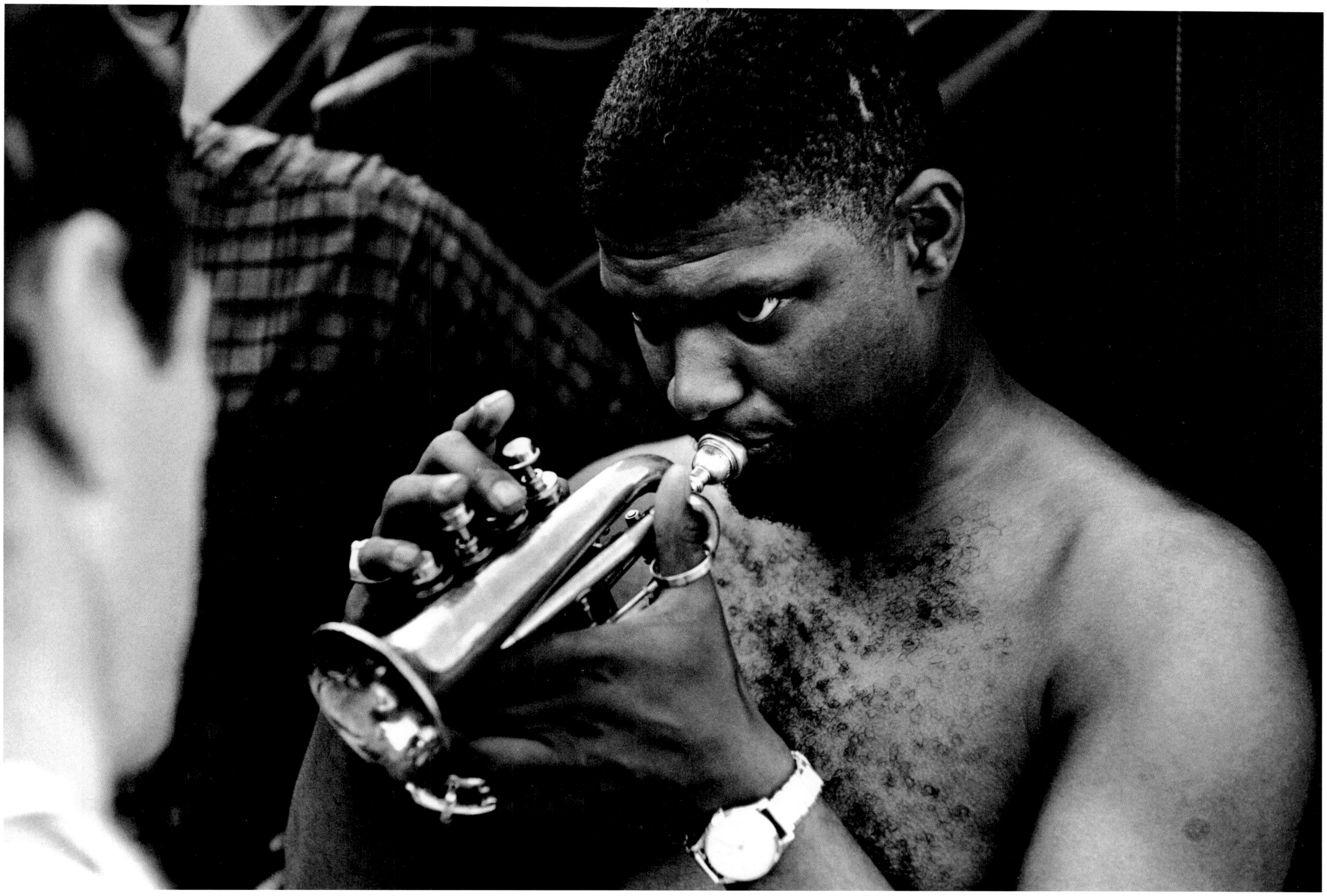

Ted Curson Newport · 1959

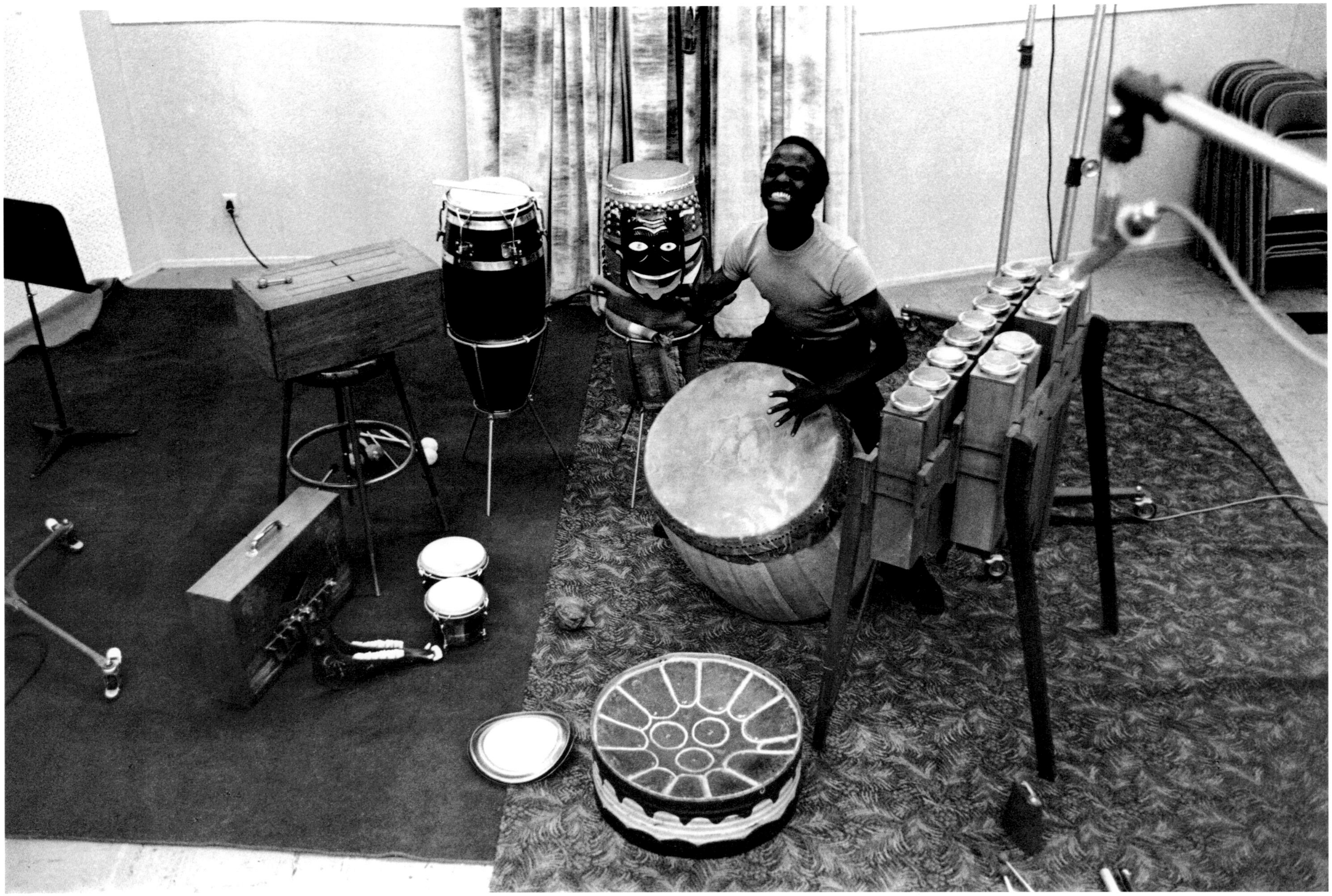

Chiano Hollywood · 1958

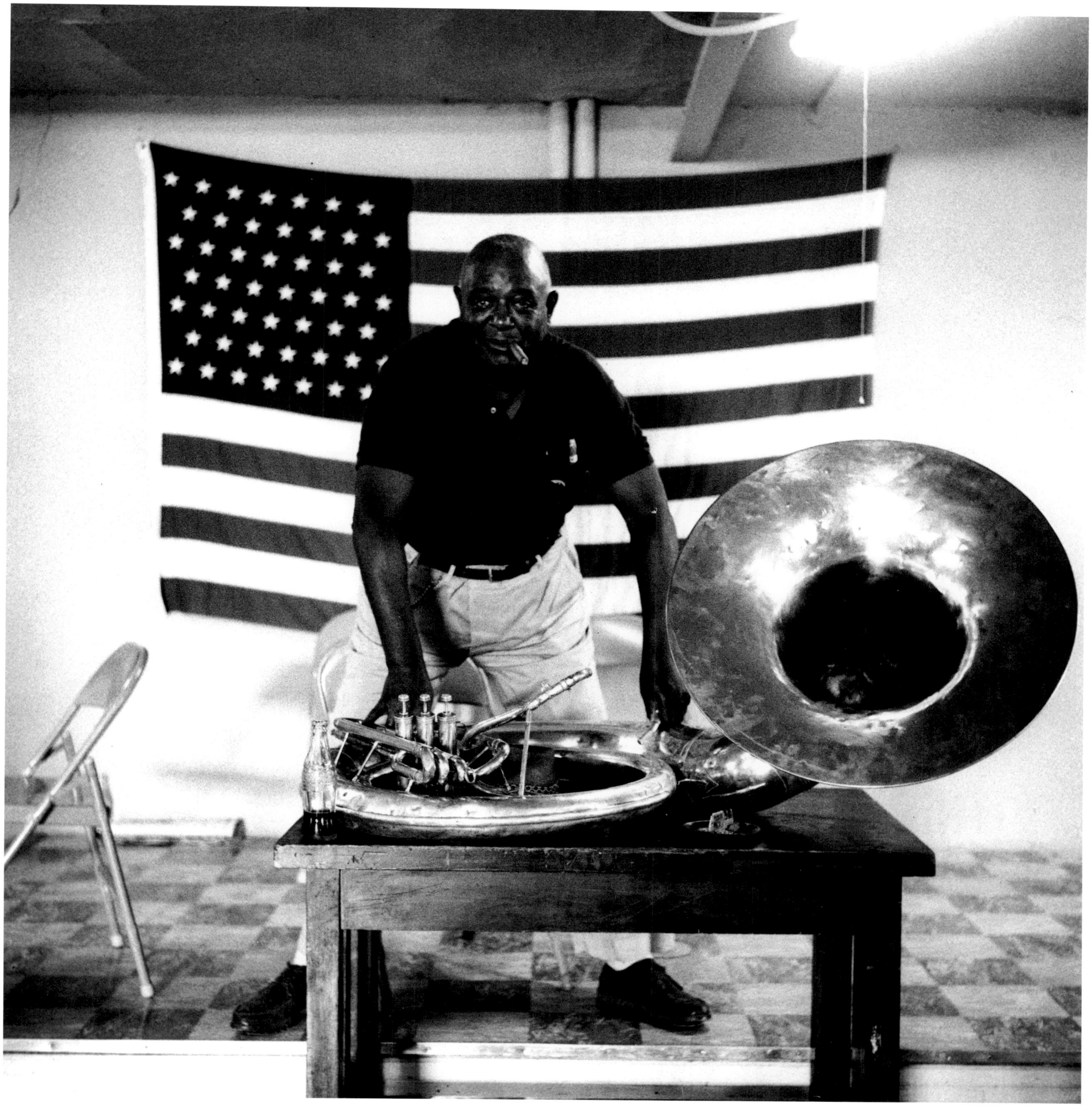

Clint "Pops" Weaver Kansas City · 1960

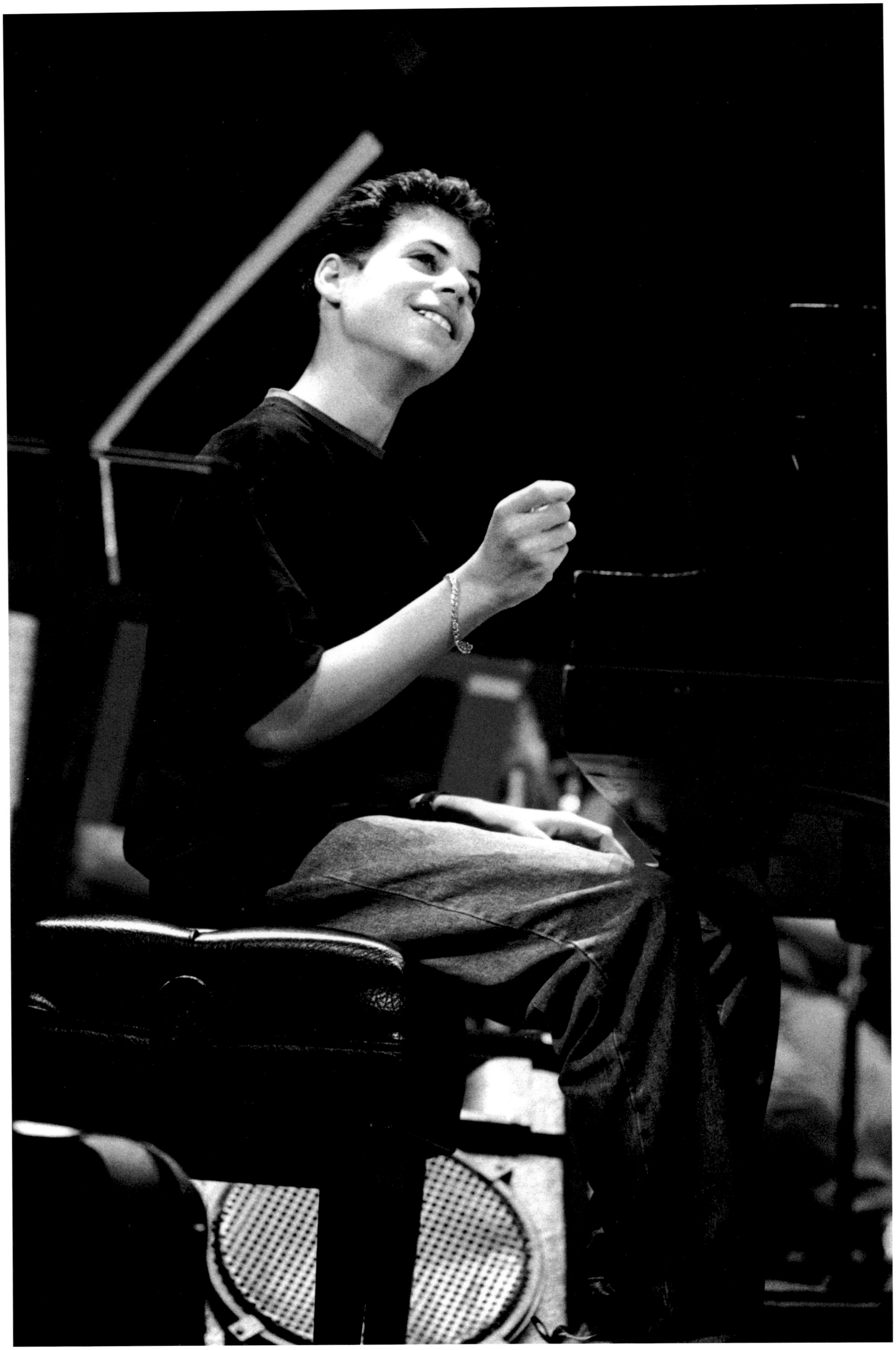

Sergio Salvatore
Los Angeles · 1994

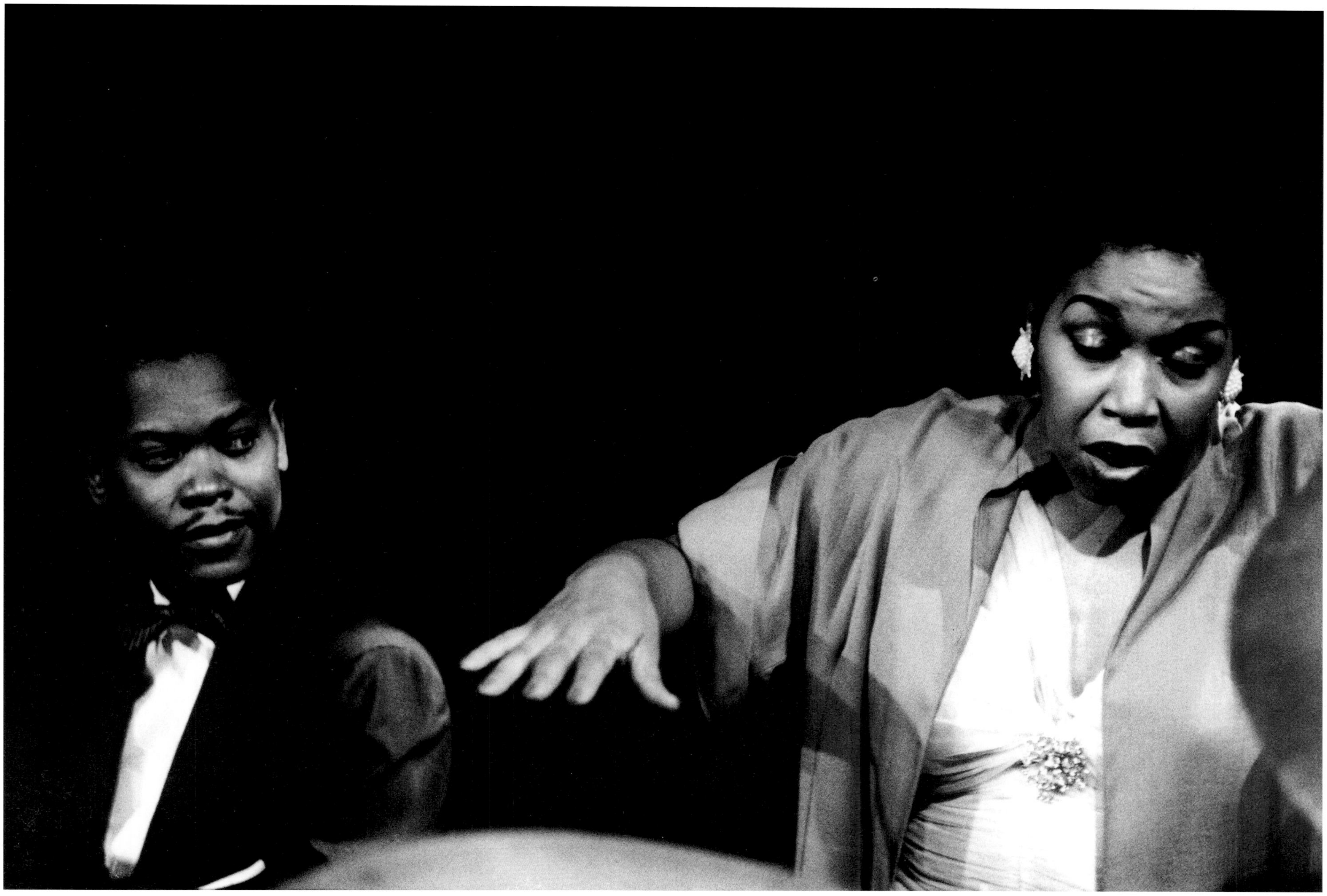

Betty Roché Hollywood · 1956

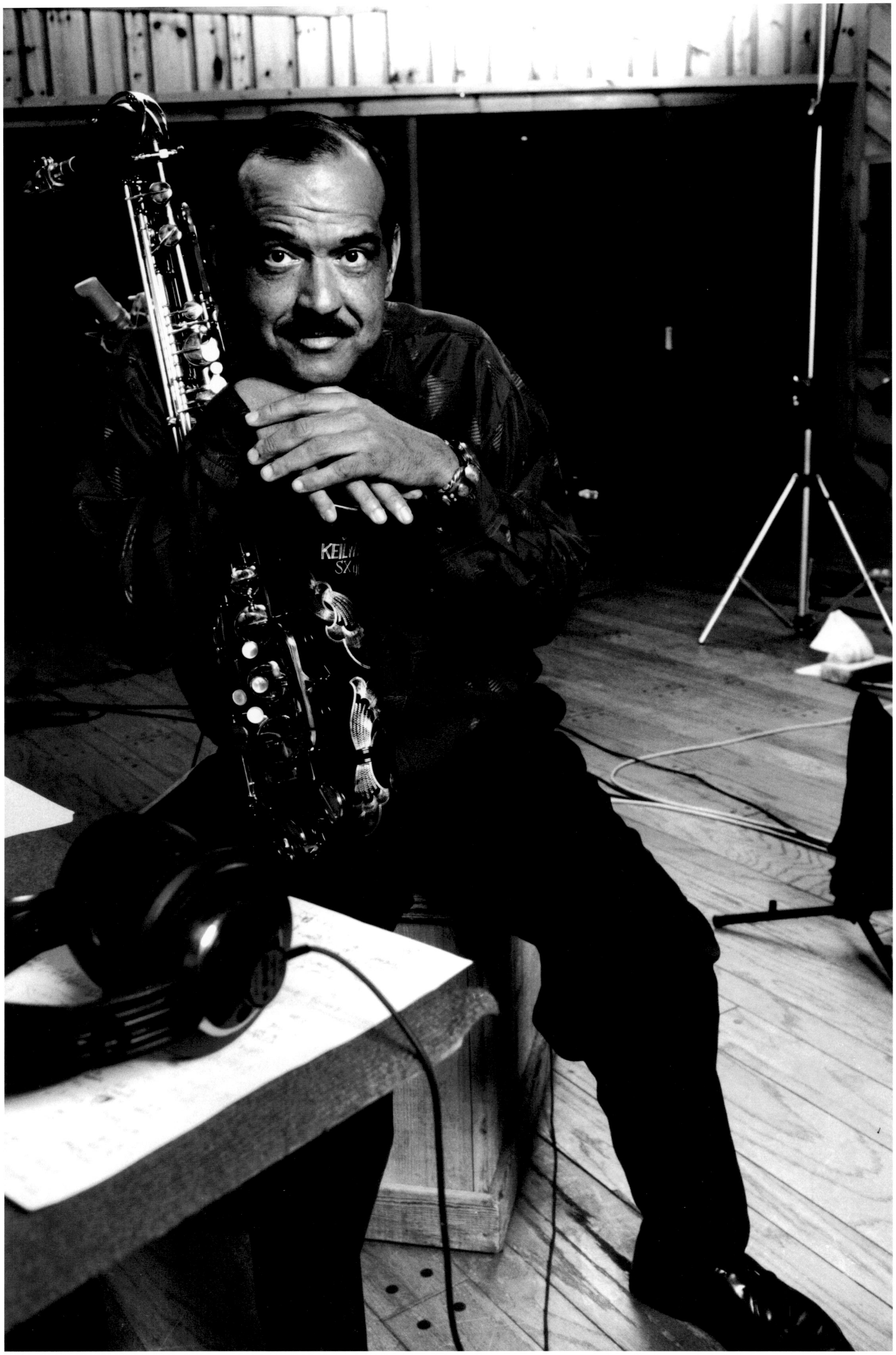

Ernie Watts
New York City · 1995

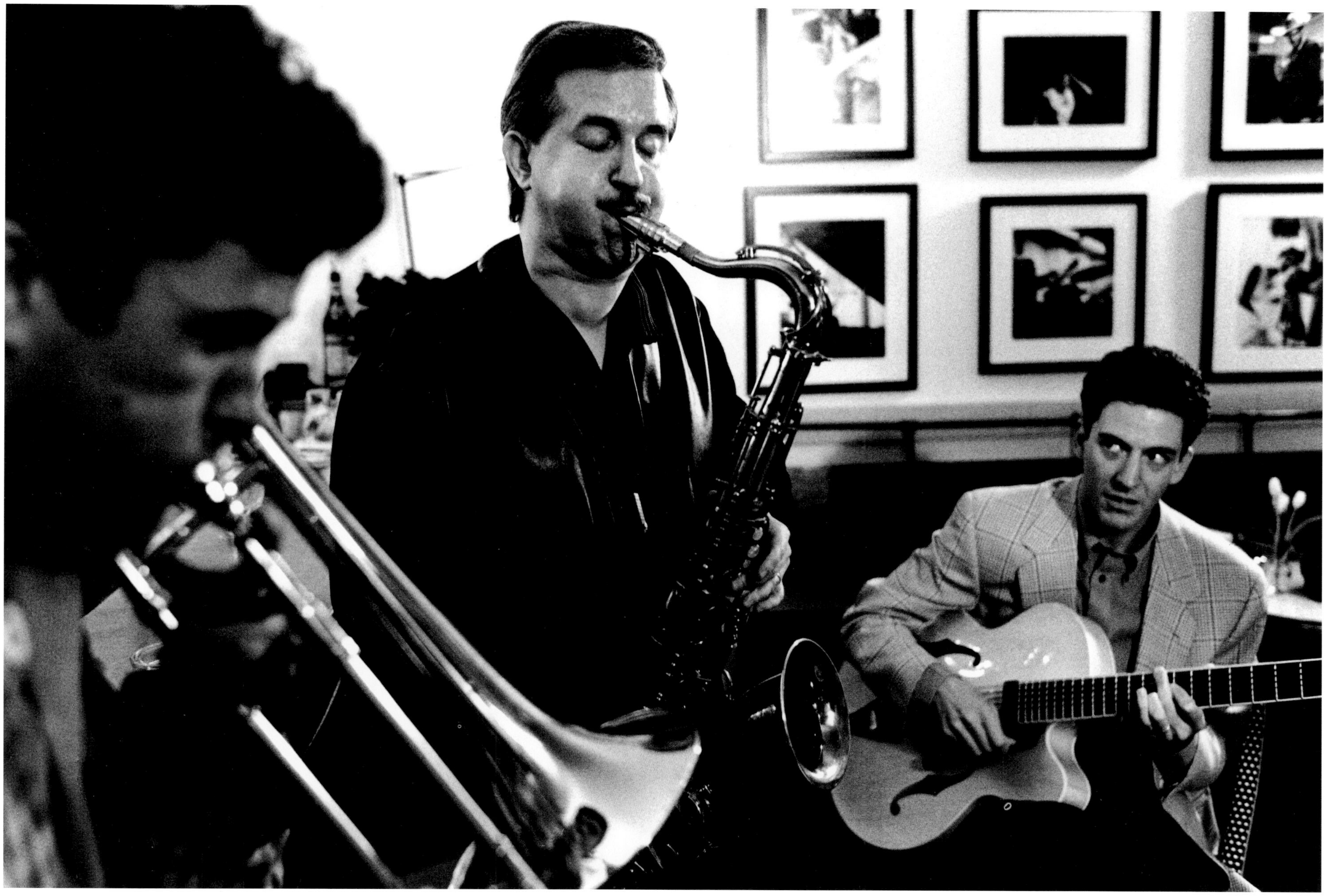

Scott Hamilton ***(tenor sax)*****, John Pizzarelli** ***(guitar)*****, Ray Anderson** ***(trombone)*** New York City · 1992

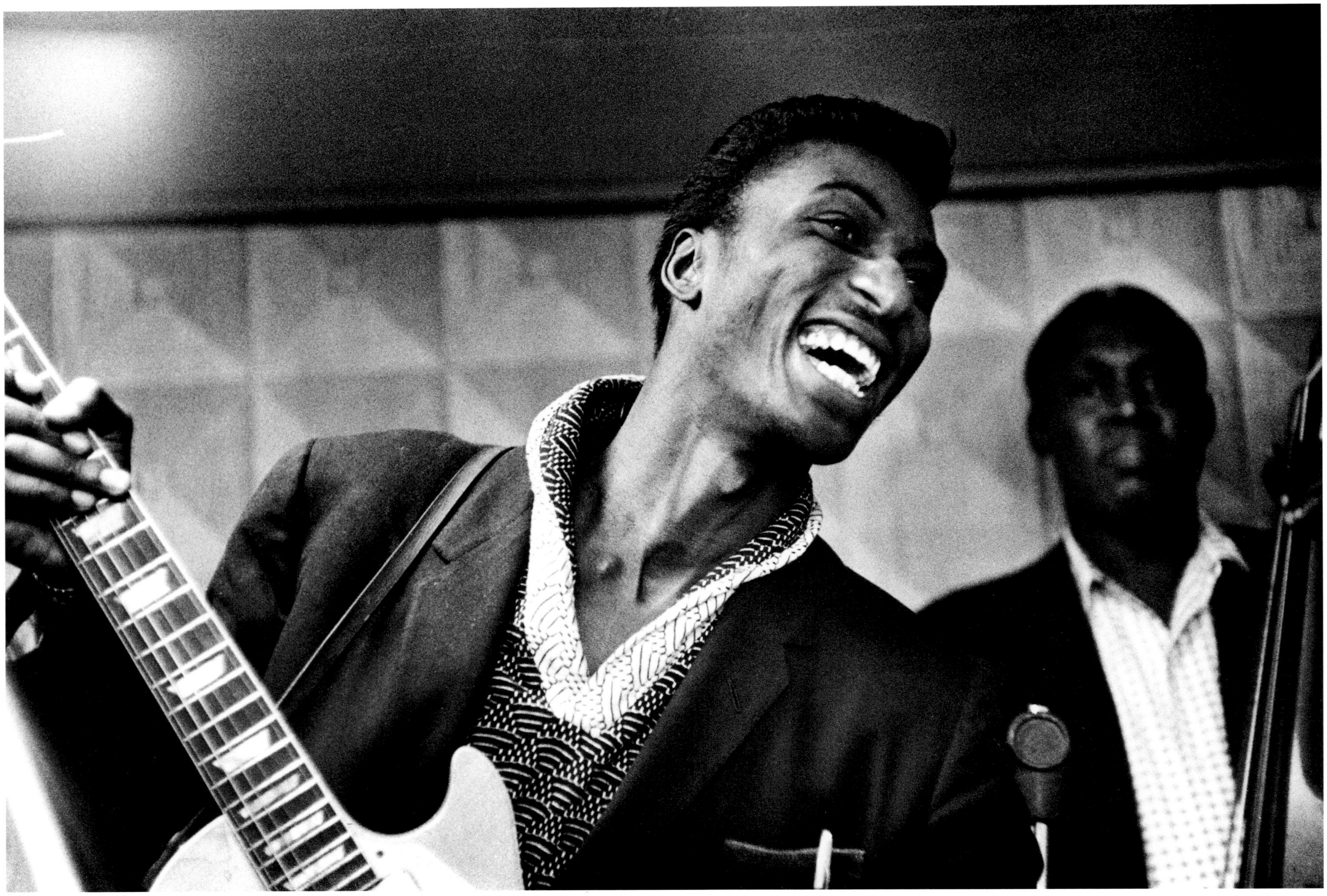

 "Clear Waters", blues party Chicago · 1960

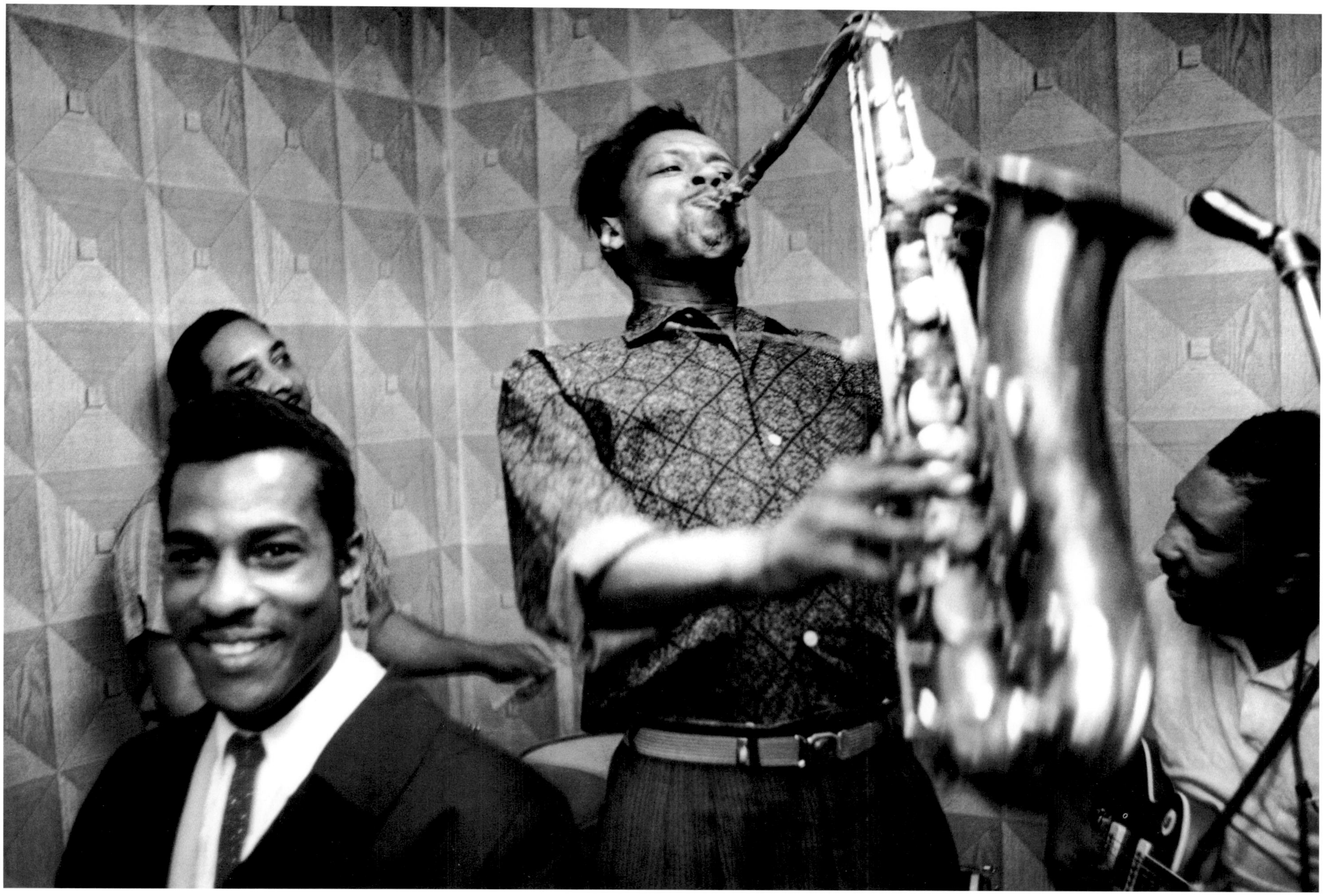

Tom Archia *(tenor sax)*, blues party Chicago · 1960

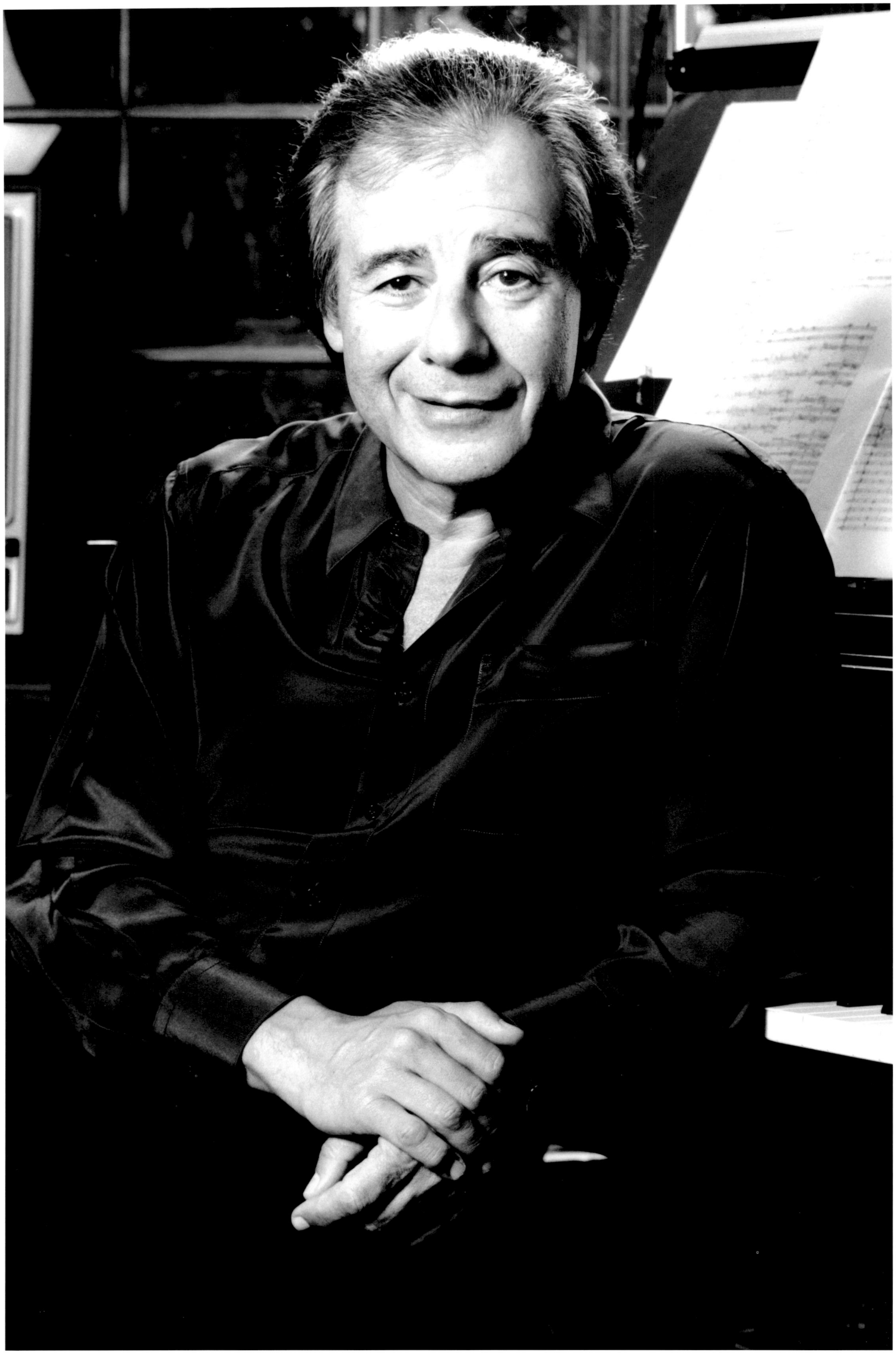

Lalo Schifrin
Beverly Hills · 1994

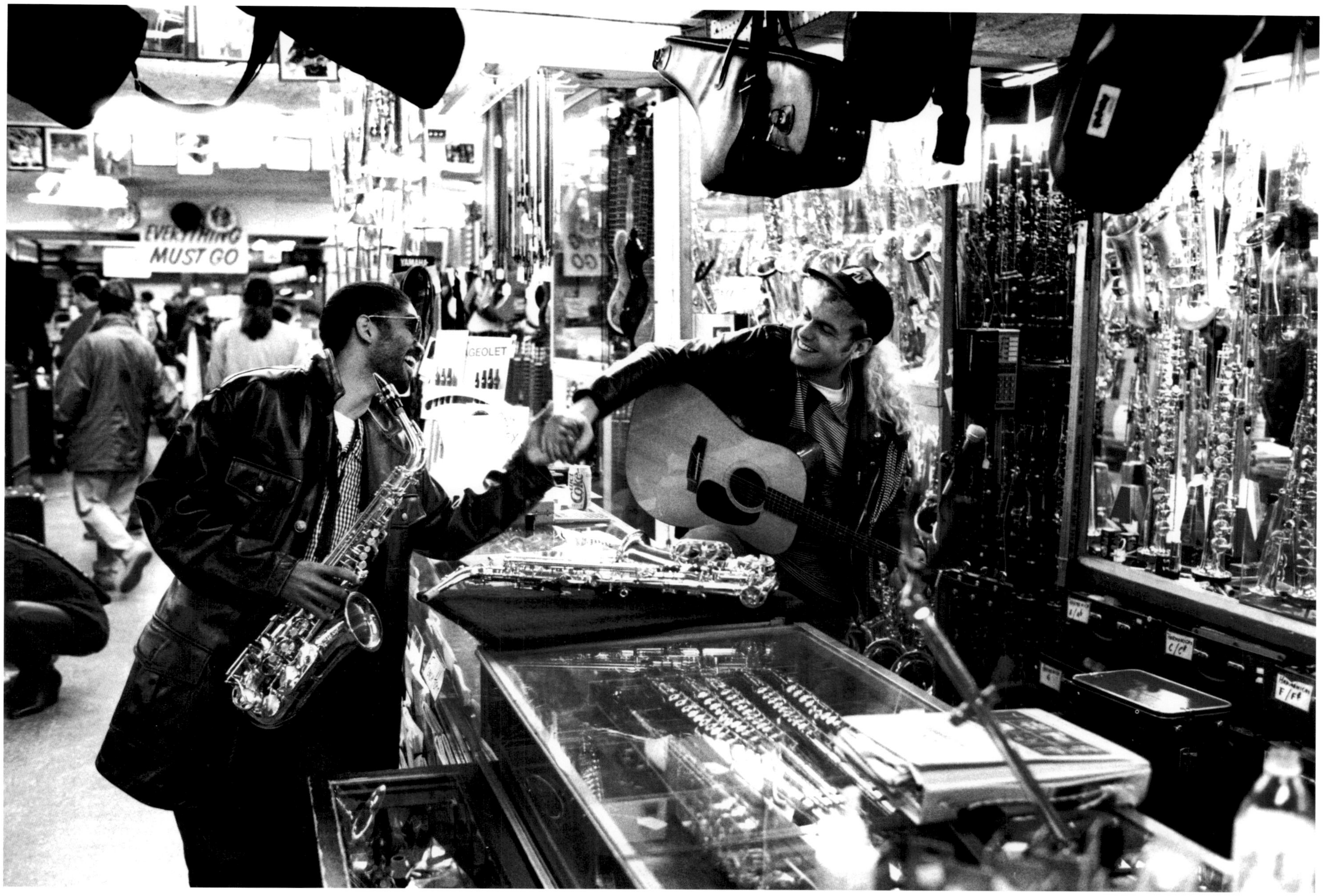

Art Porter and Chris Blackwell ***(right)*** New York City · 1993

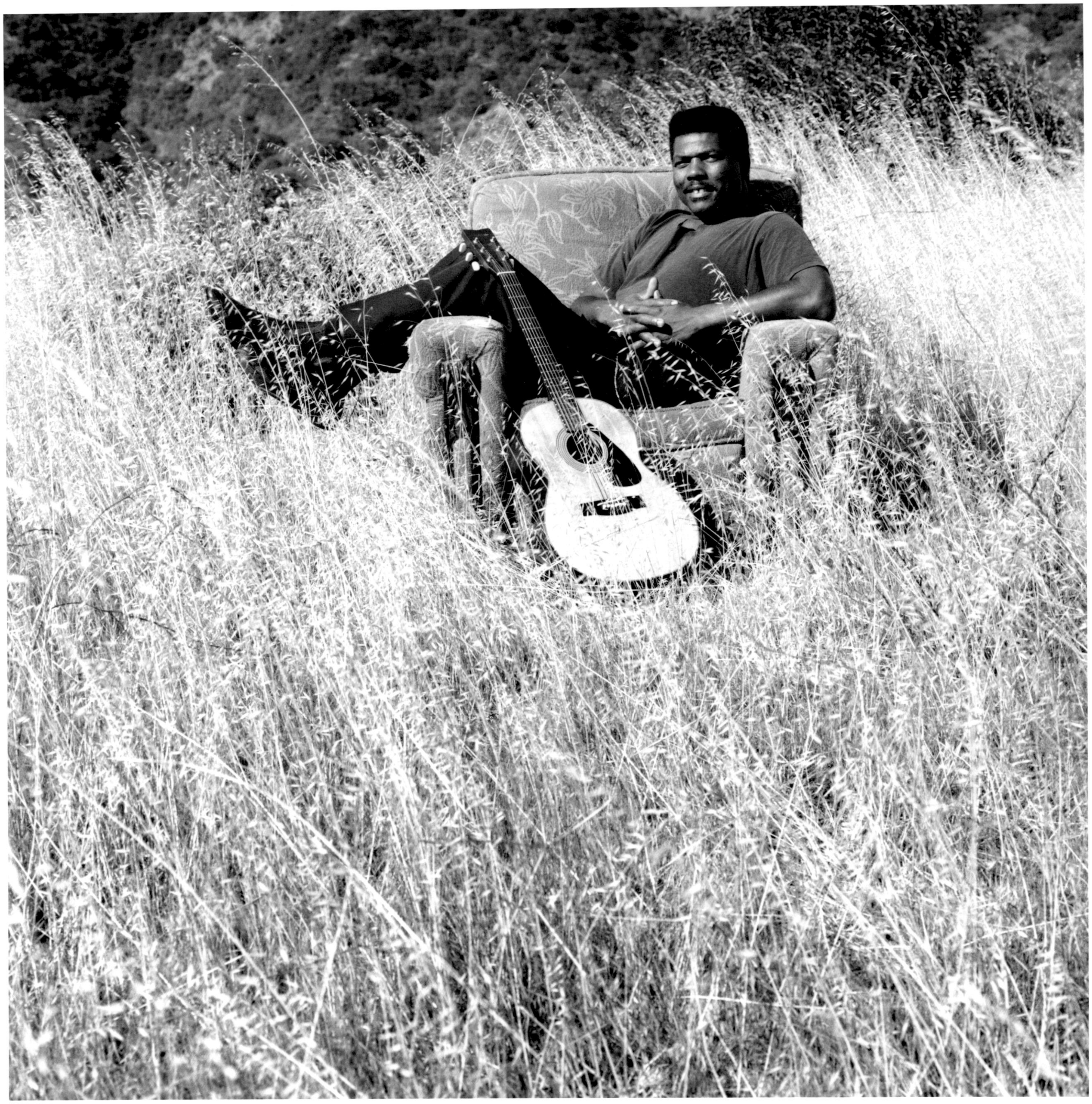

 Terry Evans Los Angeles · 1992

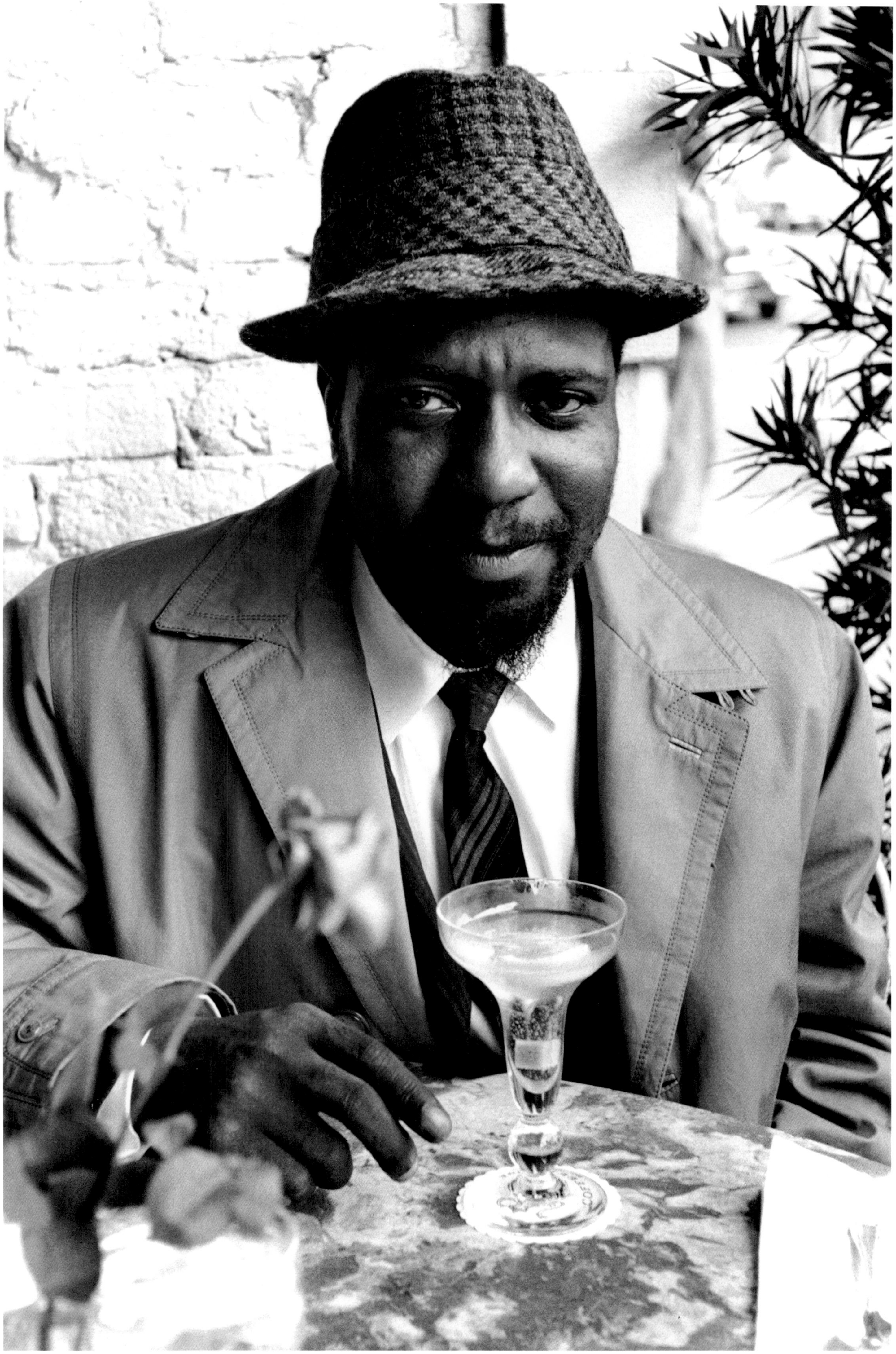

Thelonious Monk
San Francisco · 1959

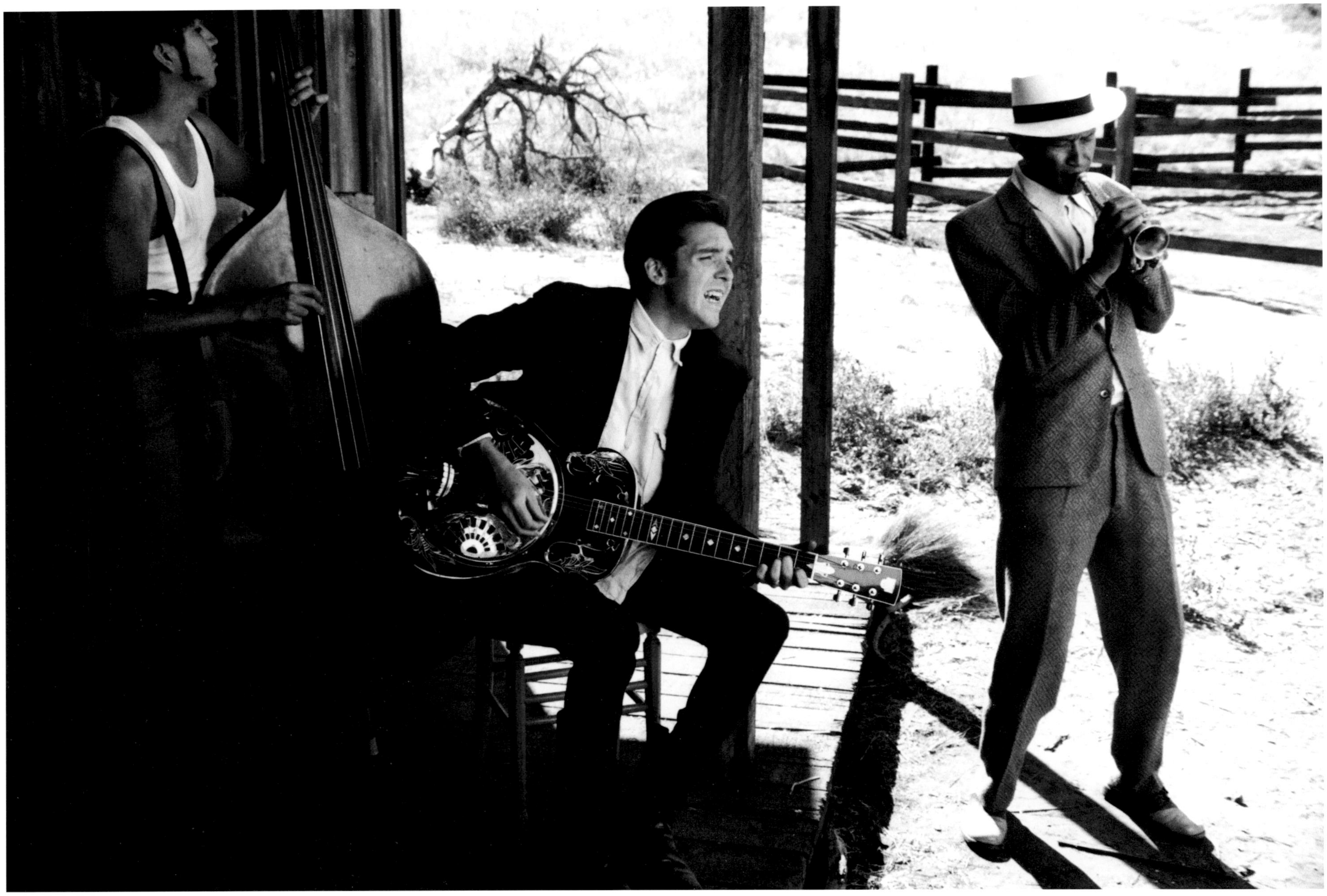

 Joe Henry, Don Cherry *(pocket trumpet)*, Ron Gomez *(bass)* Bouquet Canyon · 1989

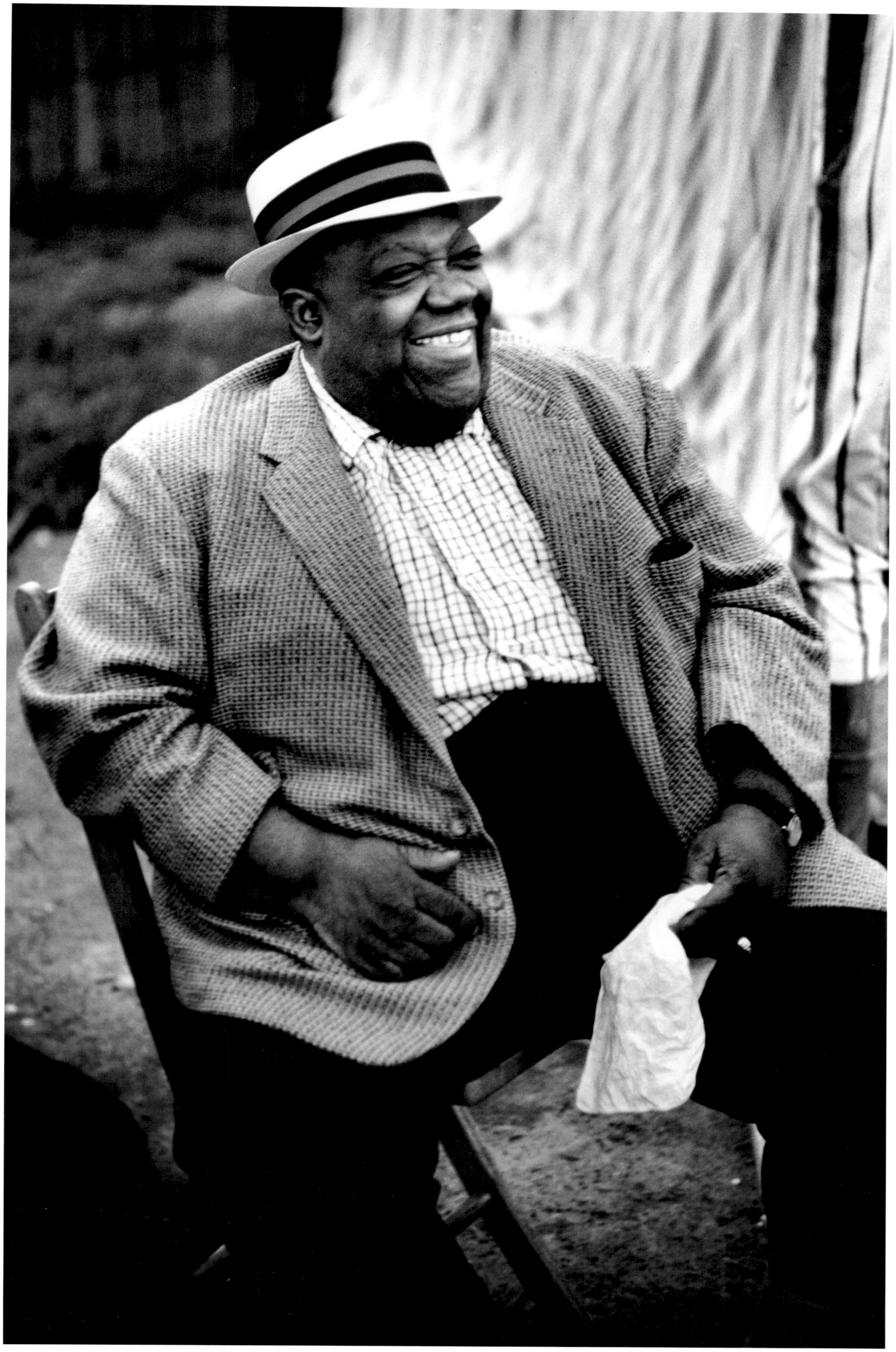

Jimmy Rushing
Newport · 1959

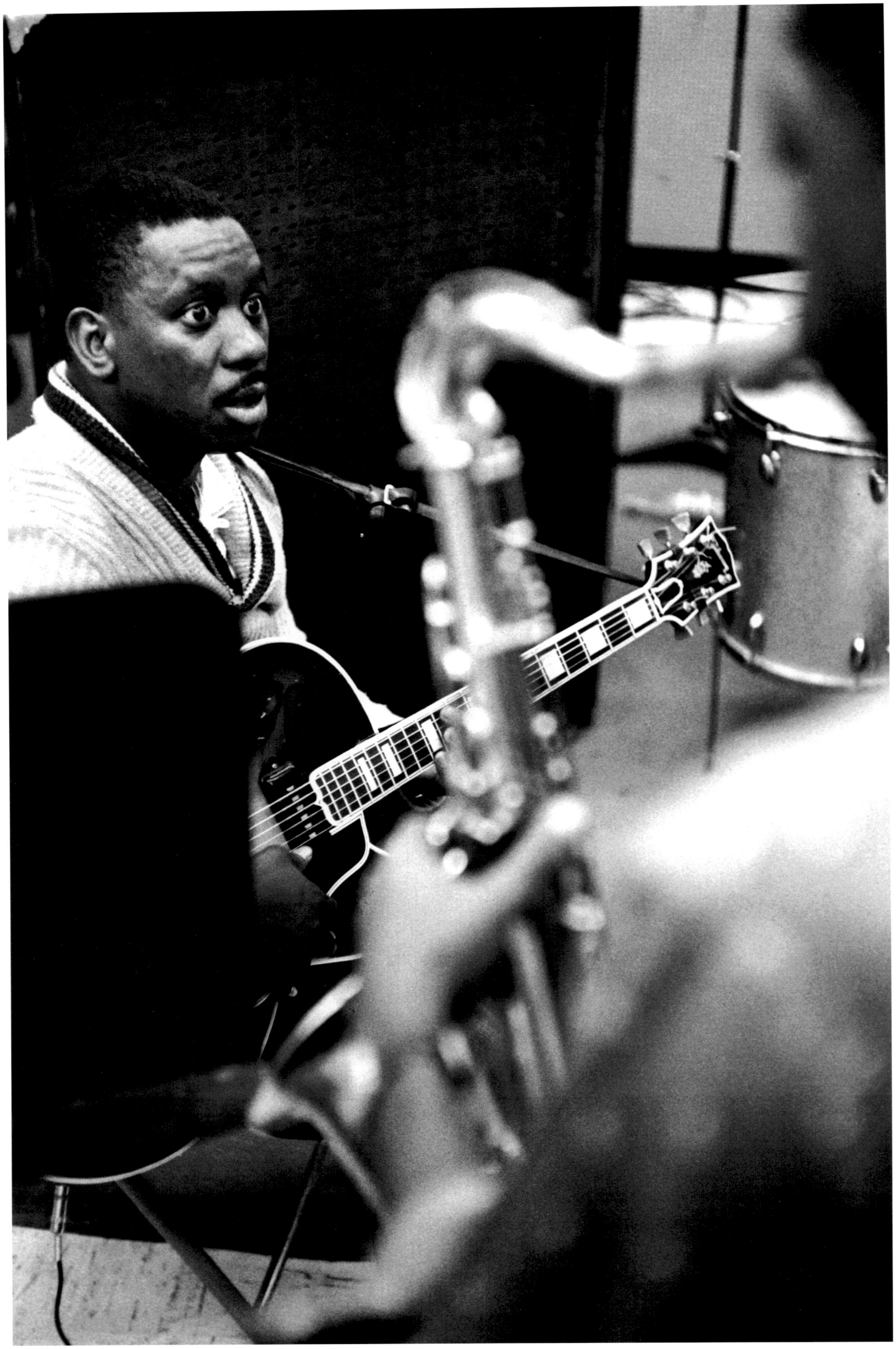

Wes Montgomery
Hollywood · 1956

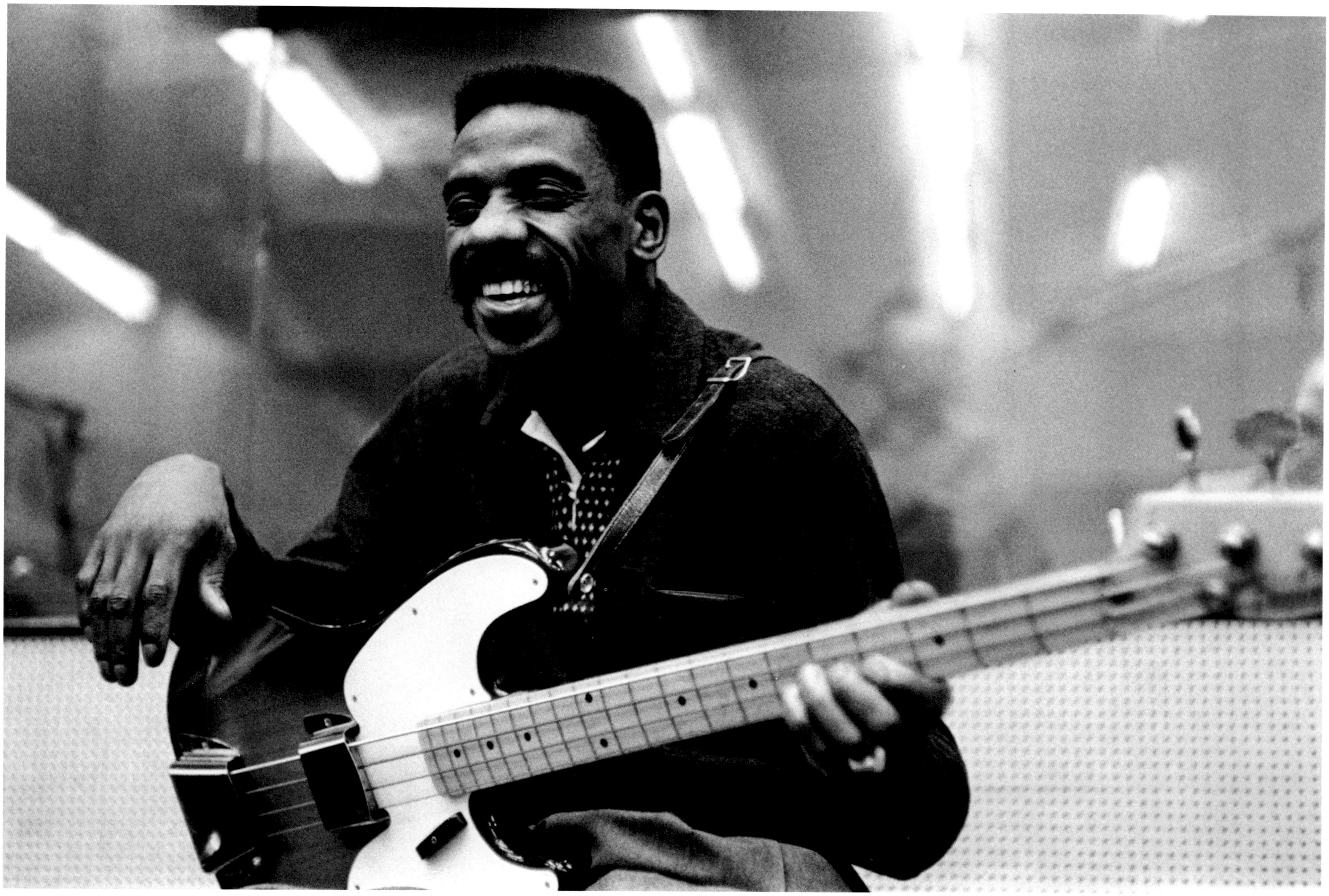

Monk Montgomery Hollywood · 1956

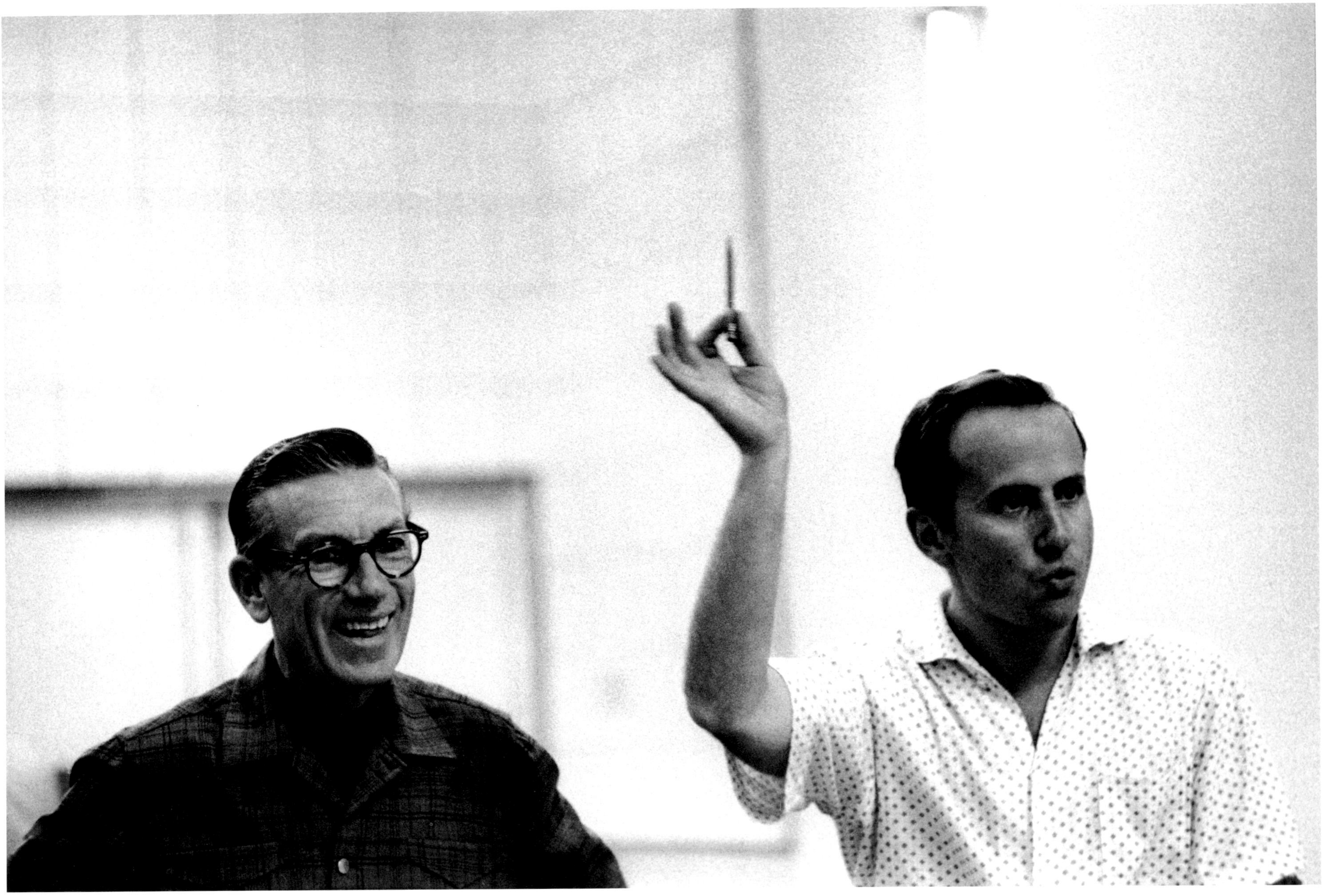

 Johnny Mandel ***(conducting)*** **and Hoagy Carmichael** Hollywood · 1956

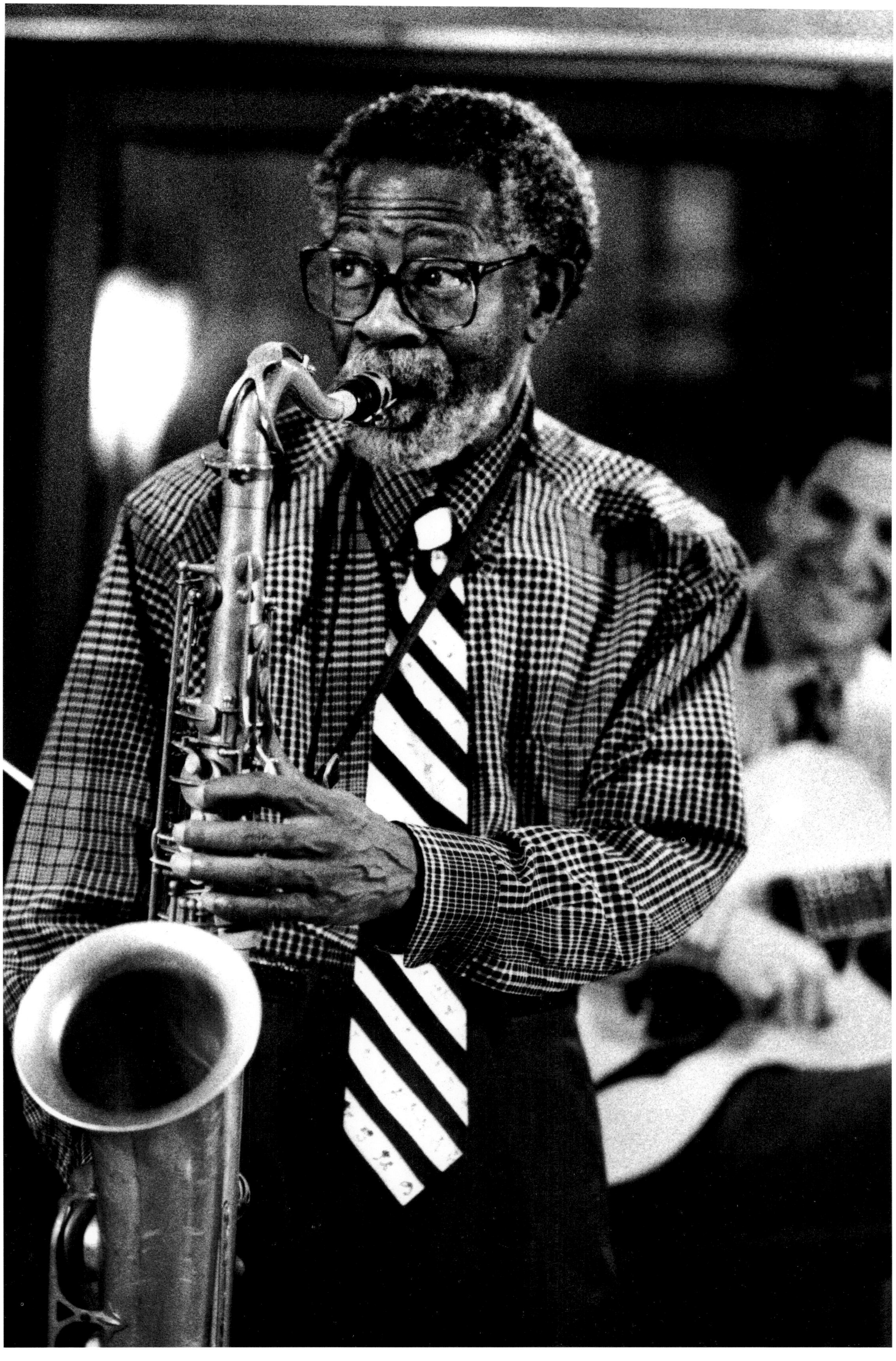

Joe Henderson
New York City · 1992

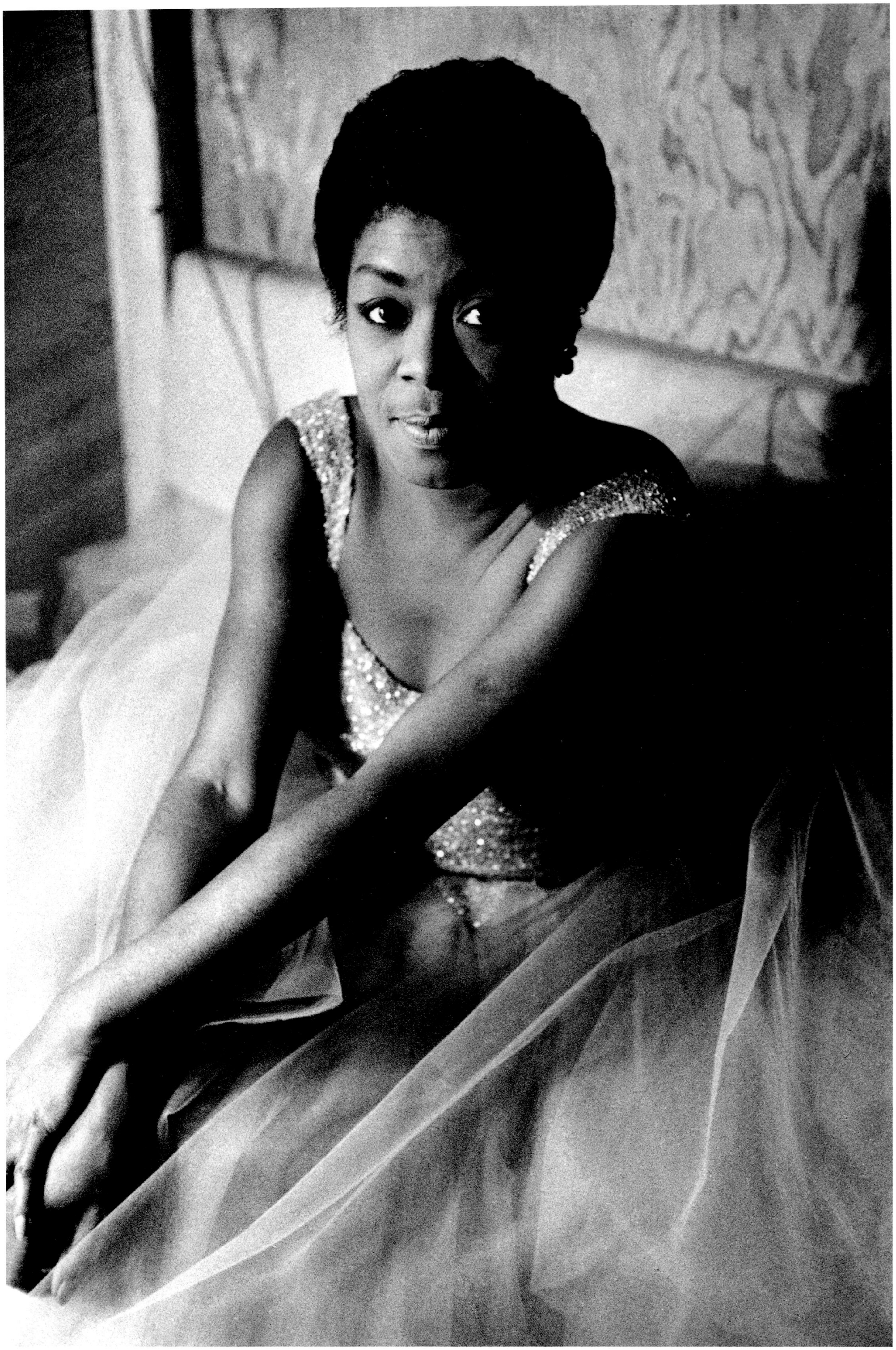

Sarah Vaughan
Brooklyn · 1960

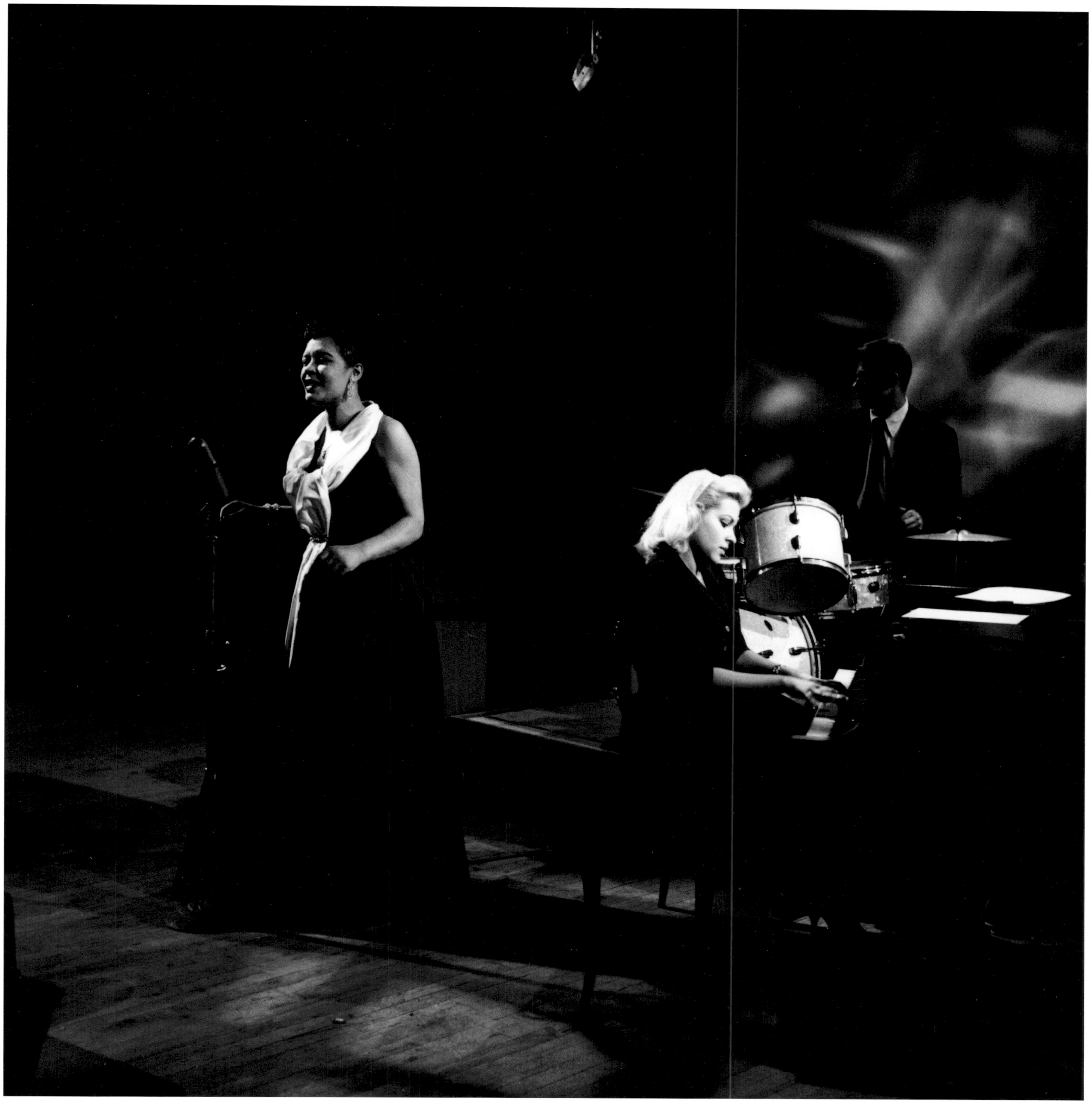

Billie Holiday, Corky Hale *(piano)*, Bob Neel *(drums)* Hollywood · 1957

As a young student, I was very interested in photography. My girlfriend was a model, and on a trip to New York she introduced me to Richard Avedon, who was an idol of mine. At the time, I didn't even own a working camera. So Avedon said, "Here, take this," and he gave me his old Rolleiflex. That camera, and my love of music, are what started me on my career.

William Claxton

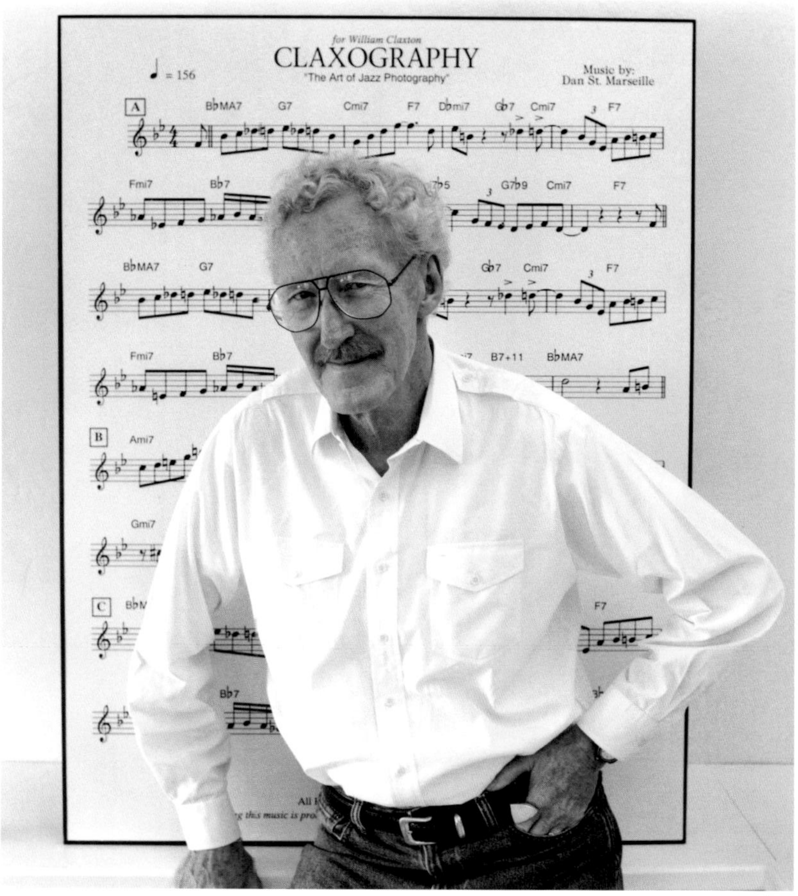

Other books by William Claxton

Jazz West Coast
Linear Publications, Hollywood · 1955
I Like What I Know
with Vincent Price; Doubleday, New York · 1962
Jazzlife
with Joachim Ernst Berendt; Burda Verlag, Munich · 1962
The Mary And Vincent Price Cookbook
with Vincent Price; Abrams Art Books, New York · 1964
Journal Of The Loved One
with Terry Southern; Random House, New York · 1965
Photostory des Jazz [Jazz: A Photo History]
with other photographers; by Joachim Ernst Berendt,
Wolfgang Krüger Verlag, Frankfurt a.M. · 1978
Jazz
Twelvetrees Press, Santa Fe · 1987
Pictures Of Peace
with other photographers; edited by Kim Caputo,
Knopf, New York · 1991
The Rudi Gernreich Book
with Peggy Moffitt; Rizzoli International, New York · 1991
The Year Of Tibet ***A Portfolio of Platinum Prints***
with other photographers; produced by Richard Gere · 1990
California Cool ***West Coast Cover Art***
with Graham Marsh / Glyn Callingham;
Chronicle Books / Collins & Brown, London-San Francisco · 1992
Jazz West Coast ***Artwork Of Pacific Jazz Records***
with Hitoshi Namekata; Bijutsu Shuppan-Sha, Tokyo · 1992
Young Chet
A Photographic Memory of Legendary Jazzman Chet Baker
Schirmer / Mosel, Munich-Paris-London · 1993

William Claxton 1995 *Photo by Peggy Moffitt*

Design and coordination Ingo Wulff, Kiel

Selection and juxtaposing of photographs William Claxton, Beverly Hills

Reproduction Litho- und Scannertechnik, Kiel
Scanner operator *Per Kristian Dehkes*
scanned with 120 lines/cm

Production Nieswand Druck, Kiel
Typesetting *Angelika Masuth*
Printing formes *Oliver Grabowsky*
Print *Manner Masuth, Lars Fenner*

Binding Fikentscher, Darmstadt

Typeface Centennial, Franklin Gothic

Paper Arctic Natura matt 170 gsm
produced by Håfreström, Sweden
supplied by Trebruk, Hamburg

Published by Nieswand Verlag
Werftbahnstr. 8, 24143 Kiel, Germany

Printed in Germany
ISBN 3 926048 67 0

Other books about music and photography by Nieswand Verlag

... Photographs Jazz by Ole Brask · 1995
ISBN 3 926048 63 8
Dizzy Gillespie by Dany Gignoux · 1993
ISBN 3 926048 60 3
Jazz Portraits by Jan Putfarcken · 1994
ISBN 3 926048 40 9
Jazz + More by Ralph Quinke · 1992
ISBN 3 926048 52 2
Jazz In LA by Bob Willoughby · 1990
ISBN 3 926048 41 7
Chet Baker In Europe edited by Ingo Wulff · 1993
ISBN 3 926048 57 3

Endpapers Shadows of the Sauter-Finegan Band Los Angeles · 1953